Basic Planning for Quality

Training in Analytical Quality Management for Healthcare Laboratories

James O. Westgard, PhD

Westgard QC, Inc.
7614 Gray Fox Trail
Madison WI 53717
Phone 608-833-4718
HTTP://WWW.WESTGARD.COM

Westgard QC

Library of Congress Card Number: 00-105531

ISBN 1-886958-13-0

Published by Westgard QC, Inc.
7614 Gray Fox Trail
Madison, WI 53717

Phone 608-833-4718

Foreword

As many of you know, I come from a long line of Vikings. Over a thousand years ago, at the turn of the first millenium, my ancestors were terrorizing the coasts of Europe in their dragon ships. Back then my relatives were famous for their ability to cause trouble.

Now, as we stand at the beginning of this new millenium, things haven't changed that much. Like my ancestors before me, I'm still stirring up trouble. Instead of using a sword, though, I use charts and graphs and statistics. I've found that there is nothing laboratorians fear more than statistics.

I have learned much from my ancestors, in particular my great-great-great-great-great-etc- grandfather Hagar the Horrible. Very early in life, he taught me that a career in Quality Control brought with it certain dangers:

There is more truth in that cartoon than we'd like to admit. Quality Control is often taught and practiced in a very simplistic manner in healthcare laboratories. Statistical QC is viewed as a "problem" because it causes repeat runs or rework. Those in charge of managing quality – Lucky Eddy, for instance – may find themselves the target of frustrated analysts who don't appreciate the importance of detecting analytical problems that cause errors in test results.

But even a Viking can do Quality Control. Look at me. I've never taken a statistics course, but I've learned how to use statistics as tools for managing Quality in the laboratory. I'll let you in on a secret: you don't have to be a statistician, or even like statistics, to do a good job of managing Quality in the laboratory. You just need the right tools.

Basic Planning for Quality will help you get started. It begins with the radical premise that if we take the time to define the Quality needed for a test, we will do a better job of selecting methods and implementing QC procedures. Careful planning will help us optimize our resources, maximize our error detection, and minimize our repeat runs, while at the same time guaranteeing the necessary quality is achieved.

Remember the old saying, *An ounce of prevention is worth a pound of cure.* The "ounce" here is time spent planning your analytical process, particularly planning QC. The "pound" is the amount of time you spend repeating runs due to false rejections and performing repeat tests that are reordered by physicians when quality isn't satisfactory.

The dawn of the 21st century has brought a new emphasis on the design or planning of healthcare processes. This is found in the general guidelines for Improving Organizational Performance (IOP) issued by the Joint Commission for Accreditation of Healthcare Organizations (JCAHO). Because the core process in a healthcare laboratory is the production of test results, the design or planning of analytical processes is an essential part of quality management in any laboratory.

Planning for quality is the area of quality management where improvement is needed in almost all laboratories. If you have any doubt about this, consider the following questions that must be addressed if a laboratory is to truly manage the quality of any testing process. What is the analytical quality that is needed for the test? What imprecision and inaccuracy are needed for the analytical method to achieve that quality? What control rules and number of control measurements are necessary to assure that quality will be achieved in routine operation of the testing process? Pick your favorite test and answer these questions.

Not so easy, is it?

Basic Planning for Quality will help you answer these questions and give you the tools to get answers quickly and easily. We will be helped by my ancestor, Hagar the Horrible, who explains things so much better than I do. With his assistance, we hope to teach you how to

- Define the quality required for a test,
- Establish the purchase specifications for imprecision and inaccuracy for new analytical methods and systems,
- Select QC procedures that maximize quality and minimize cost, and
- Formulate an overall or total QC strategy that balances statistical and non-statistical components in a quality system.

Quality-planning activities are essential in every laboratory. Recent guidelines for planning QC procedures have been issued by the National Committee for Clinical Laboratory Standards (NCCLS) in the document C24-A2: Statistical Quality Control for Quantitative Measurements. In the materials presented here, these guidelines are developed further to provide a practical quality-planning process that can be implemented in any laboratory.

Some basic knowledge of QC is assumed. Hagar has already provided us with a quick review of the basics. If you want a more thorough review of the concepts, principles, and terminology, you can refer to *Basic QC Practices* as well as our website.

One last word to wise:

There are those who are so fearful of statistical Quality Control that they want to get rid of it altogether. They'd rather assume that nothing can go wrong with today's instruments and methods. It's easier to do that than taking the time to teach people how to use statistical QC and assure that test results are correct and meaningful. When faced with numbers, charts and statistics – they ask if there isn't a magic wand, technique, or gee-whiz technology that makes everything perfect?

Alas, there isn't – except for statistical QC, which can be applied to all methods of measurement. Without statistical QC, we risk producing erroneous test results which may lead to erroneous decisions about patient treatment. With statistical QC, we have a tool that can quickly tell us whether our test results are reliable.

Just because we have to face the numbers doesn't mean it has to be hard. *Basic Planning for Quality* gives you the keys to managing methods and systems properly: a simple step-by-step planning process, a quick graphical planning tool (the OPSpecs chart). By the time you finish the book, you'll have everything you need to start planning your Quality.

And if this makes you famous for your ability to cause trouble, so much the better.

About these materials

There are 15 lessons or chapters, each beginning with a short study plan that includes the goals for the lesson, specific objectives, materials to study, and things to do. Each concludes with a short list of self-assessment questions that have answers available at the back of the book.

The quality-planning approach is developed in a systematic manner in Chapters 1 through 8. Chapter 9 provides a summary, review, or overview of the earlier chapters. Chapters 10-13 provide applications for different kinds of laboratory tests. Chapter 13 also introduces online planning tools that are available on the Internet. Chapters 14 and 15 address frequently-made-complaints about QC and frequently-asked-questions about quality-planning. There is a glossary of terms and a list of literature references and Internet materials. Appendices 1-3 provide summaries of recommendations for quality requirements. Appendix 4 describes the financial implications of quality-planning.

Fast start for QC planning

For those eager to learn practical applications and who are more concerned with "how" to do quality planning than the theory and background behind it (i.e. the "why" to do it), this accelerated syllabus is suggested:

- Begin with chapter 9 to get the overall picture.
- Study chapter 8 to learn the step-by-step quality-planning process.
- Study chapter 7 to learn how to formulate a Total QC strategy.
- Study one application chapter (10, 11, 12, or 13) that is of interest to you.
- Start your own applications.
- Refer to Appendices 1-3 for recommendations for quality requirements.
- Utilize the online QC Planner tool if you have access to the Internet.

Access to Internet materials

These materials and the online Method Planner and QC Planner tools are available to you at Westgard Web in a special directory.

Type in the address: **http://www.westgard.com/qpbook/**

Enter the username (all capitals): **QPLANNER**

Enter the password (all capitals): **BQ4P**

Table of Contents

Acknowledgments

As with all our books in the "Back to Basics" series, Sten Westgard deserves the credit for the developing the format of these materials. He makes the publication of these materials possible, first on the Internet as webmaster for Westgard Web, then in hardcopy through his desktop publishing skills. He also makes editorial contributions that add some color to what might otherwise be pretty dull material.

I continue to get critiques, comments, and suggestions from Trish Barry, Elsa Quam and Karen Mugan. They are my link to the reality of the service laboratory, the practicality of our training materials, and the utility of our quality-planning tools. They also co-authored some of the original publications that provide the basis for many of the applications that are illustrated here.

The Hagar the Horrible cartoons have been collected over a long period of time and are provided with permission from the King Features Syndicate. These cartoons speak to me and my Scandinavian heritage and I hope they convey a message to you.

James O. Westgard
Madison Wisconsin

About the author

James O. Westgard, PhD, is a Professor in the Department of Pathology and Laboratory Medicine at the University of Wisconsin Medical School, where he teaches in the Clinical Laboratory Science program. He is the Faculty Director of Quality Management Services at the Clinical Laboratories, University of Wisconsin Hospital and Clinics. He is also President of Westgard QC, Inc.

A complete profile of him is available at
http://www.westgard.com/jimbio.htm

1: Is quality still an issue in the new millenium?

Given the ongoing improvement of analytical systems by manufacturers, many laboratories assume that analytical quality is no longer a problem or even a responsibility of the laboratory. In *A Wake-up Call for Laboratory Quality Management*, Dr. Westgard provides a specific example of the FDA taking action against a manufacturer for not following Quality System Regulations and points out the need for laboratories to maintain the skills and capabilities to manage the quality of their testing process.

Objectives:

- ❍ Examine the laboratory's need to maintain an independent quality management system.
- ❍ Identify quality management activities that can't be delegated to the manufacturer.

Chapter materials:

- ❍ **A Wake-up Call for Laboratory Quality Management**

Things to do:

- ❍ Study the chapter.
- ❍ Access the FDA consent decree via the Internet.
- ❍ Review your laboratory's policy and plan for evaluating new methods.
- ❍ Review your laboratory's policy on establishing QC procedures for new methods.

Hagar the Horrible

The dragon no one wants to know about in healthcare is called "Error the Terror." Laboratory managers often don't want to know about incorrect test results or laboratory errors – there's too much else to worry about to be in compliance with all the rules and regulations and avoid charges of medicare fraud. With today's expensive instruments and expensive reagents, we hope the high price will equate with high quality. But we can't assume quality is okay, as demonstrated dramatically in this introductory chapter. As laboratory professionals, we have to assure quality, not assume it.

Hagar the Horrible is reprinted here with special permission of King Features Syndicate.

A Wake-up Call for Laboratory Quality Management

It's the start of a new millennium! Everyone is looking forward to the future and to a new and better world. Better quality healthcare is on everyone's list for this new and better world. Better quality laboratory testing should also be on the list!

Just when everyone thought the issue of quality in laboratory testing was dead and buried, a major supplier of diagnostic testing materials and systems was cited for not following the Food and Drug Administration's (FDA) Good Manufacturing Practices (GMP) or Quality System Regulations. This left laboratories scrambling to maintain testing services.

FDA action against a manufacturer

On November 2nd, 1999, the Food and Drug Administration and Abbott Laboratories entered into a legal agreement - a consent decree - to settle a dispute about manufacturing practices. This agreement required Abbott to stop manufacturing certain diagnostic test kits within thirty days (by December 2,1999) and to make corrective changes in the manufacturing processes in its Lake County IL facilities. On November 19, 1999, the Northern District Court of Illinois extended the deadline until January 10, 2000.

In the FDA "Dear Colleague Letter" (see http://www.fda.gov/cdrh/ocd/abbottletter.html), the consent decree is described as a permanent injunction that requires Abbott to discontinue sales of certain tests within thirty days because of long standing failure to comply with FDA's Good Manufacturing Practices (GMP) or Quality System Regulation (QSR) and its failure to fulfill commitments to correct deficiencies in its manufacturing operations.

In a press release, Abbott pointed out that the consent decree did not require the recall of any diagnostic products and that certain products would continue to be available (see http://www.abbott.com/news/1999news/pr110299.htm).

> "The decree allows for the continued manufacture and distribution of medically necessary diagnostic products made in Lake County, Ill., such as assays for hepatitis, retrovirus, cardiovascular disease, cancer, thyroid disorders, fertility, drug monitoring, and congenital and respiratory conditions. However, Abbott is prohibited from manufacturing or distributing certain diagnostic products until Abbott ensures the processes in its Lake County, Ill., diagnostics manufacturing operations conform with the current Quality System Regulation."

On November 3, 1999, *The Washington Post* brought the issue to the public's attention with its article on "Medical Test Maker Fined $100 Million for Poor Quality Control," in which it stated:

> "Abbott Laboratories, the nation's largest maker of medical laboratory tests, agreed yesterday to pay a $100 million fine for failing to correct defects in its manufacturing processes despite six years of warnings. The penalty was the largest ever levied by the Food and Drug Administration."

The *LA Times* also drew public attention with its article "Abbott Labs to Pay $100m to FDA."

> "The issues have to do with manufacturing processes and not with known instances of patient harm,' said FDA medical devices chief Dr. David Feigal. Under the consent decree, Abbott is permitted to continue selling only certain tests the FDA deems medically necessary... The FDA offered an important warning for laboratories, which have certain quality-control to catch glitches with products. Labs that continue to use Abbott diagnostic products should 'increase their vigilance in these areas, to make sure these tests are performing,' Feigal said."

Additional information for the laboratory community was also made available by professional organizations. AACC delivered three MANAGEMENT ALERT bulletins via fax broadcasts in the days following the consent decree and established a webpage with sources of information (http://www.aacc.org/abbott.stm). In a fax broadcast on November 9, CLMA announced it was petitioning the FDA to extend the notice before discontinuing sales of the tests. The petition would extend the thirty day period by an additional fourteen days. CLMA also established a special page on its website and organized a special audioconference November 18, 1999 to focus on practical strategies for transitioning products affected by the consent decree.

A sentinel event calling for independent analytical quality management

The FDA-Abbott consent decree sounded a warning that laboratories need to independently guarantee the quality of the test results they produce. Virtually all US laboratories have been affected because of Abbott's dominant role in supplying materials and systems for diagnostic testing. These laboratories were faced with the immediate need to validate new methods and provide better quality control of routine testing. For many laboratories, the personnel resources and skills needed to accomplish this are now very scarce due to changes in laboratory management practices and priorities during the last decade.

The need for independent laboratory quality control is fundamental! Many laboratories have become dependent on manufacturers' QC instructions and have forgotten the hard-learned lessons of the past:

- Independent QC begins by having control materials that are independent of the calibration materials.
- It is good practice to have control materials that are made by a different manufacturer than the test system, as confirmed by FDA's recommendation for "the use of quality control materials made by other companies to increase the assurance that these devices are performing successfully."
- Laboratories should establish their own means and standard deviations when implementing statistical QC procedures, rather than use bottle values provided by a manufacturer.
- Laboratories should select appropriate control rules and numbers of control measurements on the basis of the quality required by the patients and physicians they serve and the imprecision and inaccuracy observed for their methods during routine operation in the laboratory [1].

It's important to recognize that the major problem that needs to be addressed is the poor quality management practices that have evolved in laboratories during the last

decade. Laboratories aren't ready or able to exercise an independent responsibility for the quality of their own test results.

The consent decree should be a sentinel event that alerts laboratories to the serious limitations of current quality management practices which often lack independence from the manufacturer. Government agencies should reflect carefully on the state of laboratory quality management and the susceptibility of laboratory testing on a national scale to a problem from a single manufacturer. Accreditation and professional organizations also need to examine their priorities to be sure that the basic requirement for correct test results hasn't been down-played in their efforts to focus laboratory attention on utilization and outcome.

Analytical quality is not a given!

The consent decree clearly exposes the fallacy of the current thinking that "analytical quality is a given." I've been worried about the complacency that began developing in the 1990s –complacency in laboratories, complacency in professional organizations, complacency in regulatory agencies. This issue has been addressed with a discussion of *The Myths of Quality*, which is the introductory lesson in our course on *Basic Method Validation* [2]. The situation in many laboratories has deteriorated to the point that educational efforts are needed to re-establish basic quality management practices, which is why we've developed training materials for *Basic QC Practices*, *Basic Method Validation*, and *Basic Planning for Quality*. The fundamentals of quality management need to be re-established to support high quality laboratory testing in the new millennium.

Responsibility for quality can't be out-sourced!

In today's busy laboratories, managers and analysts are quite happy when they can find ways to reduce their activities. A common strategy is to bundle quality management activities into contracts when purchasing new analytical systems. For example, when a laboratory buys a new instrument, many managers negotiate to have the manufacturer not only to install the system, but also perform the method validation studies needed to satisfy CLIA validation requirements, provide the QC instructions, control materials, method manual descriptions, and in-service training. Manufacturers provide these services to satisfy the "wants" of their laboratory customers.

In effect, laboratories are out-sourcing many quality management activities by purchasing complete systems from a manufacturer. That practice is clearly dangerous. The responsibility for the quality of the test results can never be out-sourced, even if some of the activities are performed by others. Quality can be guaranteed only when the laboratory accepts its responsibility and properly manages its own testing processes!

Compliance is not enough!

"Compliance" has become the management focus as we enter this new millennium. Professional organizations tout compliance training programs. Scientific meetings feature compliance workshops. Laboratories are required to develop compliance policies and programs and may even have compliance officers. Avoiding fraud and staying out of jail are getting more management time and attention than quality. Does anyone think this inspires the laboratory staff to maintain and improve quality?

Compliance management got its start from CLIA. It wasn't mandated by the CLIA regulations, but compliance became the main response to the regulations. It is evident that management regards the minimums stated in regulations as all that need to be done, therefore these regulatory minimums have become laboratory practice maximums. For example, because the regulations say it's necessary to run two controls, bottom-line managers never run *more* than two. Some people seem to accept that the government has become very smart in the area of quality control, even though they don't think the government has a clue about anything else.

The CLIA rules might actually provide good guidance for quality management if the regulations were ever completely implemented. It would be nice to have the "final-final" CLIA document published. It would be even better if the FDA were to implement the process for clearance of manufacturers' QC instructions, as called for in the original regulations. The continual postponement of these regulations for validation of manufacturers' QC is a serious problem and compromises the overall effectiveness of CLIA.

[**Note:** The latest word at the time of printing is that the "final-final" CLIA regulations will be published in the Federal Register before the end of the year 2000. Judith Yost, Director of the Division of Laboratories and Acute Care Services at the Health Care Financing Agency (HCFA), stated *there is no provision for FDA clearance of manufacturers' QC instructions in the final regulations.* This leaves laboratories with the responsibility of providing the QC that is necessary to assure the quality of test results!]

Statistical QC can't be eliminated!

Statistical QC has been a fundamental quality management technique in industry since the 1930s and in laboratories since the 1960s because it provides an independent way of monitoring the quality of a production process. In spite of this, there have been efforts to do away with statistical QC for laboratory testing. These efforts have been initially pushed by industry to expand point-of-care markets, even though statistical QC still provides the most efficient technique for monitoring the many steps in a testing process, as well as providing a quantitative measure of operator proficiency [3]. Expanded quality management systems should rely on statistical QC, rather than attempting to eliminate it.

Minimum personnel standards and skills are not sufficient!

CLIA's minimum requirements for personnel have now been achieved in many laboratories. Again, because of the compliance mentality, the net result has been a lower level of education for laboratory analysts, a serious reduction in training programs for clinical laboratory scientists, and, of course, some reduction in personnel costs, which justifies everything for bottom-line managers.

Even some laboratory professionals have capitulated to this trend of "dumbing down" laboratory medicine. One paper published in 1997 [4] concluded that "QC is costly, and laboratorians frequently do not follow established QC practices, in part, because they are complex. To improve compliance, we believe QC practices must be simplified." In short, if the job is too complex for lower skilled people, the solution is to simplify the job. (Let's keep this little secret to ourselves – I don't want my plumber taking over for my surgeon!)

Help is available from the Internet

Laboratories that want to upgrade their skills in analytical quality management can take advantage of Internet training materials. Our course in *Basic Method Validation* provides a good starting point for understanding analytical performance. Our course in *Basic QC Practices* provides the fundamentals of statistical QC for laboratory application. *Basic Planning for Quality* builds on these fundamentals and addresses the management issues of what quality is needed and how to assure that quality is achieved in routine operation. Important elements of this course include:

The why of quality planning. A review of principles of Total Quality Management and existing regulatory, accreditation, and practice guidelines provide the background for understanding why quality planning is an essential part of laboratory quality management.

The what of quality planning. A step-by-step process provides a quantitative way for setting method performance specifications and selecting control rules and numbers of control measurements on the basis of the quality required for a test and the imprecision and inaccuracy observed for a method.

The how of quality planning. Quality-planning tools, such as the chart of operating specifications, provide an easy way to perform quality planning.

The when of quality planning. Anytime, with the quick and effective quality-planning process and tools provided here.

The who of quality planning. That's you! You have a professional responsibility for the quality of your work. Our objective here is to help you do your job better and manage quality in an appropriate way.

Independent analytical quality management still depends on manufacturers

Laboratories are dependent on manufacturers to provide the test systems needed in today's laboratories. There is a shared responsibility to deliver the test results that are needed for patient care. An important part of the laboratory's responsibility is to assure the quality of the final test results before they are released and reported. Manufacturers can help the laboratory carry out its responsibility by supplying QC materials and decision-support software that will allow the laboratory to easily implement and efficiently operate the appropriate QC procedures. However, the laboratory is still responsible to select and implement testing processes and QC procedures that will assure the quality needed for the patients it serves.

References

1. NCCLS C24-A2. Statistical Quality Control for Quantitative Measurements: Principles and Definitions; Approved Guideline - Second Edition. National Committee for Clinical Laboratory Standards, Wayne PA, February 1999.

2. Westgard JO. Myths of Quality. Lesson 1 in *Basic Method Validation.* Westgard QC, Madison, WI 1999, pp. 3-8.

3. Westgard JO. Taking care of point-of-care QC. Clin Lab News, August 1997.

4. Howanitz PJ, Tetrault GA, Steindel SJ. Clinical laboratory quality control: a costly process now out of control. Clin Chim Acta 1997;260:163-174.

Online References:

A Wake-up Call for Analytical Quality Management
http://www.westgard.com/qpbook/lesson49.htm

Myths of quality
http://www.westgard.com/essay2.htm

Remember to use the username and password provided at the beginning of this book to access the online materials.

Self-Assessment Questions:

- ❍ What is a consent decree?
- ❍ What are Quality System Regulations?
- ❍ What laboratory quality management activities are often bundled into the purchase of new methods and systems?
- ❍ How do you maintain an independent quality management system when you have to buy everything from a manufacturer?

2: Why is Quality Planning important?

In *Assuring Quality through Total Quality Management*, Dr. Westgard reviews Total Quality Management (TQM) and identifies the major components needed to manage the analytical quality of laboratory testing processes. Quality planning is identified as a critical component or activity in managing quality in the laboratory.

Objectives:

- ❍ Identify the components of a TQM process.
- ❍ Compare the TQM process to the way quality is managed in your laboratory.
- ❍ Assess your opportunity to improve quality management through implementation of a quality-planning process.

Chapter materials:

- ❍ **Assuring Quality through Total Quality Management**

Things to do:

- ❍ Study the chapter.
- ❍ Review the quality plan for your laboratory.
- ❍ Find out the quality requirement for a cholesterol test in your laboratory.

Those of you who are parents will understand this problem all too well. And if you have more than one child, the experience with the first one doesn't really allow you to avoid the problem with the next. There is a problem with the process and we, as parents, didn't plan that process – we're just line workers who have to live with the problem. The process was designed and planned by upper management, and God knows, it needs to be re-planned.

Hagar the Horrible is reprinted here with special permission of King Features Syndicate.

Assuring Quality through Total Quality Management

Quality assurance in healthcare is a modern **MYTH** – a **M**ighty **Y**earning (by the public), **T**estimony (by healthcare providers), and **H**ope (by all of us) that things will work okay if and when we need medical care. Current quality assurance practices mainly emphasize the assessment or measurement of quality, assuming (maybe hoping is a better word) that this interest and attention will work some magic to make quality happen. Unforunately, quality doesn't just happen! Production processes have to be carefully planned, monitored, and managed to assure quality is achieved.

Even the analytical quality of laboratory tests is being assumed today, rather than assured [1]. Laboratories assume that manufacturers have solved all the problems with their testing processes. Programs in quality control and quality assurance are being reduced to the minimums needed to comply with regulatory and accreditation guidelines. Today the trend is towards new management practices, such as utilization control, outcome assessment, and compliance. But have we really achieved the analytical quality that is needed? Do we even know *what* quality is needed for each of the tests we perform? If we haven't defined the quality that is needed, how can we assure that quality is being achieved by our testing processes?

Here's an assessment of what needs to be done if laboratories are to guarantee the quality of the test results they produce.

Adopt a TQM framework for quality management

Total Quality Management, or TQM, has been implemented in many healthcare organizations during the last decade. The teachings of industrial quality gurus, such as Deming and Juran, have established new principles and processes for managing quality. Personally, I have found that Deming provides the principles for what needs to be done and that Juran describes the methodologies or processes for getting it done.

Juran's quality trilogy is particularly important because it identifies quality-planning as an integral component of TQM [2]. We have shown how quality planning can be integrated with other quality management functions using the model shown in the accompanying figure [3]. This TQM framework involves quality laboratory processes, quality control, quality assessment, quality improvement, quality planning, and quality goals.

- **Quality Laboratory Processes (QLP)** refers to the policies, procedures, personnel standards, and physical resources that determine how work gets done in the laboratory. Laboratory method manuals describe the standard operating processes for producing test results.
- **Quality Control (QC)** refers to procedures for monitoring the work processes, detecting problems, and making corrections prior to delivery of products or services. Statistical process control, or statistical quality control, is the major procedure for monitoring the analytical performance of laboratory methods.
- **Quality Assessment (QA)** refers to the broader monitoring of other dimensions or characteristics of quality. Quality involves the totality of features and characteristics that bear on the achievement and satisfaction of customer needs. Characteristics such as turnaround time, patient preparation, specimen acquisition, etc., are monitored through QA activities. Proficiency testing provides an external or outside measure of analytical performance.

- **Quality Improvement (QI)** is aimed at determining the causes or sources of problems identified by QC and QA. The causes of some problems can be determined by individual analysts. Other problems may require a team of people and a team problem-solving process and team problem-solving tools (such as the flowchart, Pareto diagram, Ishikawa cause and effect diagram, force field analysis, etc) [4].

- **Quality Planning (QP)** is concerned with establishing and validating processes that meet customer needs. The selection and evaluation of new methods and instruments fits here, as well as selection and design of QC procedures.

- **Quality Goals** represent the requirements that must be achieved to satisfy the needs of customers. For analytical quality, the requirement is to provide test results that are correct within stated limits.

As shown in the figure, these components work together to provide a quality management process that functions like a feedback loop. QLP defines the best way to get the work done. QC and QA measure how well the work is getting done. When problems are detected, QI determines the root causes, which can then be eliminated through QP, in this case actually re-planning the testing processes and implementing new and better ways of doing the work (which means making changes in QLP).

This quality management framework provides a process focus for management, in contrast to the typical control structure that is usually used to organize management activities. Through this framework, continuous improvement is built into the management process by cycling through the different quality functions. Customer focus is achieved by centering the framework on quality goals, customer requirements, and quality plans. It is important to recognize that quality assurance is the outcome of this whole quality management process, rather than being a component in the process.

Another important insight is that quality planning is a *prerequisite* to quality assurance! Unfortunately, quality planning is lacking in many laboratories. The highest priority for improving laboratory quality management is to formalize a mechanism for designing or building quality into the testing processes. The benefits will be the ability to provide objective specifications for the precision and accuracy needed for analytical methods and the quality control needed to monitor the performance of those methods.

Learn the principles of quality planning from industry

Industry has learned that to guarantee quality it is necessary to specify what performance is required and how to know if that performance is achieved. An operational definition is needed to tell people what to do and how to know if they're doing it right. For example, "answer the telephone within three rings" tells a person what to do and how to know if they're achieving the desired performance.

The important message here is that bench-level specifications are needed to assure the quality of routine operations. For analytical quality, these operating specifications must describe the imprecision and inaccuracy that are allowable for the method and the control rules and number of control measurements that are necessary for routine QC. The laboratory cannot guarantee the quality of its product unless these operating specifications are achieved.

To establish operating specifications, industry has developed a technique called Quality Function Deployment (or QFD). This technique is used to translate the voice of the customer into the performance characteristics of the process AND a procedure for knowing if the process is working okay. For a laboratory test, the necessary steps include listening to the voice of the customer to understand how the test is used and the changes that are medically important, interpreting these customer needs to define quality requirements, such as the allowable total error for analytical quality or the clinical decision interval for clinical quality, and then translating these quality requirements into the operating specifications for the method, i.e., the imprecision and inaccuracy that are allowable and the QC that is necessary.

A simple example will help illustrate the key importance of the interpretation and translation steps. Anyone working in a laboratory has experienced the situation where a physician has ordered a stat or emergency test, then calls for the answer before the specimen has arrived in the laboratory. The physician is unhappy because the test result is not available and tells you to get your act together and do the test faster. Now, if you listen to the customer and do the test faster, you know that still won't satisfy the customer's needs. Doing the test faster doesn't solve the problem, which most likely is due to the acquisition of the specimen and transporting it to the laboratory. Listening to the voice of the customer doesn't mean doing what the customer says. Interpretation and translation are required to understand the problem and fix the process.

Utilize available quality-planning tools and technology

It is easy to see how this planning approach can be used to achieve the desired turnaround time for a laboratory test. A quality requirement can be defined in the form of an allowable turnaround time on the basis of discussions with the users. The steps in the process can be identified from the point of ordering the test, acquiring, transporting, and processing the specimen, analyzing

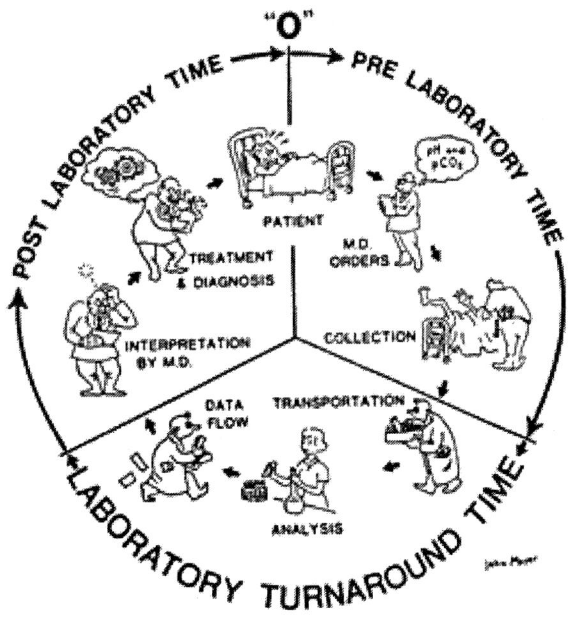

Cartoon by John Meyer, MD.

a sample, reporting the result, and receiving the result. Portions of the allowable turnaround time can then be allocated to different steps in the process, establishing specifications for each of the steps, and allowing those steps to be monitored to be sure the desired performance can be achieved.

For analytical quality, the translation is more difficult. Quality-planning models are used to convert quality requirements into specifications for the imprecision and inaccuracy that are allowable and the QC that is necessary. These models are developed by identifying the various factors or steps in the process, allocating or budgeting a portion of the quality requirement to that factor or step, building in a QC check to assure the desired quality or performance is achieved for that factor or step, then balancing the budget for the whole process and monitoring (or controlling) that budget during routine operation [5].

The analytical factors that must be considered include the imprecision and inaccuracy of the method and the sensitivity of the QC procedure. Pre-analytical factors may include within-subject biological variation, sampling variation, and specimen stability. Portions of the allowable variation or allowable error for a test need to be allocated to these different factors, as well as allocating a margin of safety to quality control the process [3,5]. For an analytical quality requirement in the form of an allowable total error, the allocations consider only analytical factors – the imprecision, inaccuracy, and QC. For a clinical decision interval requirement, a more complicated model is needed to handle both preanalytical and analytical factors.

The application of these models can be simplified by providing a graphical presentation, e.g, a chart of operating specifications (or OPSpecs chart) can be prepared for a stated quality requirement to show the inaccuracy that is allowable versus the imprecision that is allowable for different control rules and numbers of control measurements.

Implement an efficient process

We need to make quality planning quick and easy. The time to be saved is often the time of the managers, supervisors, and lead scientists who have the responsibilities for selecting laboratory methods and QC procedures. The essential process, tools, and technology will be described in later chapters, and here's a quick preview of what's to come:

- Guidelines from regulatory, accreditation, and consensus standards organizations provide a starting point for developing a quality-planning process.
- A practical quality-planning process depends on utilizing available tools and technology. Step-by-step procedures are described that can be used both to select analytical methods (by establishing purchase specifications for imprecision and bias) and to select QC procedures, i.e., specific control rules and the number of control measurements needed.
- The quality required for a test is the first step in the quality-planning process. Two types of quality requirements are practical today – allowable total error and clinical decision intervals – because quality-planning models are available to derive operating specifications for both of these types of requirements.
- A graphic tool – the OPSpecs chart – is the best and most efficient way to present operating specifications. The tool is easy to use, even though the theory is complicated. For a stated quality requirement, the OPSpecs chart provides a visual display of the imprecision and inaccuracy that are allowable for a method and the control rules and N that are needed for a QC procedure.
- A computer program – QC Validator – is available to prepare OPSpecs charts for both analytical and clinical quality requirements and to document the quality-planning process. Computer support is essential when using the clinical decision interval type of quality requirement.

- Normalized OPSpecs charts can be used to implement a manual quality-planning process that works with analytical quality requirements, such as the allowable total errors specified by CLIA proficiency testing criteria for acceptable performance. A worksheet and all the necessary charts are provided in this book.
- Internet resources are available to support the quality-planning process, including updates on quality requirements, interactive training tools, and detailed quality-planning applications.

Accept responsibility for quality

The physician can give us information about how the test is used and interpreted. This information will most likely describe the change in a test result that would cause a change in the diagnosis, treatment, or management of the patient – a medically important change. We in the laboratory have to translate the medically important change into specifications for operating our testing processes, i.e., the precision and accuracy that are allowable and the QC that is necessary. We shouldn't expect the physician to understand precision, accuracy, and QC and to be able to give us those specifications directly. We have to listen, interpret, and translate – that's our job in the laboratory.

Implementation of a quality-planning process requires that laboratories build on a solid foundation of QC, QA, and TQM, rather than replacing these management practices with new practices, such as utilization review and outcome measurements. That's a real danger with trends in management practices – we may throw out some old but useful practices because we don't have the time to do both the old and the new. It's still important to improve the technical management of analytical processes to provide a solid baseline for utilization review and outcomes assessment.

References

1. Westgard JO, QA: Are laboratories assuring, assessing, or assuming the quality of clinical testing today? Proceedings of the CDC 1995 Institute on Critical Issues in Health Laboratory Practice: Frontiers in Laboratory Practice Research. CDC, Atlanta, GA, 1996, pp 179-189.

2. Westgard JO, Barry PL. Total Quality Control: Evolution of quality systems in health care laboratories. Laboratory Medicine 1989;20:377-84.

3. Westgard JO, Burnett RW, Bowers GN. Quality management science in clinical chemistry: A dynamic framework for continuous improvement. Clin Chem 1990;36:1712-16.

4. Westgard JO, Barry PL. Beyond quality assurance: Committing to quality improvement. Laboratory Medicine 1989;20:241-247.

5. Westgard JO. Error budgets for quality management: Practical tools for planning and assuring the analytical quality of laboratory testing processes. Clin Lab Manag Review 1996;10:377-403.

Online References:

Assuring Quality through Total Quality Management
http://www.westgard.com/qpbook/lesson50.htm

Remember to use the username and password provided at the beginning of this book to access the online materials.

Self-Assessment Questions:

- ❍ What are the five components in a TQM process?
- ❍ What's the TQM process centered on?
- ❍ What is the name for the industrial approach to quality planning?
- ❍ How does "listening" to the customer differ from doing what the customer says?
- ❍ What are "operating specifications"?
- ❍ How do quality goals differ from operating specifications?

3: What guidelines exist for quality planning?

Dr. Westgard provides a review of rules that bear upon quality planning as well as recently published QC practice guidelines. *Complying with Regulations, Standards and Practice Guidelines* reviews US government regulations (CLIA), accreditation guidelines (JCAHO), and consensus practice guidelines from the National Committee for Clinical Laboratory Standards (NCCLS). The NCCLS C24-A2 document provides quality-planning guidelines for selecting QC procedures that are appropriate for laboratory applications.

Objectives:

- ❍ Review the regulatory requirements for laboratory quality management and identify those rules that influence quality planning.
- ❍ Review US practice guidelines for QC and identify those aspects related to quality planning.

Chapter materials:

- ❍ **Complying with Regulations, Standards, and Practice Guidelines**

Things to do:

- ❍ Study the chapter.
- ❍ Access the CLIA regulations on the Internet.
- ❍ Access the NCCLS website to learn about the process of developing consensus standards.

HAGAR THE HORRIBLE

Quality management is a long journey of discovery! We all have good intentions, but we also need to know what to do and how to get started. This chapter provides some guidance to get going in the right direction. That first step is critical if we're going to make any headway.

Complying with Regulations, Standards, and Practice Guidelines

Implementation of a quality-planning process should be a high priority in laboratories today to assure or guarantee the quality of laboratory tests and services. Guidelines for quality planning can be found in government regulations, accreditation standards, and national practice standards. The widespread application of quality planning is recommended in the latest inspection manual from the Joint Commission for Accreditation of Healthcare Organizations (JCAHO). A focus on analytical quality, the assessment of method performance, and the selection of appropriate quality control procedures is provided by the Clinical Laboratory Improvement Amendments (CLIA-88). A general planning methodology for quality control is outlined by the National Committee for Clinical Laboratory Standards (NCCLS). Together, these guidelines provide the basis for implementing a quality-planning process in laboratories. Here's a summary of the standards, rules, and recommendations that bear on quality planning.

JCAHO Guidelines for Improving Organizational Effectiveness

Improving Organizational Performance, or IOP, is JCAHO's latest terminology and represents an evolution of their TQM philosophy and concepts. The 2000-2001 Comprehensive Accreditation Manual for Pathology and Clinical Laboratory Services [1] states that the goal of IOP is "for the laboratory to design processes well and systematically monitor, analyze, and improve its services that affect patient health outcomes." The following are identified as essential management activities:

- Designing processes;
- Monitoring performance through data collection;
- Analyzing current performance; and
- Improving and sustaining improved performance.

Review of specific standards

More guidance is provided by specific standards. In the list that follows, I have also identified how these standards fit into the Total Quality Management framework described earlier, which is composed of quality laboratory practices (QLP), quality control (QC), quality assessment (QA), quality improvement (QI), quality planning (QP), and quality goals (QG). This additional information helps assess the relationship between IOP and TQM.

PI.1 The leaders establish a planned, systematic, organization-wide approach to process design and performance measurement, analysis, and improvement. [QP to establish QLP]

PI.1.1 The activities are planned in a collaborative and interdisciplinary manner. [QP across functions or departments to establish QLP]

PI.1.2 New or modified processes are designed well. [QP or re-planning to establish QLP]

PI.2.1 Performance expectations are established for new and modified processes. [QG or requirements for QLP]

PI.2.2 The performance of new and modified processes is measured. [QA of QLP]

PI.3 Data are collected to monitor the stability of existing processes, identify opportunities for improvement, identify changes that will lead to improvement, and sustain improvement. [QC and QA]

PI.3.1 The organization collects data to monitor its performance. [QA]

PI.3.1.1 The organization collects data to monitor the performance of processes that involve risks or may result in sentinel events. [QA]

PI.3.1.2 The organization collects data to monitor performance in areas targeted for further study. [QA]

PI.3.1.3 The organization collects data to monitor improvements in performance. [QA]

PI.4 Data are systematically aggregated and analyzed on an ongoing basis. [QA]

PI.4.1 Appropriate statistical techniques are used to analyze and display data. [QA and QI]

PI.4.2 The organization compares its performance over time and with other sources of information. [QA and QI]

PI.4.3 Undesirable patterns or trends in performance and sentinel events are intensively analyzed. [QA and QI]

PI.4.4 The organization identifies changes that will lead to improved performance and reduce the risk of sentinel events. [QI and QP or re-planning]

PI.5 Improved performance is achieved and sustained. [QP, QLP, QC, QA, QI]

IOP vs TQM

From the review of these standards and comparison to our TQM framework, the relationship between IOP and TQM is described in the accompanying figure, where the emphasis on each component is shown by the darkness of each Q. Quality Planning is strongly recommended by the JCAHO standards on the "design" of processes. Quality Laboratory Processes are pervasive throughout the standards and JCAHO's frequent reference to "processes." Quality Control and Quality Assessment provide the measure and monitor aspects that are mentioned in a large number of the standards. Quality

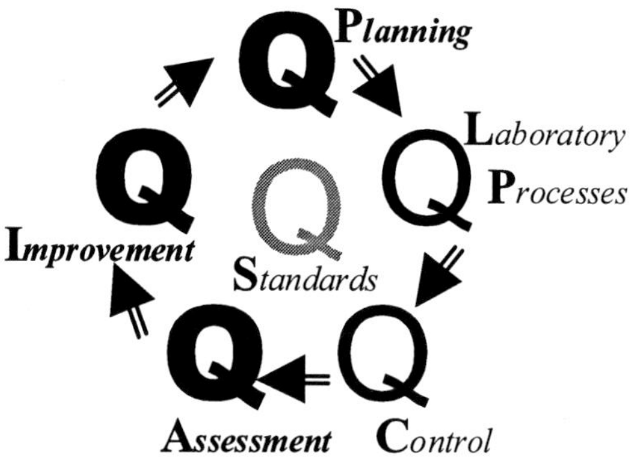

Improvement is the focus of the whole IOP approach and is specifically mentioned in several standards. Quality goals are found in the standard that recommends establishing performance expectations for new and modified processes.

In summary, JCAHO provides a broad recommendation for quality planning that applies to all laboratory processes. Given that the fundamental laboratory process is to perform tests, carefully planned testing processes should be the heart of quality laboratory processes. Performing tests is the main event in the laboratory. Other activities are important in support of testing and patient services, but none of them will matter if the laboratory can't produce correct test results.

CLIA Rules and Regulations

The strongest guidelines for analytical quality management are found in the CLIA-88 rules and regulations [2]. CLIA provides a broad focus on quality management of the "total testing process", which include the pre-analytical, analytical, and post-analytical phases. Rules for the analytical phase provide very detailed guidelines for method validation and quality control, i.e., for establishing valid testing processes and assuring the quality of the test results on an ongoing basis. CLIA also establishes specific criteria for acceptable performance in proficiency testing surveys, thereby defining the minimum quality standards that must be achieved by US laboratories.

Review of specific rules

Subpart K of the CLIA rules begins with a statement that "the laboratory must establish and follow written QC procedures for monitoring and evaluating the quality of the analytical testing process of each method to assure the accuracy and reliability of patient test results and reports." This is followed by detailed rules that can be ascribed to different components in our TQM framework, as follows:

- **Quality Goals** are defined by the proficiency testing criteria for acceptable performance which are given for immunology

[493.927], routine chemistry [493.931], endocrinology [493.933], toxicology [493.937], and hematology [493.941].

- **Quality Laboratory Processes** are defined through the facilities [493.1204], test methods, equipment, instrumentation, reagents, materials, and supplies [493.1205], and the procedure manual [493.1211], as well as detailed personnel standards [Subpart M].
- **Quality Control** is described by control procedures [493.1218], remedial actions [493.1219], and quality control records [493.1221].
- **Quality Assessment** requires the establishment and verification of method performance specifications [493.1213], calibration verification procedures [493.1217], and participation in external proficiency testing [Subpart H].
- **Quality Improvement** is not mentioned.
- **Quality Planning** for analytical methods is implied through the requirement for verification of QC.

> "For each method that is developed in-house, is a modification of the manufacturer's test procedure, or is a method that has not been cleared by FDA as meeting the CLIA requirements for general quality control, the laboratory must evaluate the instrument and reagent stability and operator variance in determining the number, type, and frequency of testing calibration or control materials and establish criteria for acceptability used to monitor test performance during a run of patient specimen(s)." [page 7166, 493.1218(b)]

Given that <u>no</u> methods have been cleared by FDA as meeting the CLIA requirements for general quality control, all QC procedures need to be carefully planned or designed to account for the variability observed for the instrument, reagents, and operators in the laboratory.

CLIA rules vs TQM

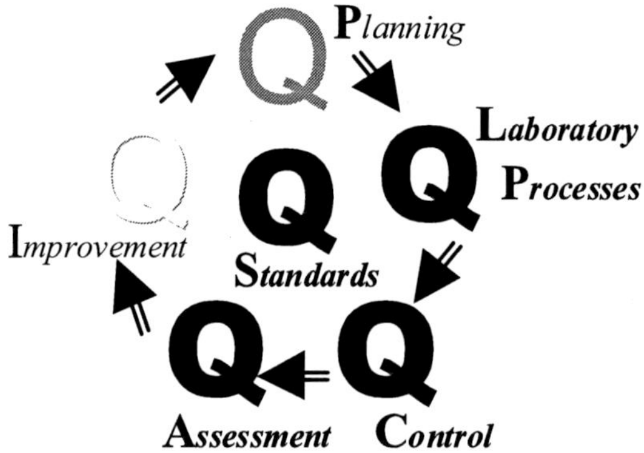

The accompanying figure summarizes the relationship of the CLIA rules to the TQM framework. CLIA provides a strong emphasis on Quality Laboratory Processes, particularly analytical testing processes, through the detailed rules that govern facilities, equipment and materials, procedure manual, and personnel. The rules for Quality Control and Quality Assessment are also much more detailed, as applied to analytical methods. There is no mention of Quality Improvement, but Quality Planning for analytical processes is implied in the rules for establishing QC procedures. Specific Quality Goals are defined for approximately 80 different tests that include some from immunology, hematology, coagulation, chemistry, endocrinology, and toxicology.

NCCLS QC Practice Guideline

Given that JCAHO provides a strong recommendation for Quality Planning and that CLIA specifies Quality Goals and requires that QC procedures account for the laboratory's own variability, laboratories must carefully plan their analytical testing processes. NCCLS provides the methodology for accomplishing this in its 1999 QC practice guideline [3] which describes a step-by-step process for selecting a statistical QC procedures on the basis of the quality required by a test and the performance observed for a method.

Review of NCCLS QC planning methodology

The NCCLS methodology appears in section 5 of the C24-A2 document. The steps recommended are shown in the figure and explained below:

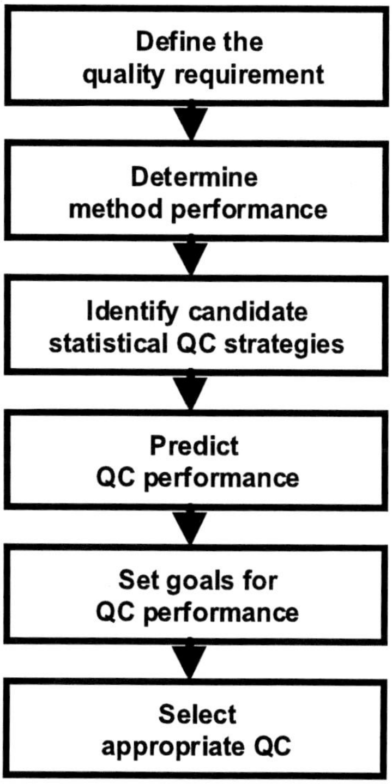

1. **Define the quality requirement.** A quality requirement may be defined in terms of an allowable total analytical error, such as often provided by proficiency testing criteria for acceptable performance. The allowable analytical error is the magnitude of analytical error that, if exceeded, would cause a test result to be of unacceptable quality [4]. It encompasses both random and systematic errors, i.e., both method imprecision and bias. There are also recommendations for medically important changes in test results that similarly include both method imprecision and bias, as well as subject biologic variation [5]. Biologic variation provides another basis for defining the allowable imprecision and allowable bias for a test [6]. Clinical treatment models can also be a source of information about the analytical quality required to assure that test results are medically useful [7].

2. **Determine method performance.** The performance characteristics of an analytical process that are critical for the proper planning of QC procedures are imprecision and bias. Estimates of these parameters should represent the stable performance of an analytical process. In addition to imprecision and bias, it would be useful to have information about unstable performance, such as the expected type, magnitude, and frequency of analytical errors, but this information is not generally available.

3. **Identify candidate statistical QC strategies.** A quality control strategy is defined by the control materials used, the number of control samples analyzed, the location of these

control samples in an analytical run, the quality control rules applied to the control sample measurements, and the time when the quality control rules are evaluated. The appropriateness of the QC strategy depends on the quality required, as well as the expected instability of the analytical method (e.g., type, magnitude, and frequency of errors). Several QC strategies may be defined and evaluated.

4. **Predict QC performance.** The performance of a quality control strategy can be predicted from probability calculations or from computer simulation studies. The most direct indicator of the performance of a quality control procedure is the expected number of unacceptable patient test results that are produced (or reported) when an out-of-control error condition exists [8]. This will depend on the type and magnitude of the out-of-control error condition, when the error condition occurs and how long it lasts, which in turn depends on how frequently quality control testing occurs and the probability that the quality control rules detect the error condition. These predictions generally assume the shape of the error distribution is gaussian, which may not account for some periodic and irregular effects observed with real laboratory systems, therefore the complexity of the prediction model needs to match the complexity of the potential error sources of the method and system.

5. **Set goals for QC performance.** Quality control performance goals set desirable targets for quality control performance. The goal will depend on the chosen quality control performance measure. Thus, one goal could be specified as a maximum allowable number of unacceptable results due to an out-of-control error condition, or a maximum allowable probability or reporting unacceptable results (maximum defect rate), or a minimum acceptable probability of detecting an out-of-control error condition. Another goal could specify a maximum allowable probability of false rejections.

6. **Select appropriate QC.** When more than one quality control strategy meets the quality control performance goals, other characteristics such as cost and ease of implementation can

be used to select the best approach. Practical approaches for selecting appropriate QC procedures have been described based on power function graphs, critical-error graphs, and charts of operating specifications [9]. Illustrative applications of QC planning are available in the literature to provide guidance in selecting appropriate QC strategies [10, 11].

Other guidelines

The College of American Pathologists (CAP) also provides detailed guidelines that focus on laboratory testing processes. CAP has "deemed status," meaning the CAP guidelines are at least as stringent as the CLIA rules. Likewise, the Commission of Office Laboratory Accreditation (COLA) has deemed status and its guidelines must comply with the CLIA rules. Therefore, the CLIA rules, JCAHO IOP standards, and NCCLS QC planning process provide a comprehensive synthesis of guidelines for managing quality in healthcare laboratories. These guidelines are also seen to be consistent with the principles from TQM.

References

1. 2000-2001 Comprehensive Accreditation Manual for Pathology and Clinical Laboratory Services. Joint Commission on Accreditation of Healthcare Organizations, Oakbrook Terrace, IL, 1999.

2. U.S. Department of Health and Human Services. Medicare, Medicaid and CLIA programs; Regulations implementing the Clinical Laboratory Improvement Amendments of 1988 (CLIA). Final rule. Fed Regist 1992;57:7002-186.

3. C24-A2. Statistical Quality Control for Quantitative Measurements: Principles and Definitions; Approved Guideline - Second Edition. National Committee for Clinical Laboratory Standards, Wayne, PA, 1999.

4. Burnett RW, Westgard JO. Selection of measurement and control procedures to satisfy HCFA requirements and provide cost-effective operation. Arch Pathol Lab Med 1992;116:777-782.

5. Skendzel LP, Barnett RN, Platt R. Medically useful criteria for analytical performance of laboratory tests. Am J Clin Pathol 1985;83:200-205.

6. Fraser CG, Hyltoft Petersen P, Ricos C, Haeckel R. Proposed quality specifications for the imprecision and inaccuracy of analytical systems for clinical chemistry. Eur J Clin Chem Clin Biochem 1992;30:311-317.

7. Hyltoft Petersen P, deVerdier C-H, Groth T, Aronsson T. Clinically based quality goals; a NORDKEM project. Eur J Haematol. 1990;45(Suppl 53):6-8.

8. Parvin CA, Gronowski AM. Effect of analytical run length on quality-control (QC) performance and the QC planning process. Clin Chem 1997;43:2149-2154.

9. Westgard JO. Error budgets for quality management: Practical tools for planning and assuring the analytical quality of laboratory testing processes. Clin Lab Manag Review 1996;10:377-403.

10. Koch DD, Oryall JJ, Quam EF, Feldbruegge DH, Dowd DE, Barry PL, Westgard JO. Selection of medically useful QC procedures for individual tests on a multi-test analytical system. Clin Chem 1990;36:230-233.

11. Mugan K, Carlson IH, Westgard JO. Planning QC procedures for immunoassays. J Clin Immunoassay 1994;17:216-222.

Online References:

Complying with Regulations, Standards, & Practice Guidelines
http://www.westgard.com/qpbook/lesson51.htm

Remember to use the username and password provided at the beginning of this book to access the online materials.

Self-Assessment Questions:

- Is quality planning explicit or implicit in the CLIA regulations?
- What specific CLIA rules relate to quality planning?
- What does CLIA mean by “clearance of QC instructions”?
- What is the NCCLS?
- How is an NCCLS standard developed?
- What are the steps recommended by NCCLS for planning a QC procedure?

4: How is quality planning performed?

The NCCLS guidelines for quality planning can be combined with available quality-planning tools to devise a step-by-step planning process that is practical in any laboratory.

Objectives:

- ❍ Review the possible applications for quality planning in laboratories, industry, and government.
- ❍ Identify five approaches for quality planning.
- ❍ Determine which approaches are available to your laboratory.
- ❍ Assess which approach will be most useful for implementing quality planning in your laboratory.

Chapter materials:

- ❍ **Devising a Practical Process**

Things to do:

- ❍ Study the chapter.
- ❍ Find out which quality-planning tools and technology are available in your laboratory.

Hagar the Horrible

We would all like to have a simple solution for achieving quality. Maybe a practical solution – something that is doable – is a more realistic goal. That's our goal in this chapter: to show you a quality-planning process that you can apply in your own work, regardless of whether you are a laboratorian, manufacturer, regulator, accreditor, or inspector.

Devising a Practical Process

The importance of implementing a quality-planning process is evident from the general principles of Total Quality Management (TQM) as embodied in the accreditation requirements of JCAHO's IOP standards [1]. CLIA provides a focus on laboratory testing processes and provides specific rules for validating the performance of methods and planning QC procedures [2]. NCCLS addresses the issue of how to perform quality-planning for QC procedures in general terms [3]. However, none of these describe a detailed process that can be easily implemented. Our objective in this chapter is to devise a step-by-step process that can be supported by available tools or technology.

Review your intended applications

An understanding of your own uses of a quality-planning process is important, particularly for assessing the practicality of different tools and technology. If you are a laboratory quality coordinator, your first interest may be in satisfying regulatory and accreditation guidelines for planning your testing processes. A rigorous and well-documented process will be important. If you are a manufacturer, your interest may be in establishing performance specifications for the precision and accuracy of new methods. If you are a laboratory inspector or a technical field specialist for a manufacturer, you may be visiting different laboratories and will need a "portable" process that you can take with you – most likely installed on your computer.

Laboratory applications. Selecting control rules and numbers of control measurements is, of course, an important application in a service laboratory. In addition, the performance needed by the method can also be determined if the QC procedures are given, which should be useful in establishing purchase specifications for methods, instruments, and systems. QC recommendations from manufacturers and QC guidelines given in the literature can be evaluated to be sure they are adequate for the quality required for the test and the analytical performance claimed for the method. It is also possible to compare allowable total errors, clinical decision intervals, and biologic goals to determine which is most demanding and should take priority in managing a testing process.

Manufacturers' applications. The design of new methods and systems should be greatly aided by a quantitative approach for setting performance specifications for imprecision and inaccuracy. QC recommendations can objectively developed and validated based on regulatory quality requirements, the design specifications for imprecision and inaccuracy, and the common QC practices in the marketplace. Customers can be supported and assisted in the proper management of analytical systems by having a better understanding of the relationships between the quality required for a test, the imprecision and inaccuracy expected from a method, and the QC procedures to be implemented.

Regulatory and accreditation applications. It is interesting that there is little documentation of the source and origin of proficiency testing (PT) criteria, such as those allowable total errors specified by CLIA. Regulatory agencies and PT providers should evaluate the practicality of proposed PT criteria by comparison with clinical decision intervals, taking into account the common QC practices and expected method performance. Manufacturers' QC product labeling should be reviewed to assess whether those QC instructions are valid for the intended users. Laboratory QC practices should be reviewed to assess whether they are valid to assure the quality needed for the patient populations and clinical applications of a healthcare organization. Laboratorians and manufacturers should be educated and supported to provide optimal management of the analytical quality of their tests and systems.

Recognize two categories of applications

The main applications involve either the (a) selection of the method of analysis or establishment of performance specifications for imprecision and inaccuracy, or (b) the selection of a QC procedure for a method in routine service. In both cases, the first step will be to define the quality requirement for the diagnostic test of interest. Then, as shown in the accompanying figure, there are two variations of the planning process, depending on whether the purpose is to select the method of analysis or to select a QC procedure:

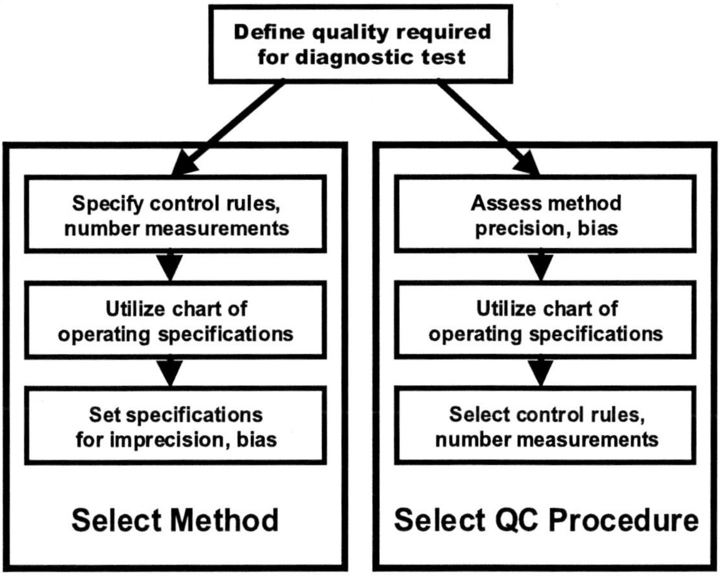

- **To select a method of analysis or set performance specifications for a method**, the quality-planning process involves specifying the QC procedure (statistical control rules, number of control measurements or N) that will be employed and then setting the developmental or purchase specifications for the imprecision and inaccuracy of the method.

- **To select a QC procedure for a method**, the process involves assessing method performance (imprecision and inaccuracy) and then selecting the statistical control rules and number of control measurements to be used.

The key step in both applications is the use of an appropriate quality-planning tool that will translate the defined quality requirement into specifications for the imprecision and inaccuracy that are allowable and the QC that is necessary.

Identify a practical quality-planning tool

A chart of operating specifications (or OPSpecs chart) is the most practical tool because it provides all of the necessary information on a single graph [4]. It is easy to use and easy to prepare using a computer program, but initially it can be difficult to understand. An analytical quality-planning model is available to translate an allowable total error requirement into the imprecision and inaccuracy that are allowable and the QC that is necessary [5]. A clinical model is available that accounts for pre-analytical factors, such as within-subject biologic variation, as well as the analytical factors – imprecision, inaccuracy, and QC [6]. The theory is in the literature [5,6]; our interest here is to demonstrate how to use the OPSpecs chart for quality-planning applications.

An OPSpecs chart is like a map!

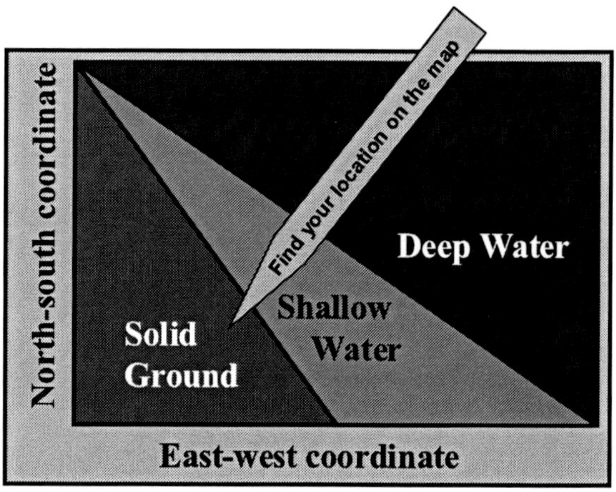

You use it to find where you are and to provide directions to get where you want to go. First you need to get the right map, which means defining the city, county, or state of interest. This is the same as defining a quality requirement for a test. There are different maps for different quality requirements, but all the maps are similar in form. As illustrated in the accompanying figure, the map identifies areas of deep water, shallow water, and solid ground. From a quality-planning point of view, the objective is to be on solid ground rather than ending up "in the drink." Given the correct map, you can find your location by knowing the coordinates on the x-axis and the y-axis, or you can look up the coordinates of where you want to be.

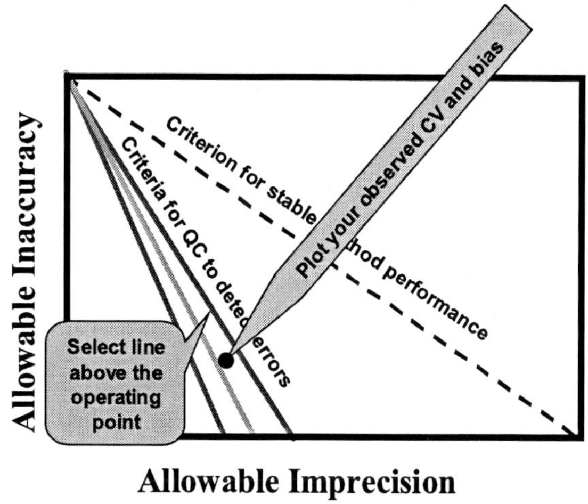

An actual OPSpecs chart will give the y-coordinate as the allowable inaccuracy (bias) and the x-coordinate as the allowable imprecision (CV), as illustrated here. The area of "deep water" is defined by a dashed line that represents a criterion for stable method performance, most commonly a total error criterion composed of the bias (method inaccuracy) plus two standard deviations (method imprecision). This is a hazardous area and must be avoided if you want to assure the quality required for a test. The solid ground is delineated by a QC procedure, i.e., the limits of bias and imprecision that are allowable for a specific control rule or combination of rules and a given number of control measurements (N). Several lines may be provided corresponding to several different QC procedures. In the figure here, three different QC procedures are depicted.

To select an appropriate QC procedure, find the location that corresponds to the imprecision and inaccuracy observed for your method. This is the "operating point" of the method in your laboratory. Then look to see if you're on solid ground for any of the candidate QC procedures. In this example, only the QC procedure corresponding to the top line could be used to assure the quality of your test results. All that remains is to look up the control rules and N that correspond to the top line (usually given by a "key" to the lines).

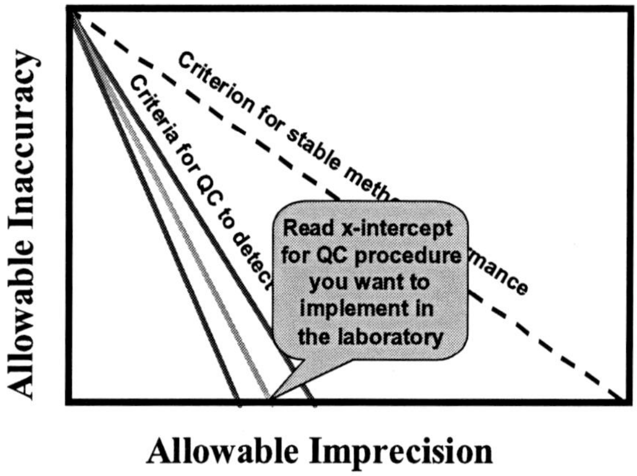

The next figure shows how an OPSpecs chart can be used to establish performance specifications for the imprecision and inaccuracy of a method. In this application, you select the QC procedure to be used in routine operation and then determine the imprecision and inaccuracy that are allowable. For example, if you pick the middle line illustrated here, then the x-intercept of that line will specify the maximum imprecision that would be allowable if bias were zero. Note that the specifications for allowable imprecision and inaccuracy are interdependent. Any allowable bias above zero will reduce the imprecision that is allowable.

Adapt the NCCLS QC planning process

Now that the general approach has been outlined and the application of the OPSpecs chart has been illustrated, we need to develop a more detailed step-by-step process. Given that the NCCLS guidelines for planning QC procedures are the most well developed, they provide a good starting point for devising a practical planning process. Note that the NCCLS term "statistical QC strategy" is replaced here with the term "QC procedure" to avoid confusion with "Total QC strategy," a term used to describe a quality system that may include non-statistical components (such as instrument function checks, patient data QC, instrument maintenance, etc). The second important point is that the NCCLS guidelines do not provide any "specifics" for how to predict (step 4) and set goals for QC performance (step 5). In devising a step-by-step planning process here, QC performance will be characterized by the probabilities of rejecting runs having different sizes of errors, therefore there are two probabilities that are of particular interest:

- **Probability of false rejection (P_{fr})**, i.e., the chance of rejecting a run when there are no errors except for the inherent random error of the method;
- **Probability for error detection (P_{ed})**, i.e., the probability or chance of rejecting a run when there is an error present in addition to the inherent random error of the method.

Therefore, to devise a practical quality-planning process, we need to add some specifics to the NCCLS process, particularly steps 3, 4, and 5.

Define a detailed step-by-step process

An eight-step quality-planning process is shown in the accompanying flowchart. Here's a description of each of the steps:

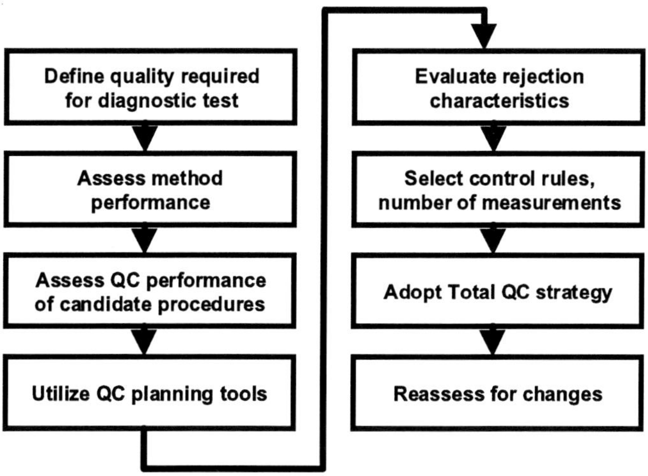

1. **Define the quality required for the test.** For practical purposes, it is easiest to get started with requirements in the form of an allowable total error, such as specified by proficiency testing or external quality assessment programs.
2. **Assess method performance in terms of imprecision and inaccuracy.** Here's where method validation experiments

are important to provide the initial estimates of imprecision (from a replication experiment) and inaccuracy or bias (from a comparison of methods experiment). Later on, the estimates of imprecision can be obtained from routine QC data and estimates of bias can be obtained from monthly peer comparison data and proficiency testing results.

3. **Assess QC performance of candidate procedures in terms of the rejection characteristics or power curves.** This information is available in the scientific literature for most of the commonly used QC procedures [7] and can be incorporated in quality-planning tools and technology to facilitate the application [8].

4. **Utilize QC planning tools.** The available tools include QC simulation programs [9], power function graphs [7], critical-error graphs [10], QC Selection Grids (QCSGs) [11], and OPSpecs charts [4]. The OPSpecs chart is recommended here because it is a quantitative tool that is easy to use and readily available.

5. **Evaluate the probabilities of rejection for the operating conditions in the laboratory.** In the quality-planning process recommended here, the probabilities for false rejection will be minimized (below 0.05 or 5%) and error detection will be maximized (0.90 or 90% and greater).

6. **Select appropriate control rules and the total number of control measurements.** A wide variety of control rules are available. The rejection characteristics of each QC procedure must be known if it is to be a candidate for implementation. Candidate QC procedures include single-rules such as 1_{2s}, $1_{2.5s}$, 1_{3s}, and $1_{3.5s}$ with Ns of 2, 3, 4, and 6; multirules such as $1_{3s}/2_{2s}/R_{4s}/4_{1s}/8_x$ with Ns of 2 and 4 and $1_{3s}/2of3_{2s}/R_{4s}/3_{1s}/6_x$ with Ns of 3 and 6.

7. **Adopt a Total QC strategy that provides an appropriate balance of statistical and non-statistical components.** This TQC strategy defines the relative amount of effort expended for statistical QC, instrument function checks, method validation tests, patient data QC, preventive

maintenance, and operator training. When HIGH error detection is obtained by statistical QC (i.e., P_{ed} of 0.90 or 90% detection of medically important errors), the HIGH TQC strategy is to depend on statistical QC and perform the minimum other QC required by regulations, accreditation, and good practice guidelines. When MODERATE error detection is obtained (P_{ed} between 0.50 and 0.90), the MODERATE TQC strategy is to balance the efforts over all the QC components. When LOW error detection is available (i.e., P_{ed} less than 0.50), the LOW TQC strategy emphasizes preventive measures because problems cannot be detected by statistical QC (see chapter 7).

8. **Reassess the control rules, N, and TQC strategy when method performance or quality requirements change.** Given a quality-planning process that is quick and easy to perform, it can be repeated whenever changes occur or when methods are periodically reviewed.

Obtain the necessary tools or technology

A laboratory's ability to do anything efficiently often depends on utilizing tools and technology to facilitate a process. Most laboratory procedures have evolved from an initial qualitative manual method (1st generation) that has then been systematized and made more quantitative with tools such as diluters and photometers, then automated through succeeding generations of technology until complete systems are available that are highly efficient and productive (such as today's 4th and 5th generation chemistry and hematology analyzers). Quality planning, likewise, must evolve from a qualitative manual method to a systematic process that utilizes standard tools to a quantitative automated process that is quick and effective.

Concerning OPSpecs charts – the quality-planning tool recommended here – different "generations" are available, as follows:

Manual from scratch: using theoretical models available in the scientific literature [5,6] with implementation via electronic spreadsheets;

Kit form: using preprinted charts in workbook form (an atlas of maps), such as the OPSpecs Manual [12], or a standard set of Normalized OPSpecs charts, which is provided in chapter 8 of this book;

Semi-automated: using online calculation tools, such as the "normalized" OPSpecs calculator, Method Planner, and QC Planner; [see http://www.westgard.com/qpbook/normcalc2.htm and http://www.westgard.com/qpbook/qptools.html]

Automated: using a PC computer program – QC Validator – that prepares OPSpecs charts for both analytical total error requirements and clinical decision interval requirements and fully automates the selection of QC procedures [13,14].

Highly automated: using a QC rule selection engine that can be embedded in QC software to support the automatic selection and design of QC procedures [see http://www.westgard.com/qcengine.html].

References

1. 2000-2001 Comprehensive Accreditation Manual for Pathology and Clinical Laboratory Services. Joint Commission on Accreditation of Healthcare Organizations, Oakbrook Terrace, IL, 1999.

2. U.S. Department of Health and Human Services. Medicare, Medicaid and CLIA programs; Regulations implementing the Clinical Laboratory Improvement Amendments of 1988 (CLIA). Final rule. Fed Regist 1992;57:7002-186.

3. C24-A2. Statistical Quality Control for Quantitative Measurements: Principles and Definitions; Approved Guideline - Second Edition. National Committee for Clinical Laboratory Standards, Wayne, PA, 1999.

4. Westgard JO. Charts of operating specifications (OPSpecs charts) for assessing the precision, accuracy, and quality control needed to satisfy proficiency testing criteria. Clin Chem 1992;38:1226-33.

5. Westgard JO, Hyltoft Petersen P, Wiebe DA. Laboratory process specifications for assuring quality in the U.S. National Cholesterol Education Program. Clin Chem 1991;37:656-61.

6. Westgard JO, Wiebe DA. Cholesterol operational process specifications for assuring the quality required by CLIA proficiency testing. Clin Chem 1991;37:1938-44.

7. Westgard JO, Groth T. Power functions for statistical quality control rules. Clin Chem 1979;25:863-869.

8. Westgard JO. Assuring analytical quality through process planning and quality control. Arch Pathol Lab Med 1992;116:765-9.

9. Groth T, Falk H, Westgard JO. An interactive computer simulation program for the design of statistical control procedures in clinical chemistry. Comp Prog Biomedicine 1981;13:73-86.

10. Koch DD, Oryall JJ, Quam EF, Feldbruegge DH, Dowd DE, Barry PL, Westgard JO. Selection of medically useful QC procedures for individual tests on a multi-test analytical system. Clin Chem 1990;36:230-233.

11. Westgard JO, Qulam EF, Barry PL. QC selection grids for planning QC procedures. Clin Lab Science 1990;3:271-278.

12. Westgard JO. Error budgets for quality management: Practical tools for planning and assuring the analytical quality of laboratory testing processes. Clin Lab Manag Review 1996;10:377-403.

13. Westgard JO, Stein B, Westgard SA, Kennedy R. QC Validator 2.0: a computer program for automatic selection of statistical QC procedures for applications in healthcare laboratories. Computer Method Programs Biomed 1997;53:175-86.

14. Westgard JO, Stein B. Automated selection of statistical quality-control procedures to assure meeting clinical or analytical quality requirements. Clin Chem 1997;43:400-3.

Online References:

Devising a Practical Process
http://www.westgard.com/qpbook/lesson52.htm

Online Quality-Planning Tools
http://www.westgard.com/qpbook/qptools.html

Normalized OPSpecs Charts (PDF for download)
http://www.westgard.com/qpbook/normcharts.html

Normalized OPSpecs Calculator
http://www.westgard.com/qpbook/normcalc2.htm

Remember to use the username and password provided at the beginning of this book to access the online materials.

Self-Assessment Questions:

- ❍ What applications are of interest in a laboratory?
- ❍ What applications are of interest to a manufacturer?
- ❍ What quality-planning tool is recommended here?
- ❍ Explain how this tool is like a map.
- ❍ How do you use this map to select a QC procedure?
- ❍ How do you use this map to set method performance specifications?
- ❍ Where can you get these maps?

5: How are quality requirements defined for a laboratory test?

Several different approaches have been recommended in the scientific literature for defining the quality required by a laboratory test. To make sense of the different concepts and formats, a system of quality standards is described to show the relationships of different types of requirements and the operating specifications that are needed in the laboratory.

Objectives:

- ❍ Identify different kinds of quality standards.
- ❍ Access Internet summaries of recommendations for quality standards.
- ❍ Assess the practical usefulness of the different kinds of quality standards.

Chapter materials:

- ❍ **Defining quality requirements**
- ❍ **Summary of CLIA Proficiency Testing Criteria for Acceptable Performance**
- ❍ **Summary of European Biologic Goals**
- ❍ **Desired Specifications for total error, imprecision, and bias derived from Biologic Variation**

Things to do:

- ❍ Study the chapter.
- ❍ Compare calculated Biologic total errors with CLIA total errors.

Is it possible that the requirements for this product weren't clear? The broom sort of looks right – it's got a long handle and is wide at the end, but obviously that's not an adequate description.

How do you define the requirements for a product like a laboratory test? If we're not clear about the requirements, how can we expect to manage the process and achieve the necessary quality? This chapter will bring you up-to-date with the current thinking on how to define quality requirements for laboratory tests.

Hagar the Horrible is reprinted here with special permission of King Features Syndicate.

Defining quality requirements

Here's a common management problem that requires quality-planning skills. You are looking at a *new! more reliable! higher-capacity! larger menu! faster! simpler-to-operate! and less costly!* analyzer (I read the advertisements too). Let's assume one of the tests to be performed is cholesterol.

What precision and accuracy are needed for a cholesterol method?

What QC procedure would you use to monitor the quality of routine results?

These are basic questions that you need to answer if you are to manage the analytical quality of the cholesterol test on this new analyzer.

Self-assessment exercise

Here's a chance to assess your quality-planning skills. Let's take our cholesterol test. The US CLIA regulations define 10% as the allowable total error for a cholesterol test [1]. The National Cholesterol Education Program (NCEP) specifies an allowable CV of 3% and an allowable bias of 3% [2]. For comparison, a European group [3] has defined a precision goal of 2.7% and a bias goal of 4.1% on the basis of the observed individual biological variation which is about 6.5%. In addition, NCEP provides test interpretation guidelines that recommend values of 200 mg/dL or lower are okay while values of 240 mg/dL and higher require additional testing to formulate a treatment plan. This defines a medically important change or clinical decision interval of 40 mg/dL, which is 20% [(40/200)*100] at medical decision level of 200 mg/dL.

What precision and accuracy do you want? What's the allowable SD or CV for the method? What's the allowable bias? These questions need to be answered before you purchase a new instrument. Ideally, you want to establish "purchase specifications" that will enable you to select the appropriate instrument.

How will you QC this test? What control rules will you use? How many control measurements are needed? These questions need to be answered before you can implement the new method in your laboratory.

Write down your answers so you can check your quality-planning skills at the end of this chapter.

Difficulties with quality requirements

These are not intended to be trick questions! Quality-planning begins with the definition of quality requirements. The selection of methods and QC procedures should follow in a logical manner. Regardless of your background and experience, my guess is that you will find it difficult to answer these questions. A major reason is that quality requirements themselves can be confusing and therefore difficult to define.

Lack of consistent concepts and terms

Part of the difficulty comes from the different types of quality goals, criteria for acceptable performance, and performance specifications that are being recommended. From the beginning, we've been plagued by conflicting concepts and terms. The first recommendations for establishing standards of quality were published by Tonks in 1963 and presented in the form of allowable total errors [4]. In 1968, Barnett described medically important changes in test results and related them to allowable SDs or CVs for laboratory methods [5]. In 1970, Cotlove et al utilized within-subject biologic variation to derive standards for allowable SDs [6].

The quality standards for cholesterol demonstrate the difficulties with inconsistent concepts and terms. Some of these are analytical outcome criteria, such as the CLIA allowable total error for proficiency testing; some are clinical outcome criteria, such as the NCEP medically important change for test interpretation. Others are method performance specifications, such as allowable CV and allowable bias defined by NCEP, and still others are quality goals, such as the recommendations for allowable imprecision and inaccuracy by the European working group.

Trying to understand and compare these different terms is like trying to compare apples, oranges, grapefruit, and bananas – they're all fruit, but they're different kinds of fruit. The allowable total error encompasses both the allowable CV or SD for method imprecision and allowable bias for method inaccuracy. A medically important change encompasses preanalytical factors, such as the within-subject biological variation, as well as analytical factors such as imprecision and inaccuracy. You will find that certain people, organizations, or agencies have a particular taste. Each selects what they like, which leaves the laboratory with a fruit-bowl of choices, rather than a coherent system of recommendations that guide the management of testing processes.

Multiple factors affecting test variability

To make sense of the different concepts and terms, you need to understand how the variability of a test result depends on pre-analytic and analytic factors. The figure here illustrates an example cholesterol situation for a patient whose true homeostatic set point is 200 mg/dL, i.e., this is the patient mean value if the patient were sampled repeatedly over a long period of time. The patient's own biologic variation is shown as BV, which in this case is illustrated as a variation equivalent to approximately 1*BV or 200*6.5% or 13 mg/dL. Note that if the test

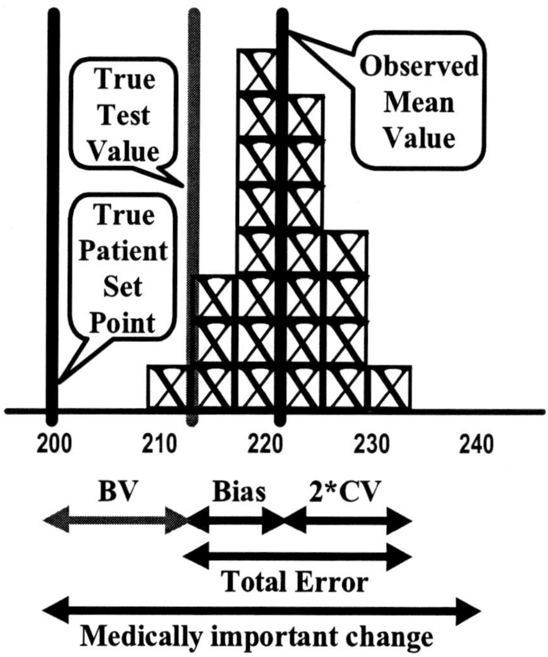

were to be repeated say a week later, the patient's true value will most likely change due to the biologic variation – and could be considerably higher or lower than illustrated here.

Method bias, or inaccuracy, is shown by the difference between the true test value and the mean that would be observed if the patient's sample were measured several times. In this illustration, the bias is approximately 3% of the true test value, which would add a systematic error of about 6 or 7 mg/dL to the true test value of 213 mg/dL, giving an observed mean of about 220 mg/dL. The distribution of repeated measurements is shown by the histogram and represents the effect of method imprecision. Method imprecision would add a random error of about another 12 or 13 mg/dL (2*3%*213 mg/dL), thus values as high as 233 mg/dL can be expected for a single measurement made on this patient.

The total error describes the net effect of method inaccuracy and imprecision. It is commonly estimated as bias + 2*CV. Note that the total error does not include the biologic variation – it only considers analytical components of error. However, biologic variation will be an important component when interpreting the cholesterol result of an individual patient. The NCEP patient treatment guidelines define a clinical decision interval from 200 to 240 mg/dL, which is a medically important change that includes both preanalytic and analytic factors. Biologic variation is a large preanalytical factor for cholesterol: 6.5% compared to NCEP's recommended method CV of 3.0%.

An unstated assumption

From my perspective, most of the recommendations are actually lemons because they provide little practical guidance for the laboratory. They don't work because they are recommendations only for the stable performance of a method, i.e., they assume everything works perfectly, no problems will occur, therefore no QC is needed. If this assumption of stable performance is not correct, then it follows that these recommendations are not correct for real laboratories where problems really do occur.

The analytical quality achieved in the daily operation of a testing process will depend on the both the stable performance of the measurement procedure (i.e., its observed imprecision and inaccuracy) and the capability of the quality control procedure to detect unstable method performance (i.e., changes in imprecision and inaccuracy). Specifications for stable imprecision and inaccuracy are incomplete and inadequate if they fail to consider QC. If you really believe in this assumption of stable performance, it should follow that you don't do any QC! If you perform QC, that's evidence you expect some method problems, therefore, the assumption of perfect method stability is wrong.

Misunderstanding performance as quality

Imprecision and inaccuracy are performance characteristics, not quality requirements. Performance certainly contributes to quality, but it's not the same thing. A given level of quality can be achieved by different combinations of imprecision and inaccuracy. Therefore, setting separate goals for imprecision and inaccuracy in the form of allowable CVs and allowable biases might conceal, rather than reveal, the total error that will be experienced by the user and consumer. Calculations can be performed to combine the maximum allowable bias with a multiple of the maximum allowable imprecision to describe the expected total error, such as done by NCEP for lipid tests, but these estimates of overall quality again are flawed because they assume stable performance and don't allow for the performance of the QC procedure.

Relevance to customers

One of the things TQM teaches is that quality is related to customer needs. To determine the customer needs for laboratory tests requires us to communicate with physicians and nurses, who usually don't think in terms of precision and/or accuracy. Here, the cartoon shows the customer's reaction to our description of quality and performance. They hear our technical words, but those words don't mean anything to them. For customer communication to work, we have to listen to their words, understand their needs, and translate those needs into our technical terms. This is the process of Quality Function Deployment where the key ideas are listening to customers and translating customer needs into process specifications. (Cartoon by John Meyer, MD)

Our customers are concerned with the total change that might occur in a test result, not components of errors such as imprecision and inaccuracy. Furthermore, their application of test results is related to certain critical changes from reference values, decision limits, or previous test results. Our customers think about medically important changes in test results; they don't think about test results with reference to imprecision and inaccuracy. The information available from our customers and relevant to their use of results from laboratory testing processes is in the form of medically important changes and total errors, not specifications for allowable imprecision and allowable inaccuracy.

Applicability for laboratory use

The practical purposes of these recommendations for quality goals, criteria for acceptable performance, and performance specifications are to help the laboratory establish, manage, and monitor a testing process to assure the analytical quality of the test results. That means these recommendations should be useful for characterizing the clinical needs of the test, setting purchase specifications for the method, evaluating method performance, establishing internal quality control, and monitoring method performance via external quality assessment or proficiency testing. A source of our difficulties is that different types or formats of quality requirements are needed at different times and for different purposes in the overall process of managing the analytical quality of laboratory tests. Each type of recommendation has its place in this system, but the system itself is not well understood.

A System of Quality Standards

The debate about the "best" type of quality requirement has overshadowed the use and application of quality requirements. Finally, in 1999 at an international conference in Stockholm, a recommendation was made to recognize a system of quality standards. This system includes different sources of information and different formats for requirements, such as the allowable total error (analytical outcome criterion), the clinical decision interval (clinical outcome criterion), or the maximum allowable standard deviation and the maximum allowable bias (analytical performance criteria).

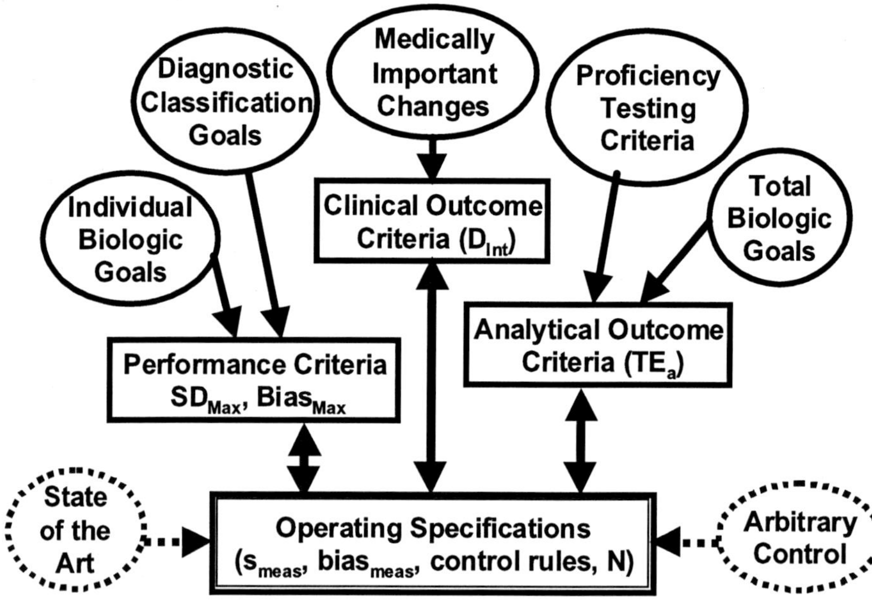

The figure above shows my view of the relationships between these different sources of information, different types of quality requirements, and the operating specifications needed for managing routine testing processes. Starting at the top of the figure, medically important changes in test results can be defined by standard treatment guidelines (clinical pathways, clinical practice guidelines, etc.) to establish clinical outcome criteria (or decision intervals, D_{int}). Such clinical criteria can be converted to laboratory operating specifications for imprecision (s_{meas}), inaccuracy ($bias_{meas}$), and QC (control rules, N) by a clinical quality-planning model [7] that takes into account pre-analytical factors, such as individual or within-subject biologic variation (s_{wsub}).

The left side of the figure shows how performance criteria for imprecision and inaccuracy can be defined as separate analytical goals for the maximum imprecision and bias that would be allowable for the stable performance of the method. Specifications for maximum imprecision and bias can be derived on the basis of within-subject biological variation [3]. The maximum allowable bias can also be derived from diagnostic classification models [8]. Laboratories can utilize these separate performance criteria by relating observed method performance to the maximum allowable value, calculating the critical-size error that needs to be detected to maintain satisfactory performance, and then selecting appropriate QC procedures by use of power function graphs.

The right side of the figure shows how proficiency testing criteria define analytical outcome criteria in the form of allowable total errors (TE_a), which can be translated into operating specifications (s_{meas}, $bias_{meas}$, control rules, N) via an analytical quality-planning model [9]. Note that the allowable total error can also be set on the basis of total biologic goals that are population-based or individual-based [10], therefore the extensive data-bank of individual biologic variation can be utilized in this situation (see http://www.westgard.com/biodatabase1.htm).

The bottom line is operating specifications. The laboratory must know the imprecision and inaccuracy that are allowable for the method and the control rules and number of control measurements that are necessary to monitor and assure the quality of the testing process. Thus, all these different forms of quality standards have some use in the context of a system for analytical quality management. However, until this system is recognized, understood, and applied, the different recommendations in the literature will continue to be incoherent, rather than useful and practical for analytical quality management. In the absence of defined quality requirements, manufacturers set performance specifications on the basis of an undefined "state of the art" and laboratories apply “arbitrary control,” not quality control.

Clinical quality requirements

Practical information can be provided in the form of a medically important change, medically significant change, or clinical decision limit, which are the commonly used terms for this type of quality requirement. One source of information about medically important changes in test values is a paper by Skendzel, Barnett, and Platt [11]. Note that the important information is found in Table 1 of this paper, which provides a summary of physicians' opinions of a significant change in test results. This paper is sometimes criticized for the rather large values recommended for medically useful CVs, which appear in Table 2 and were derived without accounting for within-subject biological variation. When Fraser's figures for within-subject biological variation [12,13] are used in a clinical quality-planning model that accounts for biological variation, the allowable CVs are much smaller [14]. The original recommendations for allowable CVs were too large because an over-simplified quality-planning model attributed the total variation to analytical variation, rather than first deducting the known biologic variation.

One major advantage of this type of quality requirement is that information is directly available from the customers, either through their description of how they use and interpret a laboratory test, through clinical pathways that detail the expected use and interpretation of tests, or through audits of clinical practices. When this information is properly translated to operating specification via a quality-planning model that accounts for pre-analytical factors, it provides a useful and valid approach for defining and managing the quality of the testing process.

Analytical quality requirements

The most useful form for these requirements is a statement of an allowable total error that encompasses both imprecision and inaccuracy. This corresponds to the industrial "tolerance specification" for process production that considers both the centering of the process on a target value and the distribution of individual products around that target. The most common sources of these type of requirements are the proficiency testing or external quality assessment programs that specify acceptability limits in the form of a target value plus/minus certain tolerances. In the US, CLIA defines such limits for approximately 80 different tests. In other countries, such as Australia and Canada, the lists and criteria may be even more extensive.

These PT limits define minimum levels of quality that must be achieved, therefore, it is always important to plan testing processes to assure PT criteria are achieved in routine operation. This can be accomplished by using an analytical quality-planning model that translates these requirements into the imprecision and inaccuracy that are allowable and the QC that is necessary.

Operating specifications

Both clinical and analytical quality requirements in the forms of decision intervals and allowable total errors can be translated into the practical specifications that are needed to manage routine operations. These operating specifications consist of the imprecision and inaccuracy that are allowable for the method and the QC that is necessary to detect unstable performance, i.e., detect analytical problems and errors that occur with the method. The exact values for the CV, bias, control rules and N are interdependent, permitting many different combinations that will still assure the desired quality will be achieved. The many possible combinations can be shown graphically by OPSpecs charts to help analysts and managers determine how to properly manage the analytical quality of a testing process.

Summaries of available recommendations

For initial guidance, see the following summaries of recommendations for different types of quality requirements:

Analytical quality requirements in the form of allowable total errors are provided by the proficiency testing criteria for acceptable performance that have been defined by the US Clinical Laboratory Improvement Amendments (CLIA). See *Appendix 1* and/or http://www.westgard.com/clia.htm. Similar information is often available from the external quality assessment programs in other countries.

European recommendations for biologic goals for imprecision and inaccuracy, as well as calculated allowable total error criteria, are based on individual biologic variation. See *Appendix 2* or http://www.westgard.com/europe.htm.

Desirable specifications for total error, imprecision and bias derived from biologic variation. An extensive databank summarizes the results of studies on biologic variation and calculates biologic goals for imprecision and inaccuracy, which in turn can be used to calculate total error criteria. See *Appendix 3* or http://www.westgard.com/biodatabase1.htm.

Clinical quality requirements can be defined from information on medically important changes in test results. Note, however, that clinical decision interval criteria and clinical quality requirements in this form require a more complicated quality-planning model to properly consider both pre-analytical and analytical components of errors. See http://www.westgard.com/clinical.htm

Answers to self-assessment exercise

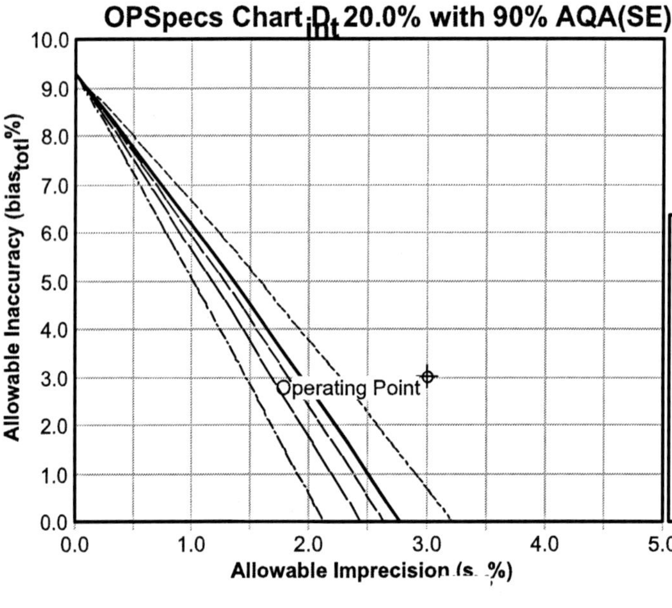

	P_{fr}	N	R
1_{2s}	0.09	2	1
$1_{2.5s}$	0.03	2	1
$1_{3s}/2_{2s}/R_{4s}$	0.01	2	1
1_{3s}	0.00	2	1
$1_{3.5s}$	0.00	2	1

For our cholesterol example, where the NCEP clinical quality requirement is 20% and within-subject biological variation is 6.5%, a clinical OPSpecs chart shows that if method bias were zero, then method CVs of 2.7% or less are needed (see the x-intercept of the bold line) if common QC procedures with N=2 are to be used and the false rejection probabilities are to be kept below 0.05 (i.e., a false rejection rate lower than 5%). A method that satisfies the NCEP 3.0% precision and 3.0% accuracy specifications will not assure the desired clinical quality, as can be seen by plotting an operating point of x=3% and y=3%, which exceeds the allowable limits of imprecision and inaccuracy for all the QC procedures with N=2.

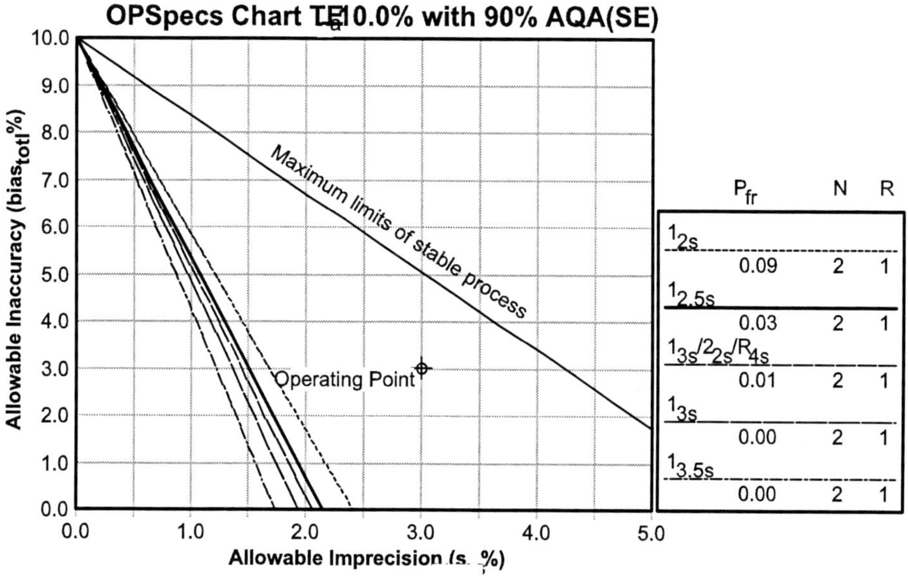

Given the CLIA analytical quality requirement of 10% for cholesterol, an analytical OPSpecs chart shows that if method bias were zero, then method CVs of 2.2% or less are needed (see the x-intercept of the bold line) if common QC procedures with N=2 are to be used and the false rejection rate is to be kept at 5% or less. Note that this OPSpecs chart also shows the operating point for a method that satisfies the NCEP 3% imprecision and 3% inaccuracy specifications and that this performance would be judged acceptable in a method evaluation study that used a bias + 2s criterion for stable performance (as shown by the line above the operating point). However, such a method cannot be adequately controlled by commonly used QC procedures with Ns of 2.

Note that these operating specifications are more demanding that the European quality goals for imprecision of 2.7% and inaccuracy of 4.1%. If bias were as large as 4.1%, then the method CV would need to be as low as 1.0 to 1.5% (as can be seen by finding 4.1% on the y-axis of the OPSpecs chart, drawing a horizontal line across, dropping a vertical line from the point of intersection with the *operating limits*, and reading the allowable imprecision from the x-axis).

In summary, a method CV from 2.0 to 2.5% would generally be required if method bias were zero and simple control procedures with Ns of 2 were to be applied. If a method with this performance were purchased, the laboratory could then implement a single-rule procedure using the $1_{2.5s}$ rule with N=2 or a multirule procedure such as $1_{3s}/2_{2s}/R_{4s}$ with N=2.

References

1. U.S. Department of Health and Social Services. Medicare, Medicaid, and CLIA Programs: Regulations implementing the Clinical Laboratory Improvement Amendments of 1988 (CLIA). Final Rule. Fed Regist 1992(Feb 28);57:7002-7186.

2. National Cholesterol Education Program Laboratory Standardization Panel. Current status of blood cholesterol measurement in clinical laboratories in the United States. Clin Chem 1988;34:193-201.

3. Fraser CG, Hyltoft Petersen P, Ricos C, Haeckel R. Proposed quality specifications for the imprecision and inaccuracy of analytical systems for clinical chemistry. Eur J Clin Chem Biochem 1992;30:311-7.

4. Tonks DA. A study of the accuracy and imprecision of clinical chemistry determinations in 170 Canadian laboratories. Clin Chem 1963;9:217-233.

5. Barnett RN. Medical significance of laboratory results. Am J Clin Pathol 1968;50:671-676.

6. Cotlove E, Marris E, Williams G. Biological and analytical components of variation in long-term studies of serum constituents in normal subjects: III. Physiological and medical implications. Clin Chem 1970;16:1028-1032.

7. Westgard JO, Hytoft Petersen P, Wiebe DA. Laboratory process specifications for assuring quality in the U.S. National Cholesterol Education Program (NCEP). Clin Chem 1991:37:656-661.

8. Klee GG. Tolerance limits for short-term analytical bias and analytical imprecision dervied from clinical assay specificity. Clin Chem 1993;39:1514-1518.

9. Westgard JO, Wiebe DA. Cholesterol operational process specifications for assuring the quality required by CLIA proficiency testing. Clin Chem 1991;37:1938-44.

10. Hyltoft Petersen P, Ricos C, Stockl D, Libeer JC, Baadenhuijsen H, Fraser C, Thienpont L. Proposed guidelines for the internal quality control of analytical results in the medical laboratory. Eur J Clin Chem Clin Biochem 1996;34:983-999.

11. Skendzel LP, Barnett RN, Platt R. Medically useful criteria for analytic performance of laboratory tests. Am J Clin Pathol 1985;83:200-5.

12. Fraser CG. Biological variation in clinical chemistry. An update: collated data, 1988-1991. Arch Pathol Lab Med 1992;116:916-23.

13. Fraser CG. The application of theoretical goals based on biological variation data in clinical chemistry. Arch Pathol Lab Med 1988;112:404-15.

14. Westgard JO, Seehafer JJ, Barry PL. Allowable imprecision for laboratory tests based on clinical and analytical test outcome criteria. Clin Chem 1994;40;1909-14.

Online References:

Defining Quality Requirements
http://www.westgard.com/qpbook/lesson53.htm

CLIA Total Error Requirements
http://www.westgard.com/clia.htm

European Biologic Goals
http://www.westgard.com/europe.htm

Desired specifications for total error, imprecision and bias derived from Biologic Variation
http://www.westgard.com/biodatabase1.htm

Self-Assessment Questions:

- ❍ What's the CLIA PT requirement for glucose?
- ❍ What's the biologic goal for the imprecision of a glucose method?
- ❍ What's the biologic goal for the inaccuracy of a glucose method?
- ❍ What's the biologic goal for the total error of a glucose test?
- ❍ What's a medically important change in results for a glucose test?
- ❍ What's the allowable imprecision for a glucose method if the allowable total error is 10% and there is no method bias?

6: How do you translate quality requirements into process specifications?

Given that a quality requirement can be defined in the form of an allowable total error (such as the CLIA PT criteria for acceptable performance), it is necessary to translate this requirement into bench-level specifications for imprecision, bias, and QC (control rules, number of control measurements). This can be done with the aid of the operating specifications chart (or OPSpecs chart) explained in this chapter.

Objectives:

- ❍ Learn how to read an OPSpecs chart.
- ❍ Understand the terms on an OPSpecs chart.
- ❍ Use an OPSpecs chart to select a QC procedure.
- ❍ Use an OPSpecs chart to set performance specifications for precision and bias.

Chapter materials:

- ❍ **Adopting the OPSpecs chart as your quality-planning tool**

Things to do:

- ❍ Study the chapter.
- ❍ Learn the terms.

It looks like it's going to be a long journey, doesn't it? We're in chapter 7 already and it seems like a long way before we'll be able get practical and actually choose QC procedures for laboratory tests. Maybe we need a smaller map, too. In our case, the map we need is a OPSpecs chart – a small map that does a big job in planning the quality of a laboratory test.

Adopting the OPSpecs Chart as your quality-planning tool

So far, these chapters have focused on the *need* for quality-planning, based on the lack of independence in past laboratory practices for analytical quality management, the emerging principles of Total Quality Management, and the existing regulatory, accreditation, and QC practice guidelines. A step-by-step quality-planning process has been described drawing on the NCCLS QC practice guidelines. The first step of this process requires definition of the quality required for a test, which can be stated in several different formats – all of which are important in a system of quality standards. The bottom line in the laboratory is knowledge of the operating specifications, which are the imprecision and inaccuracy allowable for a method and the QC needed to monitor method performance and assure the desired quality is achieved.

Operating specifications are different from quality goals or quality standards because they consider QC as an integral part for monitoring the instability of a method, whereas most quality standards assume that method performance is stable and therefore don't consider QC. In the lingo of today, this is a paradigm shift – a new perspective or a different view of the situation. QC needs to be designed *into* the testing process, in addition to analytical imprecision and inaccuracy.

This new perspective provides a more complete and comprehensive view of what is necessary to manage the analytical quality of a laboratory testing process. It's also more complicated because of the interdependence of imprecision, inaccuracy, and QC. The better the imprecision and inaccuracy, the easier it is to QC the process. The worse the imprecision or inaccuracy, the more difficult it becomes to adequately QC the process. The interactions of these three critical factors must be considered.

The best tool for showing these interactions is the chart of operating specifications, or OPSpecs chart. The concept of the OPSpecs chart has been introduced, using the idea of a map that will help you get to solid ground. Example applications of OPSpecs charts have been illustrated for a cholesterol test that has well-defined standards of quality in US national regulations (CLIA-88) and clinical practice guidelines (NCEP). Now is the time to learn the details of *how* to use OPSpecs charts. For the theory of *why* it works, see references 1 and 2.

How to read an OPSpecs Chart

Here's a figure that neatly summarizes all the information contained in an OPSpecs chart:

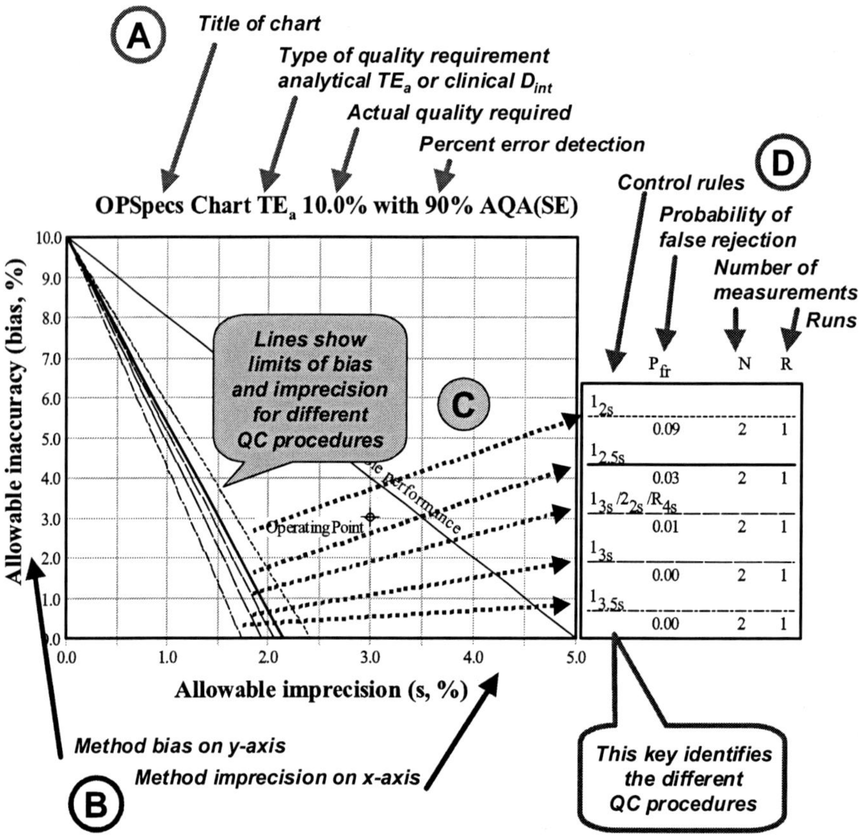

Impressive, huh? And maybe a little frightening, too. There's a lot packed into this chart. Let's explain it in words first:

An OPSpecs chart contains information about the type of quality requirement, the actual quality desired, the imprecision and inaccuracy allowable for different QC procedures, details about the control rules and number of control measurements, and information about the error detection and false rejection characteristics of the QC procedures.

Now, let's break down the chart into sections:

A. Start with the title at the top of the chart.

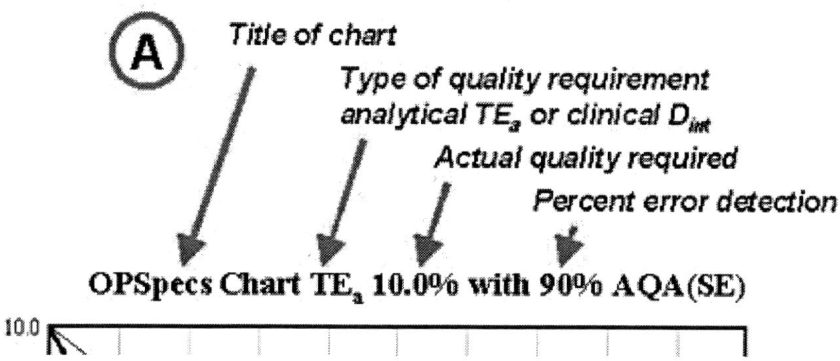

The title identifies the following:

Type of quality requirement, TE_a for an allowable total error or D_{int} for a clinical decision interval. In this example, the OPSpecs chart was prepared for an analytical total error requirement. To prepare a chart for a clinical decision interval requirement, you will need an electronic spreadsheet or computer program, such as QC Validator.

Actual quality required, in % of a medically important decision level, e.g., 10% for cholesterol in this example.

Error detection, in %, such as 90% in this example, which is the same as a probability of error detection (P_{ed}) of 0.90. The AQA(SE) stands for Analytical Quality Assurance for Systematic Error.

Charts are also available for 50% AQA(SE). With the aid of the QC Validator computer program, charts can also be prepared for 25% AQA and also for random error (RE).

B. Look at the axes of the chart.

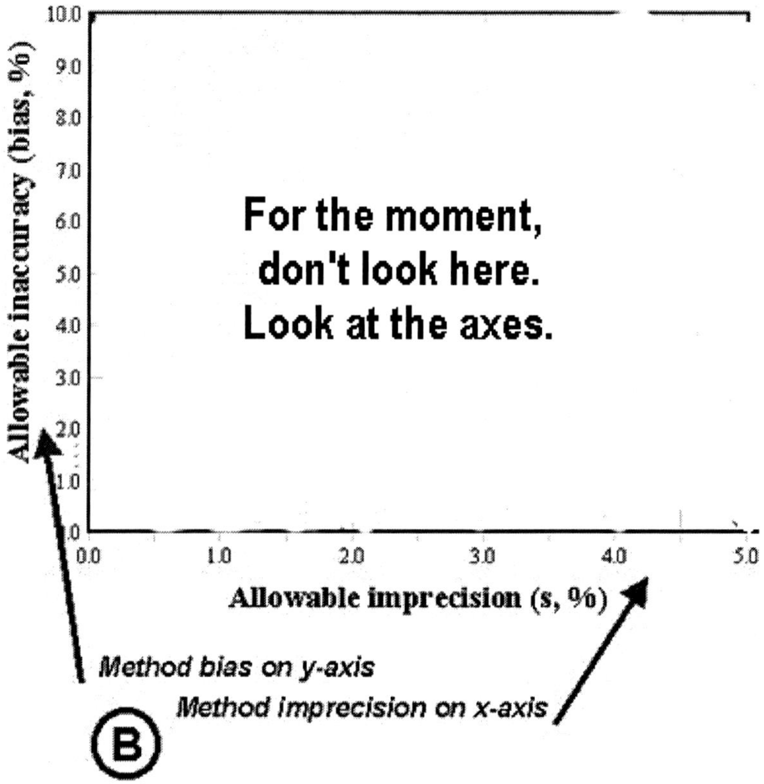

The y-axis shows allowable inaccuracy, or the method bias in units of %, i.e., relative to the medical decision level of interest.

The x-axis shows allowable imprecision, or the standard deviation (s) in units of %, which is the same as the coefficient of variation or CV.

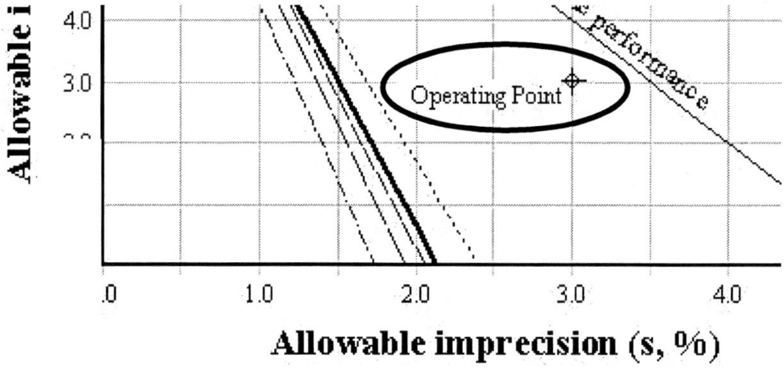

The actual performance of a method can be displayed by plotting an **Operating Point**, as shown in the middle of this chart (y-coordinate of 3.0% and x-coordinate of 3.0% representing conditions of 3.0% bias and 3.0% CV).

C. Inspect the lines that describe the limits of allowable bias and allowable imprecision, i.e., define the solid ground.

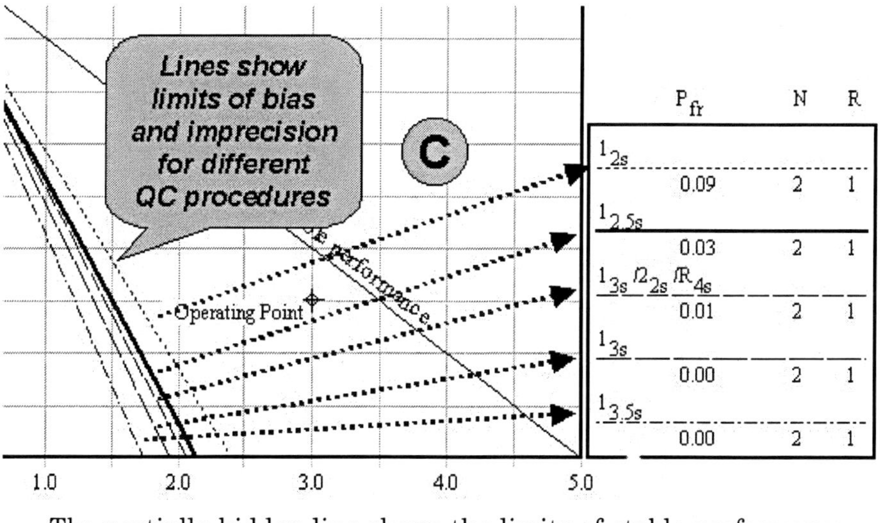

The partially hidden line shows the limits of stable performance that correspond to a total error criterion of bias + 2s, which is commonly used as a criterion for acceptable performance in the initial evaluation or validation of a method. Remember that this criterion assumes stable method performance and does not consider the need for QC – that's why this line is the highest.

The other lines correspond to certain control rules and numbers of control measurements, which are identified in the key at the right side of the chart. Follow the arrows across to find the details of individual QC procedures. Note that the order of the lines – top to bottom on the chart – corresponds to the order of the lines top to bottom in the key at the right.

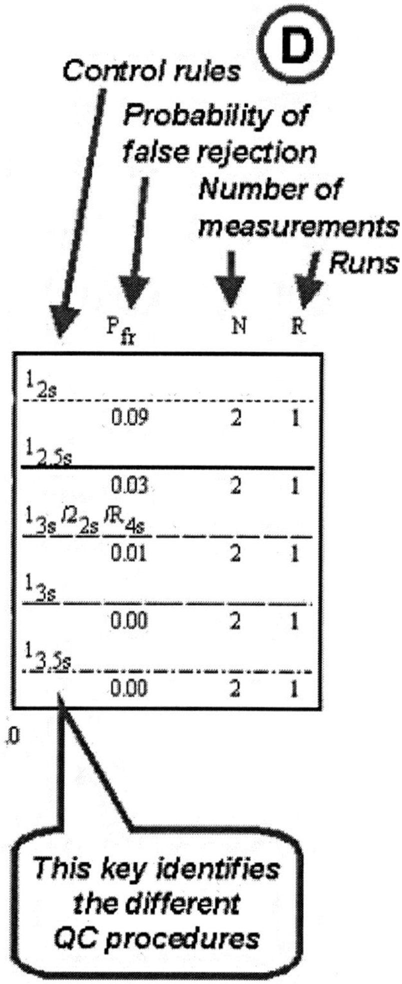

D. Match the lines in the key of the graph to get the details about each QC procedure.

The dots and dashes in the lines in the graph match the dots and dashes in the lines in the key. For example, the solid line on the graph corresponds to the solid line in the key. Often it is easier to match up the lines based on their top-to-bottom order on the graph and in the key.

The **control rule or rules** are shown in the first column of the key. The abbreviations are of the form A_L, where A is the symbol for a rule or the number of control measurements and L is the control limit. For example, the top line is for a 1_{2s} rule and indicates a run is to be rejected when 1 control measurement exceeds a 2s control limit. This corresponds to a Levey-Jennings control chart having control limits set as the mean ± 2 standard deviations.

The probability of false rejection, P_{fr}, is listed in the second column. Ideally, this figure should be less than 0.05, or 5%, to minimize the false alarms from the QC procedure. Note that for the 1_{2s} rule with N=2, the probability for false rejection (P_{fr}) is 0.09, which means a 9% chance of falsely rejecting each run. The use of 2s control limits with N=2 should be generally discouraged because they cause a 9% waste in the production of a testing process, even when the process is working perfectly. It gets even worse for higher Ns (14% for N=3, 18% for N=4).

N is the total number of control measurements per analytical run. An N of 2 could refer to 2 measurements on a single control material or 1 measurement on each of two different materials. Remember that N is the "total number" of control measurements that can be spread over different control materials being used.

R is the number of runs over which the control rules are applied. In this example, all the rules are applied only in the 1st run. However, if a 4_{1s} rule were added to the multirule procedure, the rule could only be applied if there were 2 runs each having 2 control measurements to give the total of 4 needed to apply the rule. Likewise, if a 10_x rule were added, there would need to be 5 runs to accumulate the 10 measurements.

How to determine method performance specifications

Recall the steps in the planning process when the intent is to determine the imprecision and inaccuracy that is needed by a method:

1. Define the quality required for the test, e.g., a 20% clinical decision interval for cholesterol on basis of NCEP treatment guidelines.

2. Obtain the OPSpecs chart for a 20% D_{int}, as shown in the accompanying figure. Note the title of the OPSpecs chart states D_{int} 20% with 90% AQA(SE), indicating it has been prepared for a clinical quality requirement of 20% and 90% detection of medically important systematic errors.

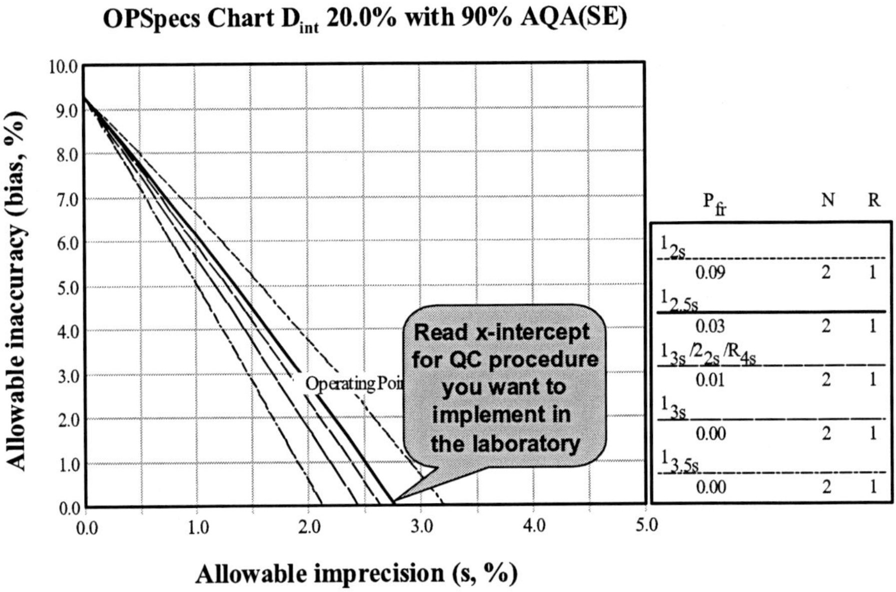

3. Specify the laboratory's preferred QC procedure, e.g., $1_{2.5s}$ with N=2 as shown by the solid line. Note that the 1_{2s} procedure with N=2 is being avoided here because of its high false rejection rate of 9%.

4. Read the x-intercept for the solid line that corresponds to the preferred QC procedure, in this case the line for $1_{2.5s}$ with N=2. In this example, it looks like a method CV of 2.7-2.8% is needed if method bias is zero. If method bias were 1.0%, then a CV of about 2.5% would be needed; if method bias were 3.0%, then a CV of 1.9% would be needed.

How to select a QC procedure

Again, let's go through this application step-by-step to illustrate how OPSpecs charts are used:

1. Define the quality required for the test, in this case, an allowable total error of 10% according to the CLIA criterion for acceptable performance for a cholesterol test.

2. Obtain the OPSpecs chart for 10% TE_a, as shown in the accompanying figure. Again, start by reading the title of the chart which indicates TE_a of 10% for 90% AQA(SE). Note that this chart is for N=2 QC procedures which are preferred to keep the cost of QC low.

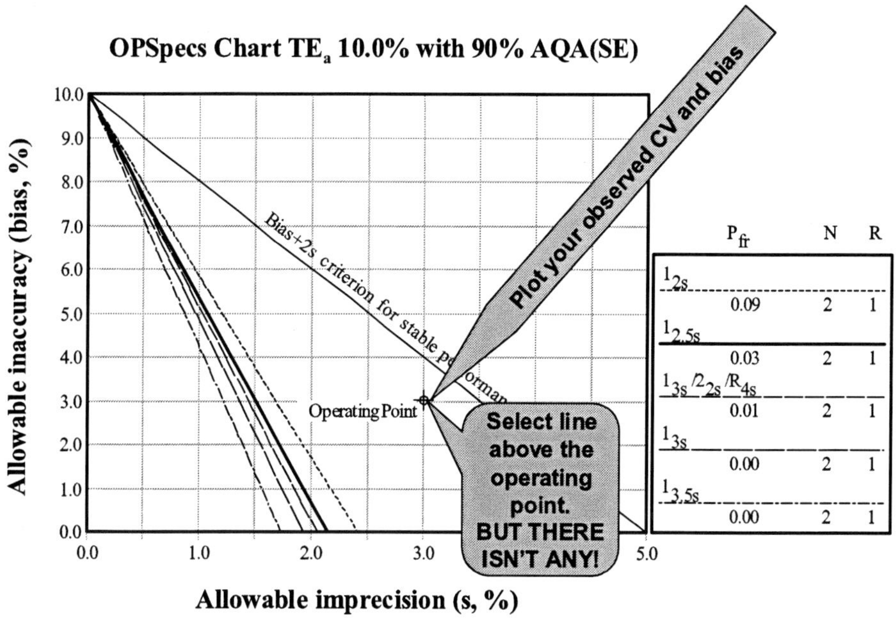

3. Plot the operating point for the method, i.e., the observed standard deviation or CV (in %) is the x-coordinate and the observed bias (in %) is the y-coordinate.

4. Inspect the lines showing the allowable limits of imprecision and inaccuracy for different QC procedures. Select a line

above the operating point. If none is available, as in this example, it will be necessary to consider other QC procedures having higher Ns or to settle for lower error detection, perhaps 50% AQA(SE).

5. Utilize other OPSpecs charts if necessary. If selecting a QC procedure to work with 2 control materials, the strategy is to inspect OPSpecs charts in the following order:

   N=2 with 90% AQA
   N=4 with 90% AQA
   N=2 with 50% AQA
   N=4 with 50% AQA

If using 3 control materials, the strategy is to inspect OPSpecs charts in the following order:

N=3 with 90% AQA
N=6 with 90% AQA
N=3 with 50% AQA
N=6 with 50% AQA

The objective is to select a QC procedure having 90% error detection with 5% or less false rejection and the lowest number of control measurements possible. If necessary, settle for 50% error detection and compensate by beefing up other non-statistical control procedures as part of the overall or Total QC strategy. In the example here, it's not possible to achieve 50% AQA even with multirule QC procedures and Ns up to 6, as shown by the OPSpecs chart on the next page titled "50% AQA(SE)". The operating point for a 3% CV and 3% bias is still above all the lines for the QC procedures given in the key here, which now include single-rule and multirule procedures with Ns of 2, 4, and 6.

The last step here is to formulate a Total QC strategy that provides an appropriate balance of statistical and non-statistical procedures (such as preventive maintenance, instrument function checks, method validation tests, patient data QC, in-service training, staffing with operators who have maximum experience and minimal rotations). This TQC strategy can depend primarily on statistical QC when a solution is obtained from a 90% AQA chart.

A balanced strategy is needed when the QC selection is made using a 50% AQA chart. If less than 50% AQA, the maximum statistical QC that is practical should be selected, but in addition, efforts should be made to maximize other non-statistical components and to improve the performance of the method. It may even to advisable to acquire a new method having better imprecision and lower bias, rather than expend so much effort trying to control a method that does not provide the necessary analytical performance.

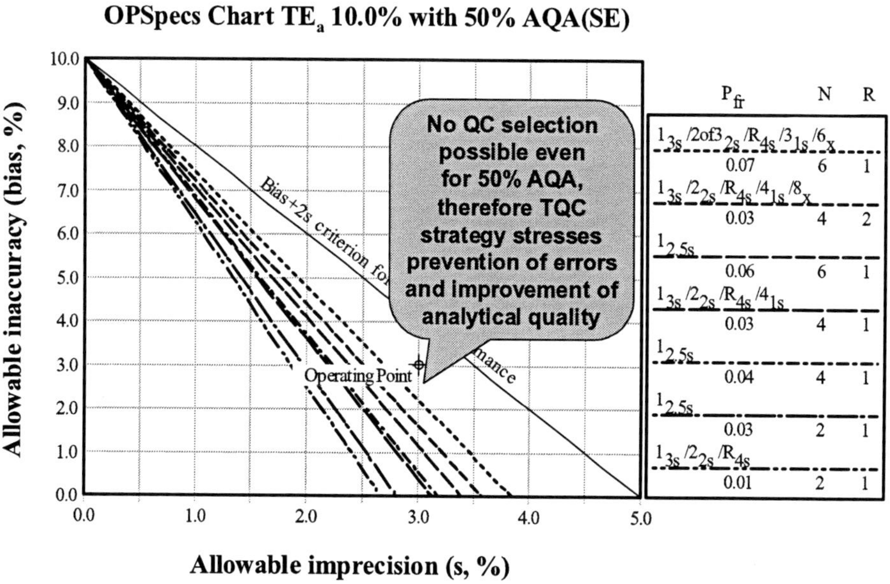

How to assess need for quality improvement

Another useful application of the OPSpecs chart is to assess the improvements in analytical quality that are needed to simplify QC and reduce the number of control measurements. For example, the cholesterol application considered on the next page is shown on the OPSpecs chart for a TE_a of 10%, 90% AQA(SE), and QC procedures with Ns from 2 to 6.

The effect of reducing method bias is shown by the vertical arrow located at 3.0% on the x-axis. If method bias were reduced to zero, then a method with a CV of 3.0% could be controlled using a multirule QC procedure with an N of 6. That's a costly QC procedure, but at least the necessary analytical quality would be assured.

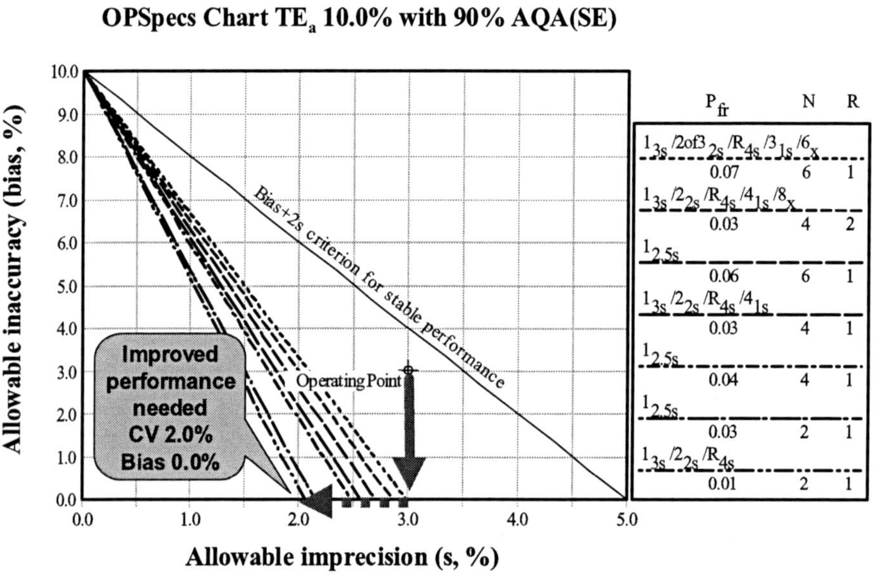

The additional benefit of improving method imprecision is shown by the dotted horizontal arrow. If the method CV were improved to 2.5%, adequate control is possible with single-rule or multirule QC procedures having Ns of 4. If the method CV were improved to 2.0%, QC procedures with Ns of 2 would be adequate.

The ability to assess the benefits of improvements in method performance is one of OPSpecs chart's real advantages. Of course, this cycles back to its earlier application for setting performance specifications. If the necessary analytical performance were achieved initially through careful selection and evaluation of the method, then QC will turn out to be simple and easy to perform. However, when the QC selection application leads to costly QC with high N, you have the information to help you assess the benefits from any improvements in method performance.

Note also that the demands of different quality requirements can be compared by having OPSpecs charts for both the clinical requirement (1st figure, NCEP clinical decision interval of 20%) and the analytical quality requirement (last figure, CLIA allowable total error of 10%). As shown earlier, to achieve the quality needed for a cholesterol test that will be interpreted according to the NCEP treatment guidelines, a method should be selected that has a CV of 2.7% or less (when bias is 0.0 and the laboratory intends to monitor performance with only 2 control measurements per run). Compare this with the demands of the CLIA proficiency testing requirement where the method needs a CV of 2.0% or better (when bias is 0.0). The clinical requirement for patient treatment is less demanding than the regulatory requirement for method performance.

It makes no sense to have a more demanding requirement for analyzing proficiency testing samples than for analyzing patient samples! This inconsistency is due to a lack of understanding of the nature of these quality requirements and the inherent difficulty of comparing apples and oranges. However, the OPSpecs charts translate both requirements into equivalent terms (operating specifications) that can be compared – another advantage of the tool.

References

1. Westgard JO. Assuring analytical quality through process planning and quality control. Arch Path Lab Med 1992;116:765-769.

2. Westgard JO. Charts of operational process specifications ("OPSpecs Charts") for assessing the precision, accuracy, and quality control needed to satisfy proficiency testing performance criteria. Clin Chem 1992;38:1226-1233.

Online References:

Adopting the OPSpecs Chart as your planning tool
http://www.westgard.com/qpbook/lesson54.htm

Mapping the Road to Quality with OPSpecs Charts
http://www.westgard.com/scotland.htm

Remember to use the username and password provided at the beginning of this book to acces the online materials.

Self-Assessment Questions:

- ❍ What's the meaning of 90%AQA(SE)?
- ❍ Where do you find the probability of false rejection?
- ❍ How do you match the different lines to the different control rules?
- ❍ Given a 10% TE_a, recommend a QC procedure for a glucose method that has a CV of 1.5% and a bias of 2.0% (Hint: use the last OPSpecs chart in this chapter).
- ❍ Given a 10% TE_a, recommend the maximum CV for a glucose method if you are to implement a Levey-Jenning's control chart having 3 SD control limits and a minimum of 2 controls per run (Hint: use the OPSpecs chart on page 79).

7: What do you do when quality isn't good enough?

The most cost-effective testing process is one where statistical QC can detect medically important errors and alert analysts to problems with the method. In situations where high error detection cannot be achieved by statistical QC, additional efforts should be made to prevent problems from occurring and to utilize other non-statistical techniques to alert analysts to problems. The appropriate combination of these statistical and non-statistical techniques provides a Total QC strategy.

Objectives:

- Identify different Total QC strategies.
- Identify non-statistical components of Total QC strategies.
- Learn how to develop appropriate Total QC strategies for testing processes.
- Assess the need for improving method performance as part of the Total QC strategies.

Chapter materials:

- **Formulating a Total Quality Control Strategy**

Things to do:

- Study the chapter.
- Review your laboratory's strategy for deploying personnel on the basis of skill and experience.
- Review your laboratory's strategy for cross-training in relation to QC and Total QC strategies.

Hagar the Horrible

Our quality-planning process is pretty well defined, except for one last step. What do we do if our plan doesn't work out the way we hope? What's the backup plan? The answer is the Total Quality Control strategy described in this chapter. The TQC strategy provides guidance for developing a quality system that defines the right balance of statistical QC, instrument function checks, performance tests, preventive maintenance, patient data QC, etc. In cases where statistical QC can't do the job, our alternative is to spend more time and effort on these other components of the quality system.

Formulating a Total QC Strategy

Optimal management of analytical quality depends on individualizing the QC procedures for each test and method in the laboratory. The quality-planning process provides the methodology for (a) setting method performance specifications that are appropriate for the analytical or clinical quality required for a test and (b) selecting statistical QC procedures appropriate for the actual imprecision and inaccuracy observed for methods in routine operation in a laboratory. Ideally, the QC procedure should provide at least a 90% chance of rejecting an analytical run having medically important errors. At the same time, the QC procedure should have less than a 5% chance of falsely rejecting a run that contains only the random errors due to the inherent (stable) imprecision of the method. And, for practicality and low cost, the QC procedure should require only 2 to 6 control measurements per run – the lower the better.

Review of CLIA regulations

US government regulations (CLIA-88) define a set of standards for quality control that include method performance specifications, statistical quality control, preventive maintenance, instrument function checks, and method performance tests [1,2]. These CLIA rules may be viewed as separate requirements for individual components of Quality Control (QC), or as a requirement for developing a Total Quality Control (TQC) strategy that incorporates these components in a manner appropriate for controlling individual testing processes. The latter view would seem to be more desirable for assuring the quality of laboratory testing because of the need to individualize the QC designs for the many different analytical methods for performing those tests.

The responsibility for establishing a TQC strategy initially belongs to the manufacturers of medical testing systems, devices, or kits. If a manufacturer's QC instructions were cleared by FDA as meeting CLIA requirements for quality control, the CLIA rules require that a laboratory does the following:

"demonstrate that, prior to reporting patient test results, it can obtain the performance specifications for accuracy, precision, and reportable range of patient test results, comparable to those established by the manufacturer [2, p. 5230, par. 493.1213(b)(1)],

"perform maintenance as defined by the manufacturer and with at least the frequency specified by the manufacturer," [2, p. 5231, par. 493.1215(a)(i)],

"perform function checks as defined by the manufacturer and with at least the frequency specified by the manufacturer" [2, p. 5231, par. 493.1215(b)(i)],

"follow the manufacturer's instructions for calibration and calibration verification procedures using calibration materials specified by the manufacturer" [2, p. 5231, par. 493.1217(a)], and

"follow the manufacturer's instructions for control procedures" [2, p. 5232, par. 493.1218(a)].

For a test method whose QC instructions *have not been cleared* by the FDA, the laboratory itself assumes responsibility for formulating an appropriate strategy for quality control that includes these same components. Note that as of the year 2000, a QC clearance process has NOT yet been implemented in accordance with the CLIA regulations, thus *the laboratory is primarily responsible* for selecting appropriate QC procedures and for implementing appropriate TQC strategies.

General TQC Guidelines

The starting point for formulating a TQC strategy is the quality-planning process and the error detection available from the selected statistical QC procedure. Testing processes will be classified into one of three categories: **high error detection** when a QC procedure can be selected from an OPSpecs chart with 90% AQA; **moderate error detection** when a QC procedure is selected from an OPSpecs chart with 50% AQA; **low error detection** when 50% AQA is not obtainable, in which case a maximum QC procedure should be defined as the default selection. The recommendations for maximum QC selections here are to use a multirule procedure such as $1_{3s}/2_{2s}/R_{4s}/4_{1s}/8_x$ with the maximum of N=4 (for 2 control materials) and $1_{3s}/2of3_{2s}/R_{4s}/3_{1s}/6_x$ with N=6 (for 3 control materials).

The general TQC strategies for these three classes are shown in the this table, where SQC refers to Statistical QC, Other QC includes preventive maintenance (PM), instrument function checks (FC), performance validation tests (PV), and patient data quality control (PD). QI means quality improvement and refers to improving the precision, accuracy, and stability of the measurement procedure.

HI-Ped Strategy 	MOD-Ped Strategy 	LO-Ped Strategy 
SQC	SQC	SQC
Other QC	**Other QC**	**Other QC**
QI	QI	**QI**

HI-Ped strategy. When SQC is able to provide high error detection, then the TQC strategy is to depend primarily on SQC and perform the minimum requirements for other QC components.

MOD-Ped strategy. When SQC provides moderate error detection, the TQC strategy is to balance the emphasis on SQC, Other QC, and QI.

LOW-Ped strategy. When SQC provides low error detection, the TQC strategy cannot rely on SQC, but must emphasize Other QC and QI.

(Note that Ped stands for probability of error detection.)

Step-by-step guidelines

The flowchart shows a more detailed process for developing a TQC strategy for an individual method. When SQC provides high error detection (90% AQA), the emphasis is on minimizing the costs of statistical and non-statistical QC. When SQC provides moderate error detection (at least 50% AQA), then the emphasis is on maximizing statistical and non-statistical components, as well as improving measurement performance. If SQC provides low error detection (less than 50% AQA), the efforts also include optimizing QC for process stability, improving the skills of the analysts, and adding patient data QC. In all cases, the final step is to document the QC system.

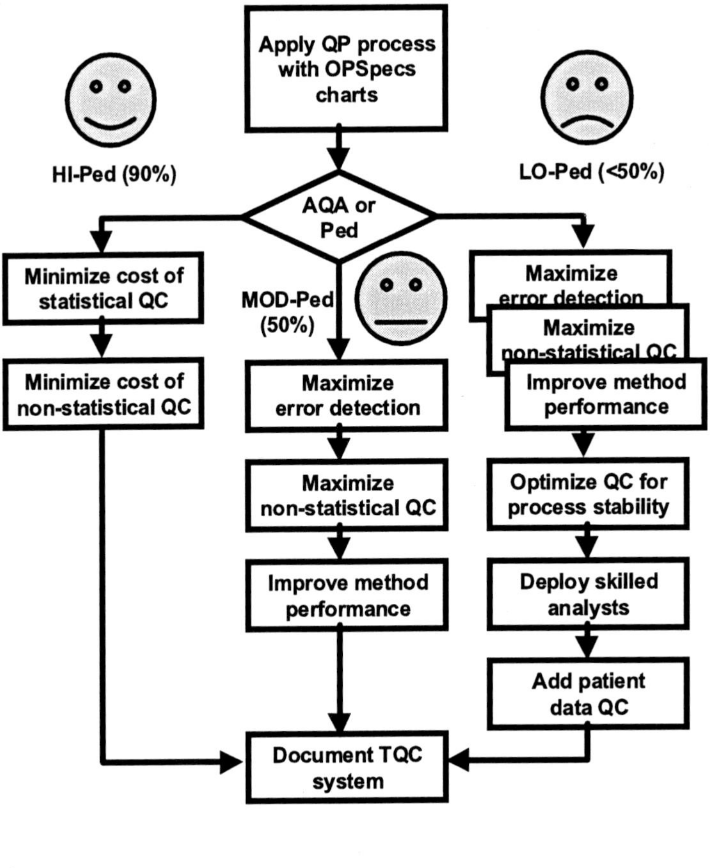

HI-Ped Strategy

Minimize the cost of statistical QC. Use as few control measurements as needed. Reduce N to a minimum of 2 whenever possible. Use single-rule rather than multirule procedures. Use control limits as wide as 3.5s when possible to minimize false rejections. Aim for 1% or lower false rejection. Increase run length to maximize test yield, i.e., the ratio of patient samples to control and calibration samples.

Minimize cost of non-statistical QC. Recognize the limitations of control materials and their matrices when minimizing non-statistical QC. Weigh the clinical needs and risks carefully. Then identify the minimum frequency of system function checks, performance validation tests, and preventive maintenance, as required by regulations, manufacturer's instructions, and good laboratory practice.

Document the TQC strategy. The last step for any of the TQC strategies is documentation, including the QC acceptability criteria (control rules, N) for assessing the control status of an analytical run. Document the expected rejection characteristics of the statistical QC procedure. Establish the schedule for performing non-statistical QC checks and document the procedures for performing those checks.

MOD-Ped and LO-Ped Strategies

Maximize error detection. Increase N from a minimum of 2 up to at least 4 control measurements per run when using two control materials and increase N from 3 to 6 when using three control materials. Increase run length as a way of increasing N, being careful to satisfy the turnaround time requirements for the test. Narrow the control limits and tolerate higher false rejections, up to 6-7% for the N=6 procedures. Change from single-rule to multirule QC procedures. Use look-back rules to effectively increase N by inspecting control data from the previous run. Implement multistage QC procedures that have a startup design with higher N and/or more sensitive control rules to maximize error detection, then switch to a monitor design having lower N and/or less sensitive control rules that minimize false rejections. Switch back and forth between the startup and monitor designs as necessary.

Maximize non-statistical QC. Perform preventive maintenance, calibration, instrument checks, and performance verification tests that are required by CLIA, recommended by the manufacturer, and appropriate for the susceptibility of the method and the clinical application of the test. Adopt a more aggressive schedule to minimize problems.

Improve method performance. Reduce analytical bias by selecting appropriate standards, calibrating properly, and by selecting proper comparison groups in proficiency testing surveys. Reduce imprecision by identifying and minimizing the major component of variance, standardizing operator techniques, and mechanizing manual steps in the process. Reduce frequency of errors by identifying and eliminating sources of problems, increasing the preventive maintenance schedule, increasing function checks and performance verification tests, reducing operator variables, and increasing operating training and expertise. When necessary, change measurement procedures or analytic systems to obtain better accuracy, precision, and stability.

Additional steps for LO-Ped strategy

Optimize QC for process stability. Document the frequency of errors by careful study of the analytical process. In general, a 50% error detection rate will be satisfactory for stable processes that have <2% frequency of errors and even a 25% detection rate may be sufficient for extremely stable processes that have <1% frequency of errors.

Deploy skilled analysts. Assign highly skilled analysts to testing processes that are problematic and difficult to control. Provide thorough in-service training. Increase technical skills and experience. Improve problem-solving capabilities. Improve statistical skills for method validation and quality control. Reduce the rotation schedule for personnel to maintain operator experience and continuity.

Add patient data QC. Perform between-system comparisons on patient samples. Check patient data with consistency algorithms, such as delta checks, anion gap, etc. Utilize population statistics, such as mean of normals, Bull's algorithm, etc. Perform clinical correlations to check test results with patient diagnosis and condition.

Cost of quality control vs cost of quality improvement

The costs of quality control are ongoing and never-ending, month after month, year after year (see *Appendix 4*). This figure illustrates the relative costs for different TQC strategies.

HI-Ped Strategy	MOD-Ped Strategy	LO-Ped Strategy
$	$$$	$$$$ $$$$$
SQC	SQC	SQC
Other QC	Other QC	Other QC
QI	QI	QI

HI-Ped TQC costs. When 90% detection of medically important errors can be achieved with statistical QC, the cost of ongoing quality management is lowest. The better the analytical performance, the lower number of control measurements needed, the wider the control limits, the lower the false rejection rate, and the less non-statistical QC is needed. This demonstrates Deming's principle that improved quality leads to lower costs.

MOD-Ped TQC costs. When moderate error detection is achieved – greater than 50% detection of medically important errors, all the costs go up, including the cost of statistical QC. There is a need for more control measurements, more preventive maintenance, more frequent instrument checks, etc., which means more time and effort by laboratory personnel.

LO-Ped TQC costs. When error detection is low – less than 50% detection of medically important errors, costs become even greater. There is a need for more training, more operator experience, and more review and correlation of patient data.

At some point, the costs for MOD-Ped TQC and LO-Ped TQC should justify efforts to improve the performance of an analytical method. Begin your quality improvement efforts by reducing the inaccuracy or bias of the method. Next try to reduce the imprecision or CV of the method. Try to gain enough improvement to change the TQC strategy, moving from LO-Ped to MOD-Ped to HI-Ped strategies. If this is not successful, consider replacing the method with one that has better analytical performance.

References

1. Health Care Financing Administration (HCFA) and Public Health Service (PHS), US Dept of Health and Human Services (HHS). Medicare, Medicaid and CLIA Programs. Regulations implementing the Clinical Laboratory Improvement Amendments of 1988 (CLIA) and Clinical Laboratory Improvement Act program fee collection. Fed Regist 1993;58:5215-37.

2. U.S. Dept. of Health and Human Services. Medicare, Medicaid, and CLIA Programs: regulations implementing the Clinical Laboratory Improvement Amendments of 1988 (CLIA). Final Rule. Fed Regist 1992;57:7002-186.

Online References:

Formulating a Total Quality Control Strategy
http://www.westgard.com/qpbook/lesson55.htm

Remember to use the username and password provided at the beginning of this book to access the online materials.

Self-Assessment Questions:

- ❍ What is the key parameter for deciding which TQC strategy to use?
- ❍ How can you minimize the cost of statistical QC?
- ❍ When might you reduce the amount of QC being performed?
- ❍ When is it appropriate to utilize multirule QC procedures with look-back rules?
- ❍ How can you identify methods or systems where staff can be rotated without any effect on the quality of testing?
- ❍ When should you reduce staff rotations in order to improve quality?

8: Can you do quality planning by hand?

This chapter provides everything you need to start a "manual" quality-planning process for your own applications. You can do this manual process "by hand" in the sense that you don't need any computer software or sophisticated support – everything you need is provided in this book or online. Normalized OPSpecs charts are introduced and provide a generic set of charts that can be applied with any total error requirement

Objectives:

- ❍ Implement a manual quality-planning process in your laboratory.
- ❍ Utilize "Normalized" OPSpecs charts.

Chapter materials:

- ❍ **Using Normalized OPSpecs charts**
- ❍ **Quality-planning worksheet**
- ❍ **Normalized OPSpecs charts**

Things to do:

- ❍ Study the chapter.
- ❍ Make copies or download the quality-planning worksheet.
- ❍ Make copies or download the Normalized OPSpecs charts.
- ❍ Work through the examples in the chapter using your own charts.

There are certain manual skills that are critical to get the job done. In our case, it's the quality-planning job and you can get it done manually by using normalized OPSpecs charts. Don't choke on the word "normalized." It's just a different way of scaling the charts so you only need a handful of charts for all your quality-planning applications. This chapter will show you how to use normalized charts and also provide you with a set of charts, a worksheet, and a flowchart with directions – everything you need but the pencil. (You'll need the pencil to plot an operating point on the normalized OPSpecs chart, but if you access the online quality-planning tools, you won't even need to do that.)

Using Normalized OPSpecs charts

You can start a manual quality-planning process *now* – using the normalized OPSpecs charts presented in this chapter. With a few additional calculations, you can plan quality with just a handful of charts for all your QC applications. These normalized charts work for the allowable total error type of requirement, such as given by the CLIA acceptability criteria in proficiency testing surveys. This type of quality requirement is the essential starting point for quality-planning applications in US laboratories.

Concept of a normalized OPSpecs chart

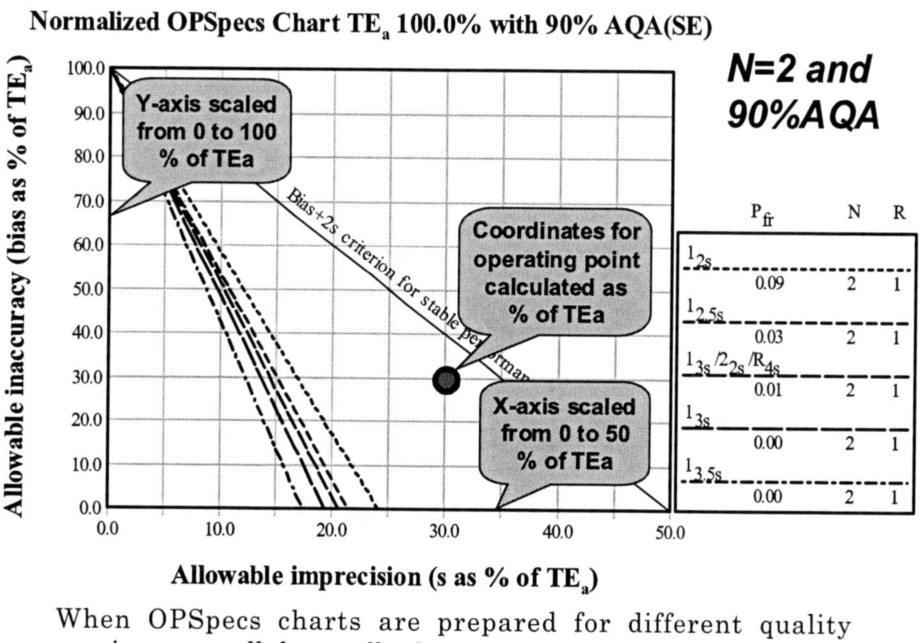

When OPSpecs charts are prepared for different quality requirements, all that really changes are the scales on the X and Y axes. The y-axis is scaled from 0 to TE_a and the x-axis is scaled from 0 to $0.5*TE_a$. The actual operating limits for different QC procedures occupy the same positions relative to the axes, i.e., all the charts look exactly the same except for the scaling of the axes.

The idea for a *normalized OPSpecs chart*[1] is to make the scaling be the same, i.e., the y-scale becomes 0 to 100% TE_a and the x-scale becomes 0 to 50% TE_a. The operating point will then have to be expressed as a percent of TE_a. For example, TE_a was 10% for cholesterol in an earlier application, the method CV was 3.0%, and method bias was 3%. The normalized OPSpecs chart is shown on the previous page, with the operating point located at 30% of TE_a on the y-axis and 30% of TE_a on the x-axis, i.e, the original 3% figures are now expressed as 30% of TE_a [(3/10)*100 which is 30%]. Note that the chart looks exactly the same as in the earlier chapter that illustrated quality requirements and operating specifications for cholesterol (OPSpecs for TE_a=10% with 90% AQA(SE) for N=2 QC procedures on page 79).

Step-by-step procedure

These steps follow the general procedure described earlier in the book, but with adaptations to use normalized OPSpecs charts.

1. **Define the quality requirement** for the test in the form of an allowable total error (TE_a), such as given by CLIA proficiency testing criteria.

2. **Determine the imprecision (CV) and inaccuracy (bias) of the method.** Present these estimates in units of percent, i.e., %CV and %bias relative to a medical decision concentration of interest.

3. **Calculate the normalized operating point** by dividing the method %CV or %bias by the defined TE_a, multiplying by 100 to express as percent of TE_a.

   3a. **X-coordinate:** method CV in percent divided by defined TE_a in percent, then multipled by 100, e.g., 3% CV divided by 10% TE_a multiplied by 100 gives 30%;

   3b. **Y-coordinate:** method bias in percent divided by defined TE_a in percent, then multiplied by 100 to express as percent, e.g., 2% bias divided by 10% TE_a, multiplied by 100 gives 20%.

4. **Use normalized OPSpecs charts** for the number of control materials of interest in the application, i.e., for two control materials, use the charts for Ns of 2 and 4; for three control materials, use the charts for Ns of 3 and 6.

5. **Plot the normalized operating point on the normalized OPSpecs chart.**

6. **Inspect OPSpecs Charts** in the following order and select a QC procedure whose operating limits are above the operating point.

   6a. First, try the low N chart with 90% AQA.

   6b. If no solution can be found on the low N chart and *if N cannot be doubled*, then try the low N chart with 50% AQA. If N can be doubled, move on to step 6c.

   6c. If no solution can be found on the low N and low AQA chart, try doubling N and use the high N chart with 90% AQA.

   6d. If no solution can be found on the high N chart, try the high N chart with 50% AQA.

   6e. If still no solution can be found, then use a maximum QC procedure such as $1_{3s}/2_{2s}/R_{4s}/4_{1s}$ with N=2 or $1_{3s}/2_{2s}/R_{4s}/4_{1s}/8_x$ with N=4 for two control materials; $1_{3s}/2of3_{2s}/R_{4s}/3_{1s}/6_x$ with N=3 or N=6 for three control materials.

7. **Establish the Total QC strategy** on the basis of which OPSpecs chart gives the solution.

   7a. Use HI-Ped TQC when the solution is found on 90% AQA chart;

   7b. Use MOD-Ped TQC when the solution is found on 50% AQA chart;

   7c. Use LO-Ped TQC when no solution is found on the 90% or 50% AQA charts.

8. **Reassess for changes when appropriate.**

Materials for manual quality-planning:

Quality-planning worksheet: For documenting the steps of this process, a worksheet is available in this chapter and also in PDF file format at

http://www.westgard.com/qpbook/qcplanworksheet.html

The PDF can be downloaded to your computer and printed repeatedly as you wish.

The worksheet describes the steps of the planning process and allows you to "fill in the blanks" for your test and method and also shows you how to calculate the normalized operating point. The steps for inspecting the normalized OPSpecs charts involve the sequential use of a series of charts, inspecting the low N 90% AQA chart first to assess whether a QC procedure can be selected, and if not, moving on to the high N 90% AQA OPSpecs chart to repeat the assessment, and if necessary moving on to the high N 50% AQA OPSpecs chart to repeat the assessment for a third time. If no solution is found, then a maximum QC procedure must be defined as the default procedure to be implemented. This max QC procedure should represent the most QC that the laboratory can afford to do to monitor method performance. Any method where the maximum QC procedure is employed should also be targeted for improvement or replacement.

Normalized OPSpecs charts for two and three control materials: A total of eight normalized OPSpecs charts are needed, four for use with two control materials (N=2 90% AQA, N=4 90% AQA, N=2 50%AQA, N=4 50%AQA) and four for use with three control materials (N=3 90%AQA, N=6 90%AQA, N=3 50%AQA, N=6 50%AQA).

To calculate a normalized operating point, you can calculate by hand using the instructions in this chapter, or use a Javascript calculator on Westgard Web to perform the calculations for you:

http://www.westgard.com/qpbook/normcalc2.htm

To obtain Normalized OPSpecs charts, these charts are available in PDF file format on Westgard Web:

http://www.westgard.com/qpbook/normcharts.html

Worksheet for Selecting a QC Procedure

Test	
Method	
System	
Analyst	
Date	

1. Define quality requirement %TEa ☐ at Xc ☐

2. Determine method performance %CV ☐ %bias ☐

3. Calculate normalized operating point

   a. y-coordinate = (%bias/%TEa)100 ☐ ☐

   b. x-coordinate = (%CV/%TEa)100 ☐ ☐

4. Select normalized OPSpecs charts for 2 or 3 control materials

5. Plot normalized operating point

6. Inspect OPSpecs chart and select QC procedure

   ☐ a. Solution found on lo-N 90% chart
   ☐ b. Solution found on lo-N 50% chart
   ☐ c. Solution found on hi-N 90% chart
   ☐ d. Solution found on hi-N 50% chart
   ☐ e. No solution, use max QC

   RULES ☐

   Total N ☐

7. Adopt a Total QC strategy

   ☐ a. Solution on 90% chart - Hi-Ped
   ☐ b. Solution on 50% chart - Mod-Ped
   ☐ c. No solution - Lo-Ped

   TQC ☐

Start with top chart (use bottom only if max N=2)

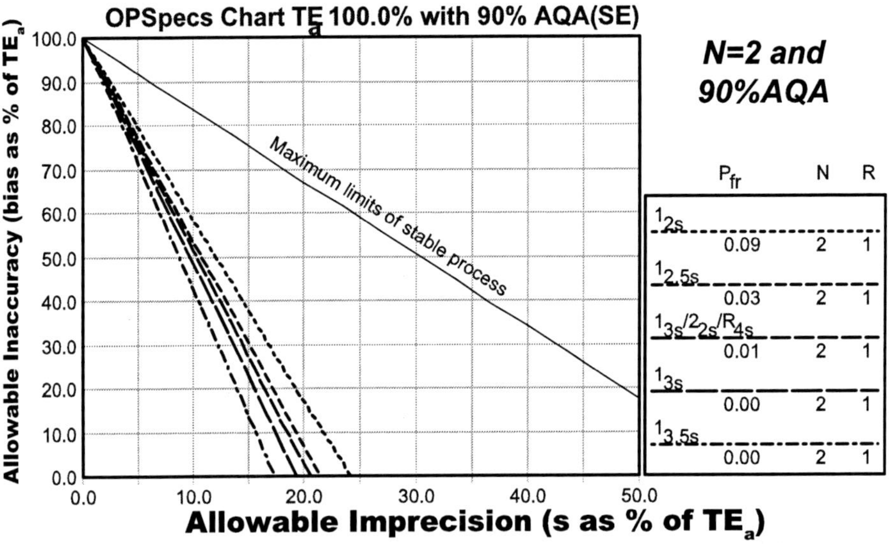

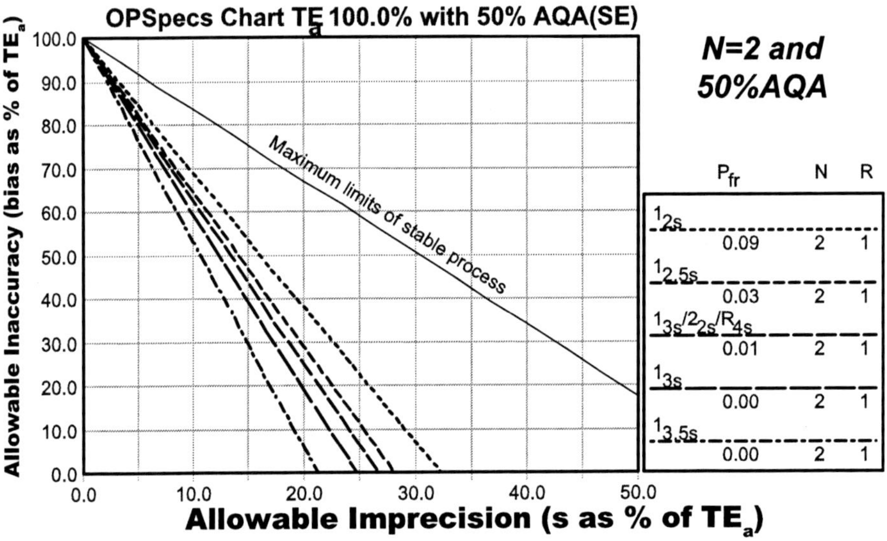

Next, try these charts – top then bottom

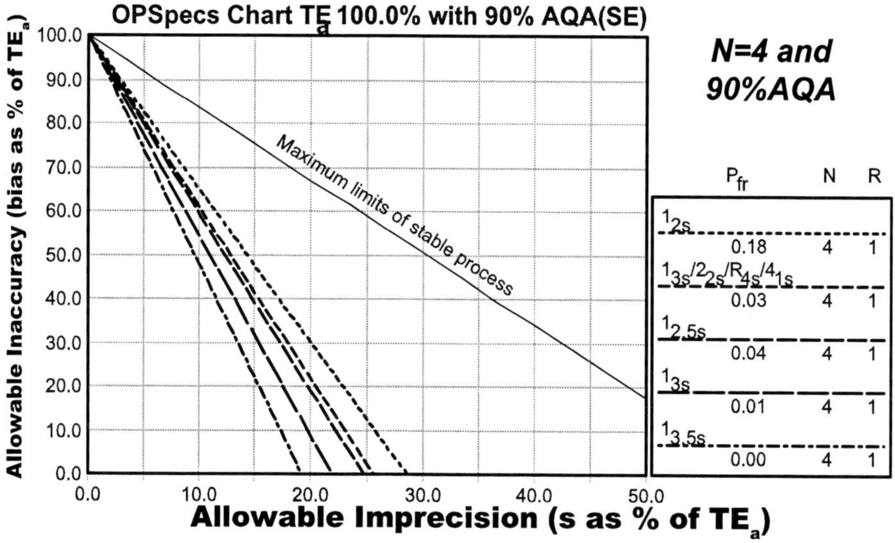

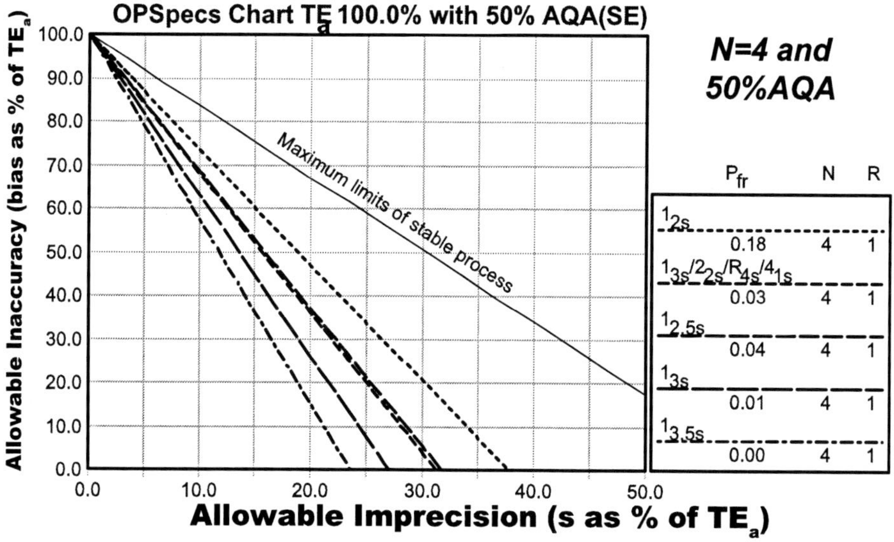

Start with top chart (use bottom only if max N=3)

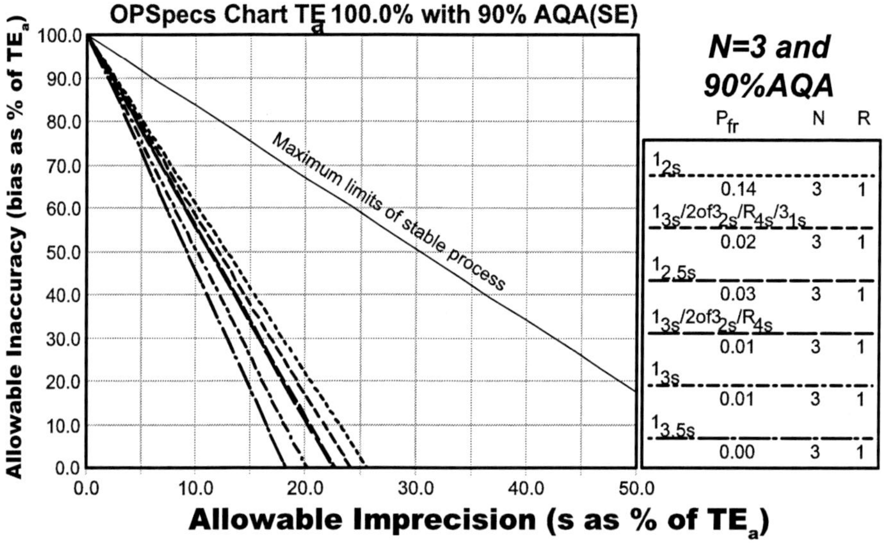

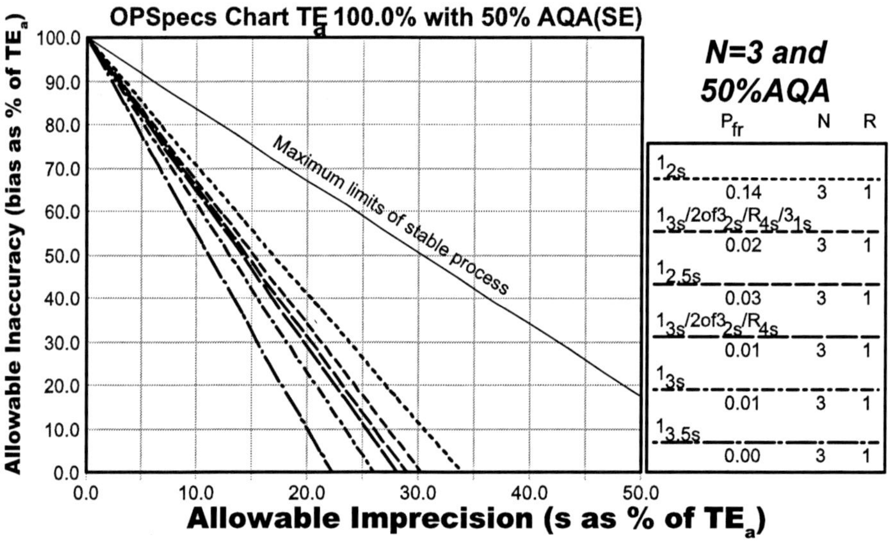

Next, try these charts – top then bottom

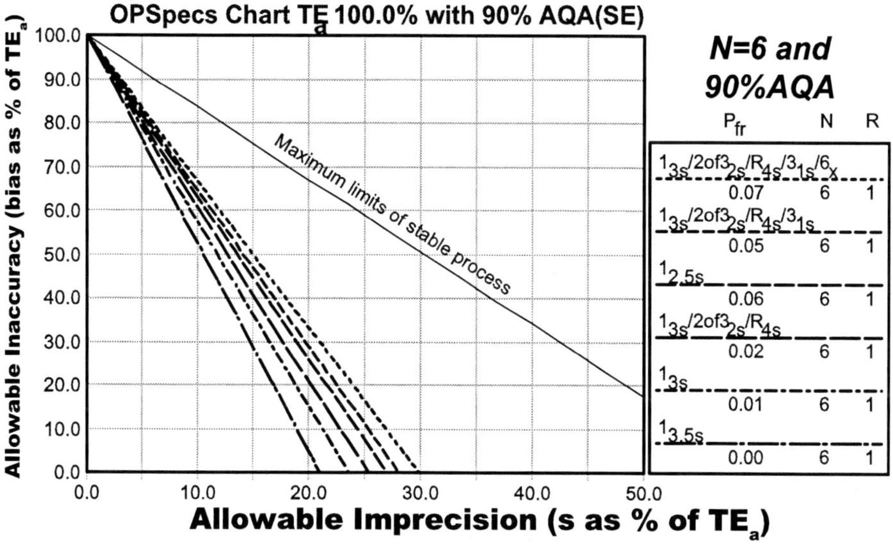

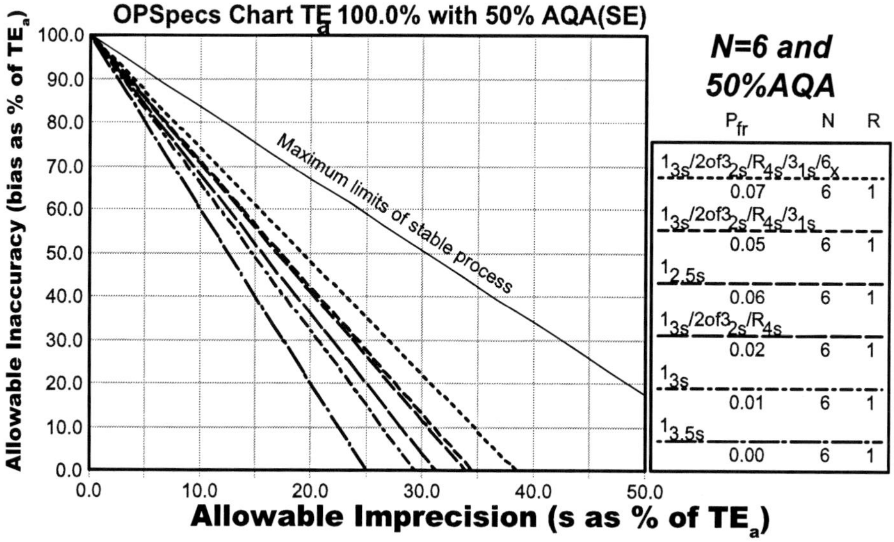

Flow chart for manual quality-planning process using normalized OPSpecs charts

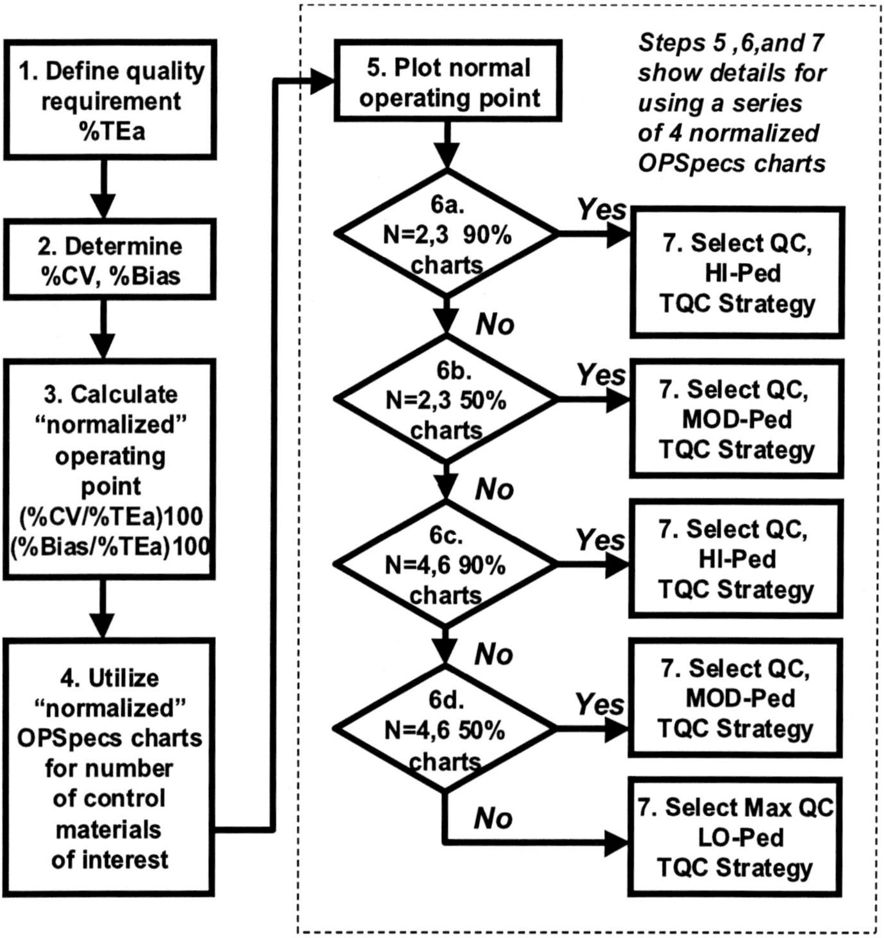

This flowchart shows the steps of the quality-planning process and illustrates in detail the methodology for inspecting the OPSpecs charts and selecting both the QC procedure and the Total QC strategy.

Example applications

Here are three chemistry examples that show how to select QC procedures and TQC strategies using normalized OPSpecs charts. The input parameters describe the quality requirement, observed bias, observed CV, and number of control materials to be assayed. The normalized operating point is calculated, plotted on the OPSpecs charts, and the chart giving the solution is shown. Using that chart, the QC procedure and TQC strategy are selected.

Glucose

Input parameters: TE_a of 6 mg/dL or 10%, whichever greater; observed bias of 1.0% at 120 mg/dL; observed CV of 1.7% at 120 mg/dL; use two control materials.

Calculated operating point: Y-coordinate is 10% [(1/10)*100]; X-coordinate is 17% [(1.7/10)*100];

Normalized OPSpecs Chart TE_a 100.0% with 90% AQA(SE)

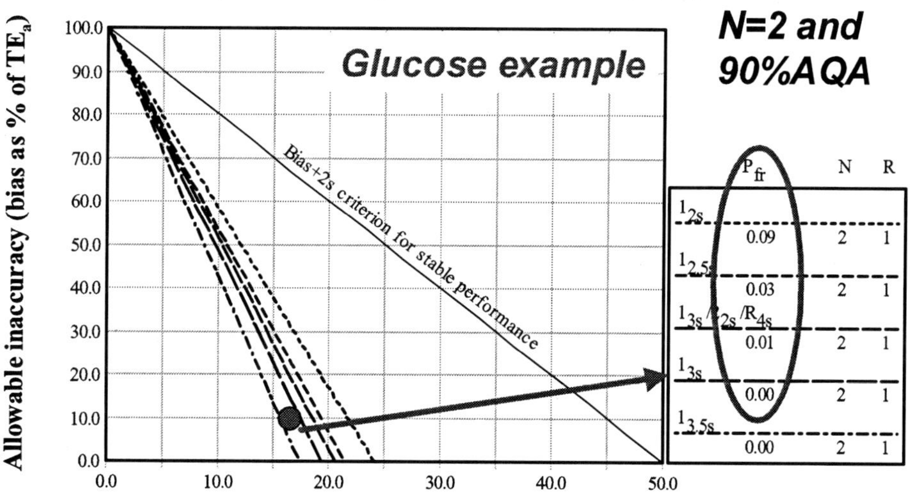

Allowable imprecision (s as % of TE_a)

Solution found on N=2 90% AQA chart; four possibilities of which the 1_{3s} with N=2 offers 90% AQA, the simplest rule, and the lowest false rejection rate (0%); select HI-Ped TQC strategy.

Cholesterol

Input parameters: TE_a 10.0%, observed bias 2.0%, observed CV 2.0%, use two control materials.

Calculated operating point: Y-coordinate is 20% [(2/10)*100]; X-coordinate is 20% [(2/10)*100]

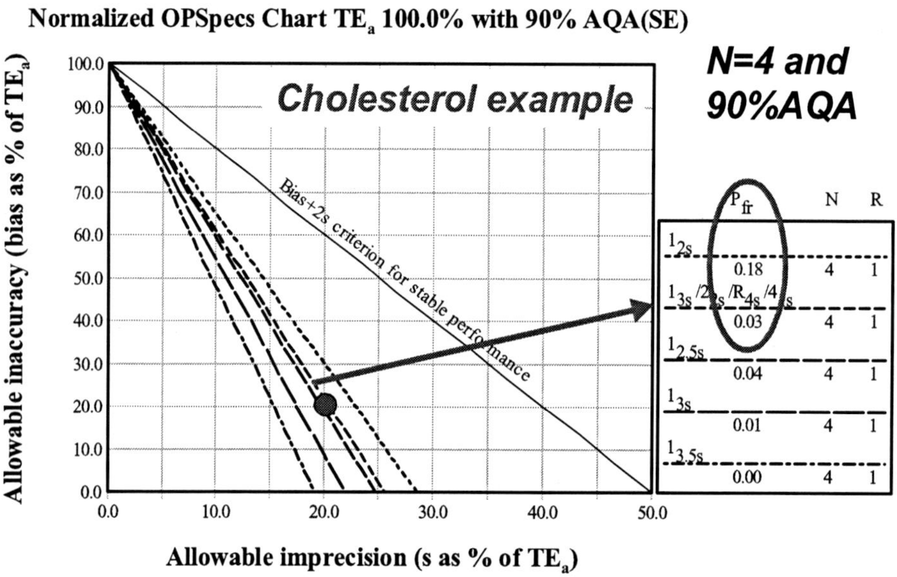

Solution found on N=4 90% AQA OPSpecs chart, which means that each of the two controls should be analyzed twice to give a total N of 4: $1_{3s}/2_{2s}/R_{4s}/4_{1s}$ with N=4 will provide 90% detection of medically important systematic errors with only 3% false rejections; HI-Ped TQC strategy is appropriate. *Avoid* 1_{2s} with N=4 because of expected 18% false rejections.

Calcium

Input parameters: TE_a of 1.0 mg/dL or 9.0% at a decision level of 11.0 mg/dL; observed bias of 1.5%; observed imprecision of 2.2%; use two control materials.

Calculated operating point: Y-coordinate of 17% [(1.5/9.0)*100]; X-coordinate of 24% [(2.2/9.0)*100].

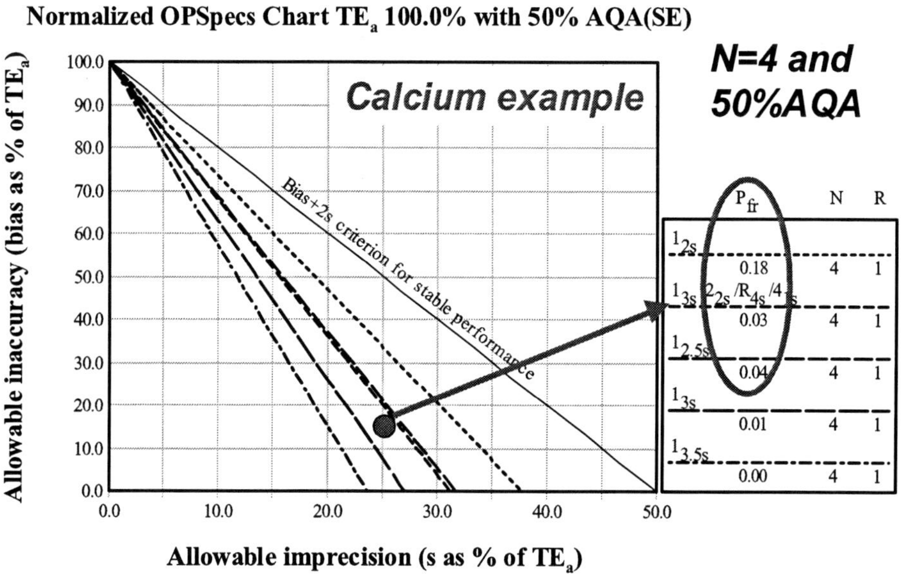

Solution found on N=4 50% AQA chart, which means each control material should be analyzed twice to give a total of 4 control measurements per run; $1_{3s}/2_{2s}/R_{4s}/4_{1s}$ with N=4 will provide somewhat greater than 50% detection of medically important systematic errors with only 3% false rejections; prefer multirule procedure over single-rule procedure in this situation and would even be better to add an 8_x rule to look-back at control measurements in the previous run; MOD-Ped TQC strategy is appropriate.

Try it!

Here are three more examples for you to try on your own. These examples are for hemoglobin, leukocyte count, and erythrocyte count to demonstrate that this planning process can also be applied to tests in hematology. Look up the quality requirement using the CLIA PT criteria for acceptability (see Appendix 1). Use three control materials. Select an appropriate QC procedure and TQC strategy.

Hemoglobin

Given an observed bias of 0.0%, an observed imprecision of 1.3%, and three levels of control materials:

What is the CLIA quality requirement?

What is the calculated Y-coordinate for the operating point?

What is the calculated X-coordinate for the operating point?

Which normalized OPSpecs chart is used for the selection?

What control rules and N are selected?

What error detection is expected?

What false rejection is expected?

What TQC strategy should be used?

Leukocyte Count

Given an observed bias of 0.0%, observed imprecision of 3.9%, and three levels of control materials:

What is the CLIA quality requirement?

What is the calculated Y-coordinate for the operating point?

What is the calculated X-coordinate for the operating point?

Which normalized OPSpecs chart is used for the selection?

What control rules and N are selected?

What error detection is expected?

What false rejection is expected?

What TQC strategy should be used?

Erythrocyte count

Given an observed bias of 0.0%, an observed imprecision of 2.0%, and three levels of control materials:

What is the CLIA quality requirement?

What is the calculated Y-coordinate for the operating point?

What is the calculated X-coordinate for the operating point?

Which normalized OPSpecs chart is used for the selection?

What control rules and N are selected?

What error detection is expected?

What false rejection is expected?

What TQC strategy should be used?

Answers for hematology applications

Hemoglobin

Input parameters: TE_a of 7%; observed bias of 0.0%; observed imprecision of 1.3%; use three control materials.

Calculated operating point: Y-coordinate is 0.0%; X-coordinate is 18.6% [(1.3/7.0)*100].

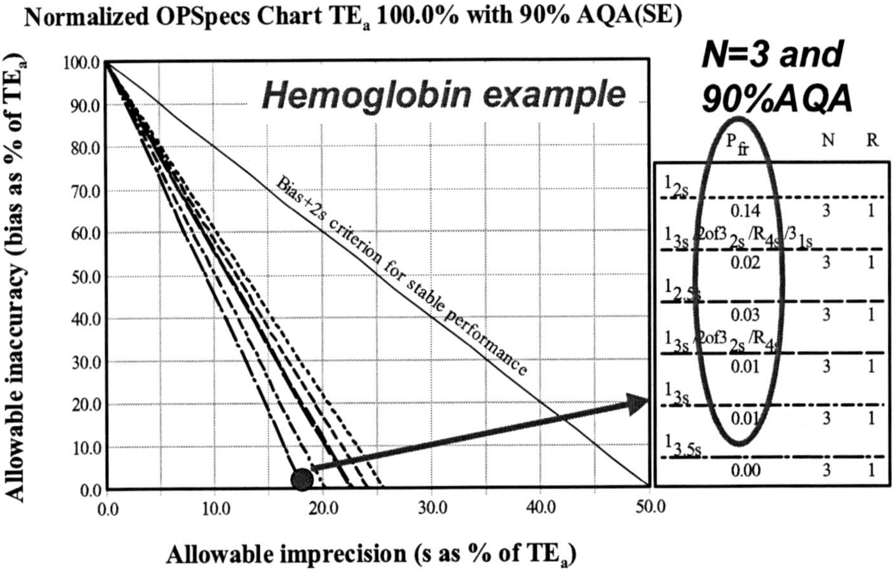

Solution found on N=3 90% AQA OPSpecs chart: any of 5 different QC procedures are possible, but 1_{3s} with N=3 would be the simplest and have the lowest false rejections (0.0%); HI-Ped TQC strategy is appropriate.

Leukocyte Count

Input parameters: TE_a of 15%; observed bias of 0.0%; observed imprecision of 3.9%; use three control materials.

Calculated operating point: Y-coordinate is 0.0%; X-coordinate is 26% [(3.9/15)*100].

Normalized OPSpecs Chart TE_a 100.0% with 90% AQA(SE)

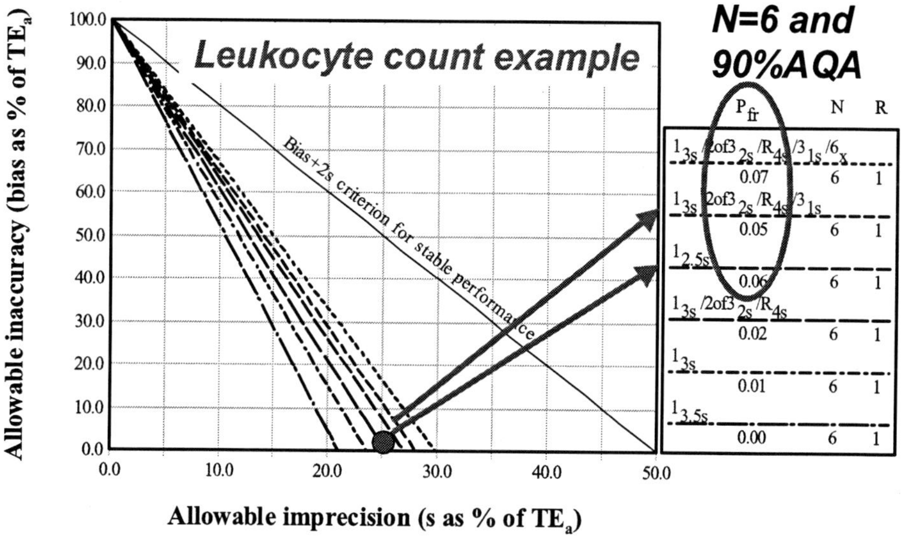

Solution found on N=6 90% AQA chart, which means that each of the three controls should be analyzed twice to give the total N of 6; any of the top three QC procedures are possible, but it would be best to choose between the multirule without 6_x rule or $1_{2.5s}$ single-rule procedure, both of which provide 90% error detection with 5-6% false rejections; HI-Ped strategy is appropriate.

Erythrocyte count

Input parameters: TE_a of 6.0%; observed bias of 0.0%; observed imprecision of 2.0%; use three control materials.

Calculated operating point: Y-coordinate is 0.0%; X-coordinate is 33.3% [(2/6)*100].

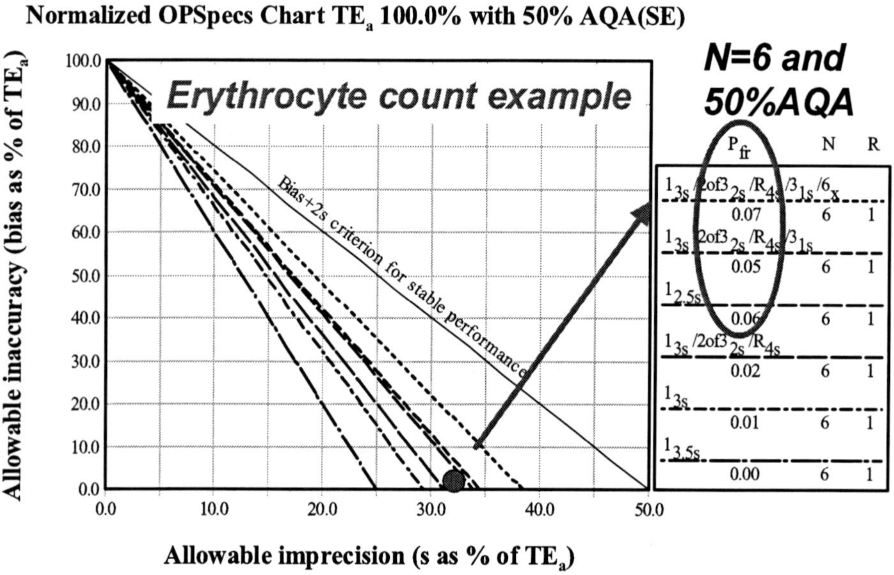

Solution found on N=6 50% AQA chart: note that each of the three control materials would have to be analyzed twice to give a total N of 6; the multirule procedure with the most error detection should be used here (includes the 6_x rule), even though the false rejection rate is a little bit higher (7% vs 5 or 6% for the other two choices); need to use MOD-Ped TQC strategy here.

References

1. Westgard JO. Charts of operational process specification ("OPSpecs charts") for assessing the precision, accuracy, and quality control needed to satisfy proficiency testing performance criteria. Clin Chem 1992;38:1226-1233.

Online References:

Using Normalized OPSpecs charts
http://www.westgard.com/qpbook/lesson56.htm

Quality-planning worksheet (PDF Download)
http://www.westgard.com/qpbook/qcplanworksheet.html

Normalized OPSpecs charts (PDF Download)
http://www.westgard.com/qpbook/normcharts.html

Normalized OPSpecs calculator
http://www.westgard.com/qpbook/normcalc2.htm

Remember to use the username and password provided at the beginning of this book to access the online materials.

Self-Assessment Questions:

- ❍ What's the advantage of using "normalized" OPSpecs charts?
- ❍ Given a quality requirement of 10% for a cholesterol test, and a bias of 1% and a CV of 2%, what are the coordinates for plotting a normalized operating point?
- ❍ Given a triglycerides method with a CV of 5%, a bias of 4%, and two control materials, what control rules and N should be used?
- ❍ What performance is needed for a triglcerides method in order to use 2 control measurements and a Levey-Jennings chart with 3 SD control limits?

9: How do you become proficient at quality planning?

This chapter gives an overview of the whole quality-planning process and sets the stage for your own applications. To become proficient with the quality-planning process, you need to practice on the tests and methods in your laboratory.

Objectives:

- ❍ Review the needs, approach, and methodology for planning the quality of a laboratory test.
- ❍ Apply the quality-planning process to tests of interest in the laboratory.

Chapter materials:

- ❍ **Practice makes Proficient**

Things to do:

- ❍ Study the chapter.
- ❍ Choose a few tests in your laboratory and apply the quality-planning process to select QC procedures.

HAGAR THE HORRIBLE

The biggest obstacle to planning quality is "timing." Today's busy laboratories don't seem to have enough time to do everything. Just keeping the lab running consumes the entire effort of the managers and analysts. If we're lucky, we have a few minutes to spare at the end of the day.

Well, what if you could plan quality in a minute or less? You can, if you learn to use the quality-planning tools in this book. This chapter reviews the whole quality-planning process and prepares you to implement it in your own laboratory. Use the examples in the following chapters for practice.

Practice makes proficient

This chapter provides an overview of needs, approach, and methodology for quality planning in healthcare laboratories. This overview should be useful as a preview, review, or quick refresher of the quality-planning process and the training materials available to support your applications. Because we all learn best from tests and methods that are of interest to ourselves, the remaining chapters present a variety of example applications for automated chemistry tests, blood gas measurements, immunoassays, and coagulations tests. Use these applications to master the steps of the quality-planning process and become proficient in performing the process. Proficient means you should be able to select a QC procedure and identify the TQC strategy in one minute or less. Even the one-minute manager can perform quality planning with support of the tools and technology available today!

Quality planning overview

The fifteen chapters of this book are designed to support your understanding and application of quality planning for laboratory tests. Included in this book are all the necessary tools for a manual quality-planning process so that you can readily implement quality-planning in any healthcare laboratory. Mini-courses, short courses, and workshops may utilize only a subset of these lessons, so you may find it useful to know about all the lessons that are available.

The first three chapters focused on the WHY or need for quality planning. The next two [4-5] described WHAT should be done to plan the quality of laboratory tests. The following three chapters [6-8] provide the HOW or practical methodology for performing quality planning quickly and easily. This chapter summarizes important points about the quality-planning process and provides additional discussion about WHEN to do quality planning and WHO should be involved and responsible. The remaining chapters provide example applications for different areas of the laboratory.

The WHY of quality planning

1. The laboratory must provide a final and independent assurance of quality for the test results it produces. This need for an independent quality management process is described in *A Wake-up Call for Laboratory Quality Management*, which discussed the limitations of current laboratory management practices that bundle many of the essential quality management activities into the services provided by manufacturers of analytical systems.

A recent FDA action against a major manufacturer exposed several fallacies in current management and revealed some hard truths :

- Analytical quality is not a given!
- Responsibility for quality can't be out-sourced!
- Compliance is not enough!
- Statistical QC can't be eliminated!
- Minimum personnel standards and skills are not sufficient!

2. The principles of Total Quality Management (TQM) point out the importance of defining quality standards and establishing a quality-planning process that builds the desired quality into daily production processes. *Assuring Quality through Total Quality Management* describes a quality management framework that is constructed from components – Quality Laboratory Processes, Quality Control, Quality Assessment, Quality Improvement, and Quality Planning – and assembled in a loop or cycle that provides continuous improvement of quality (as shown in the accompanying figure).

This quality management framework should be centered on, or

Laboratory TQM Process

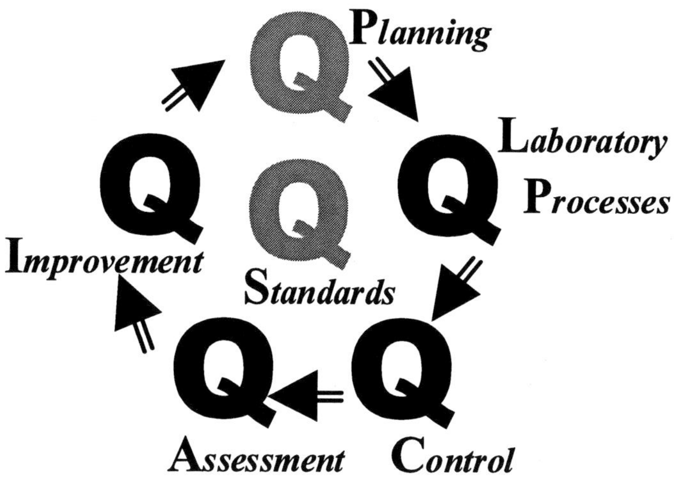

guided by, quality goals or standards. In most laboratories, implementation places a priority on the following:

- Defining quality goals or standards
- Establishing a quality-planning process

3. Current regulatory and professional practice guidelines identify the need for quality planning and provide guidance for implementing a quality-planning process. In *Complying with Regulations, Standards, and Practice Guidelines* [3], the TQM framework is compared with JCAHO IOP guidelines (Joint Commision for Accreditation of Healthcare Organizations, Improving Organizational Performance) CLIA regulatory rules (Clinical Laboratory Improvement Amendments), and NCCLS QC practice guidelines (National Committee for Clinical Laboratory Standards), which reveals that:

- JCAHO IOP strongly recommends quality assessment, quality improvement, and quality planning.
- CLIA rules emphasize quality standards, quality laboratory processes, quality control, and quality assessment.
- JCAHO and CLIA together support the complete framework identified earlier from principles of TQM.
- NCCLS provides guidelines for planning QC procedures as shown in the accompanying figure. The planning process includes steps for defining the quality required for a test, determining method performance, identifying candidate statistical QC strategies, predicting QC performance, setting goals for QC performance, and finally, selecting an appropriate QC procedure.

NCCLS C24-A2 QC Planning Process

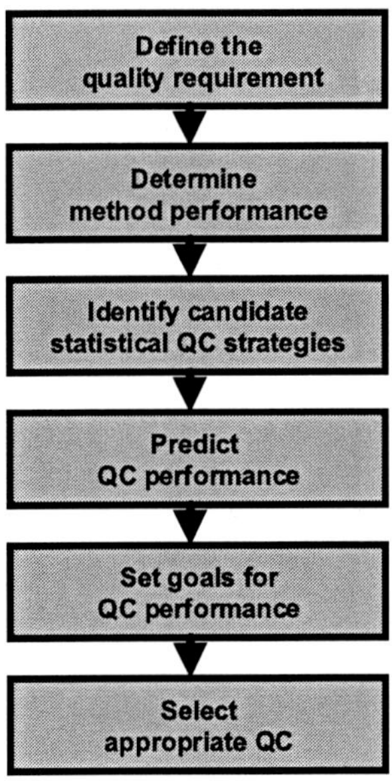

The WHAT of quality planning

4. A detailed quality-planning process can be developed by building on the NCCLS QC planning guidelines and introducing a quality-planning tool that provides information about the performance of different QC procedures. *Devising a Practical Process* [4] describes the steps of a quality-planning process that utilizes a graphical quality-planning tool – the chart of operating specifications, or OPSpecs chart. As shown in the accompanying figure, the two major areas of application are:

- Setting specifications for imprecision and bias when selecting a new analytical method, and
- Selecting control rules and numbers of control measurements when selecting a new QC procedure.

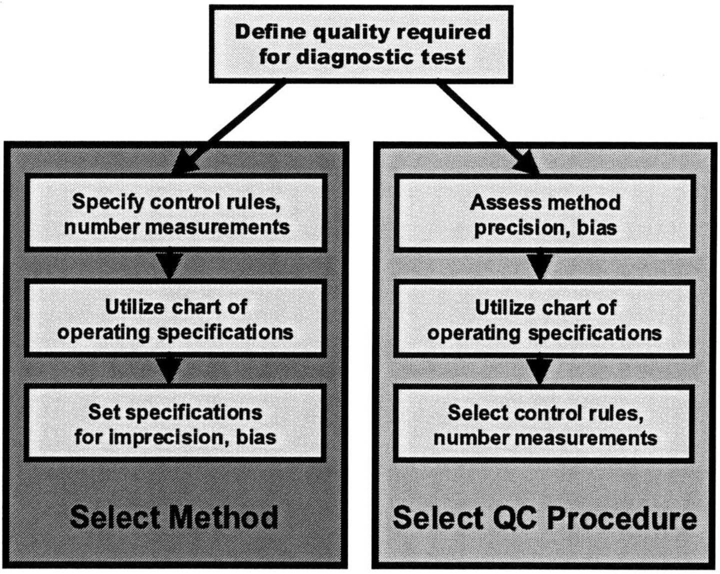

Quality planning for a laboratory test

5. The first and most important step in the planning process is to define the quality required for the test. Unfortunately, this is not a trivial pursuit! *Defining Quality Requirements* describes the difficulties and the solution:

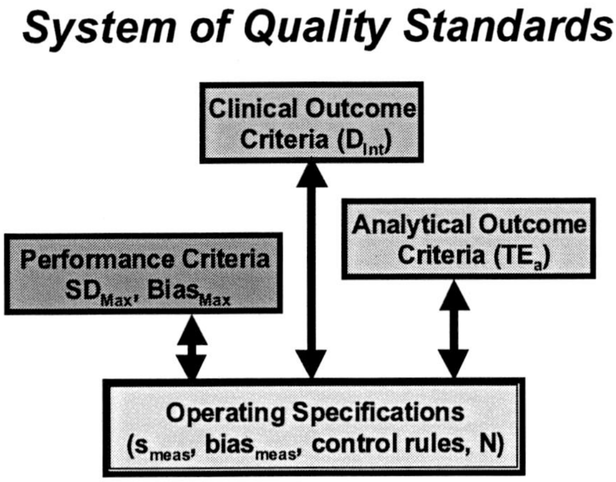

- Concepts and terms are not consistent in the literature on requirements for quality, so there are many formats: a medically important change in test results, an allowable total error, or a maximum allowable standard deviation and a maximum allowable bias.

- Multiple factors affect test variability and different factors are included in different concepts or formats of quality requirements.

- A system of quality standards must be recognized to understand the relationship between the different types and formats of quality requirements. The accompanying figure illustrates a system involving clinical outcome criteria, analytical outcome criteria, and method performance criteria.

- All current quality standards assume that method performance is stable and do not consider the need for QC to detect unstable performance.

- Quality standards must be converted into operating specifications for the imprecision and inaccuracy that are allowable and the control rules and number of control measurements that are necessary to detect medically important errors – the bottom line in a system of quality standards.

The HOW of quality planning

6. A practical tool for translating quality requirements into operating specifications is needed to make quality planning quick and easy to perform. *Adopting the OPSpecs Chart as your quality-planning tool* provides the basic details about a graphical tool called the OPSpecs chart, including:

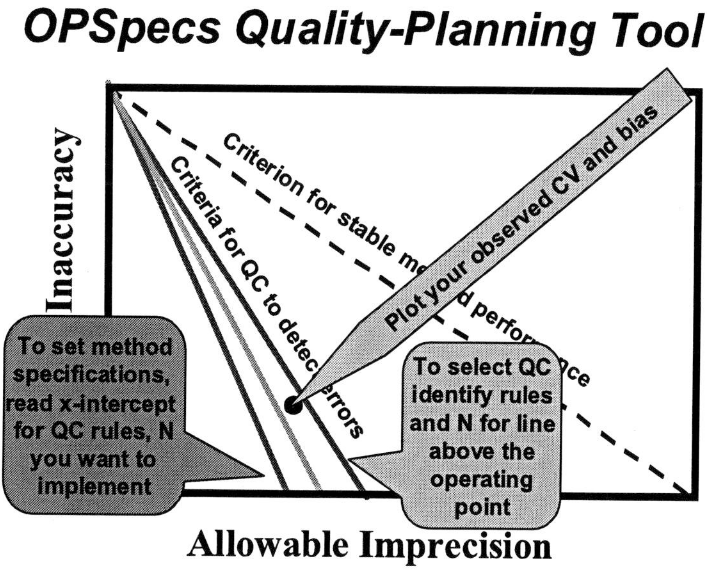

- How to read an OPSpecs chart and recognize the imprecision and inaccuracy that are allowable for different QC procedures.
- How to determine method performance specifications from the x-intercept of the operating limits of different QC procedures
- How to select a QC procedure by plotting the operating point of your method (observed bias as y, observed imprecision as x).
- How to assess the need for quality improvement by identifying changes in imprecision and inaccuracy that would lead to better and easier quality control.

7. Cost-effective operation of testing processes depends on individualizing the QC procedures for each test and method in the laboratory. QC is a technical management strategy and statistical QC is one component of the broad or Total QC strategy. *Formulating a Total Quality Control Strategy* describes how to establish the appropriate balance between statistical and non-statistical components (preventive maintenance, instrument function checks, performance validation tests, patient data QC, in-service training) on the basis of the error detection capability of the statistical QC procedure for the application of interest. Three general strategies are described:

- A HI-Ped strategy is appropriate when statistical QC provides 90% detection of medically important errors. Costs are minimized by selecting QC procedures that have a low number of control measurements and a low probability or chance of false rejections.

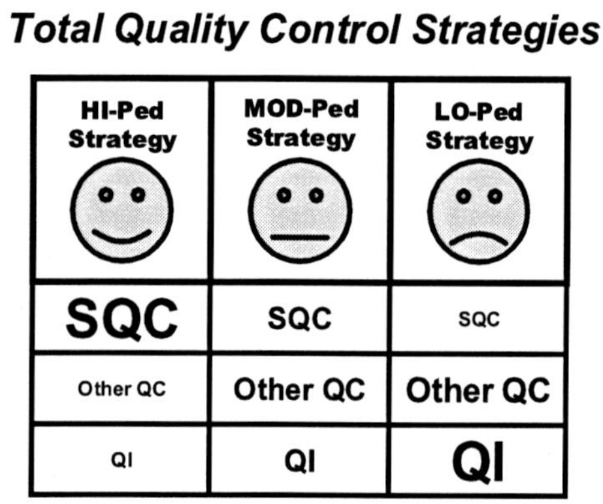

- A MOD-Ped strategy is appropriate when statistical QC provides at least 50% detection of medically important errors. Costs increase to achieve the maximum error detection possible with the maximum amount of statistical QC that is practical. Preventive efforts and non-statistical QC increase.

- A LO-Ped strategy is needed when statistical QC provides less than 50% detection of medically important errors. The emphasis must be on prevention of errors through operator training, preventive maintenance, verification of individual performance factors through instrument function checks and method validation tests, and monitoring patient test results by correlation with other diagnostic information or by patient data QC procedures. Cost is high and efforts should be made to improve analytical performance.

8. Normalized OPSpecs charts provide a practical tool for doing quality planning by hand. *Using Normalized OPSpecs Charts* describes how OPSpecs charts can be scaled to be used with any quality requirement. As shown here, the y-axis is scaled from 0 to 100 and the x-axis is scaled from 0 to 50. The operating point is then calculated as a percent of the quality requirement and plotted on the normalized chart. By using this approach, only eight charts are needed to select a QC procedure for any test. Everything you need to get started is available in this book and from the Internet:

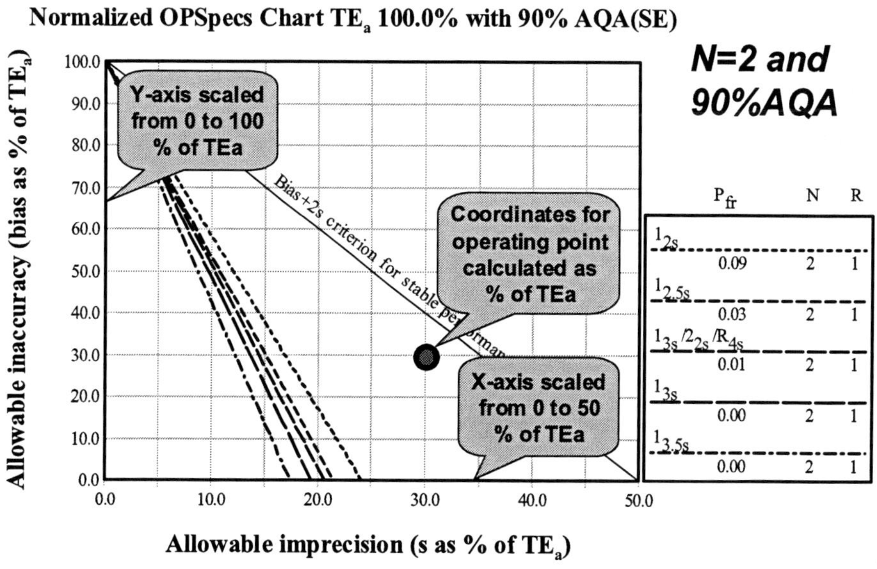

- Normalized OPSpecs charts can be photocopied from this book or a PDF file can be downloaded from the Internet. These are the tools that allow you to choose QC procedures for tests.
- The Worksheet for Selecting a QC Procedure can also be photocopied from this book or a PDF file can be downloaded from the Internet. It allows you to document your applications.
- A Normalized Operating Point calculator is also available on the Internet to calculate the operating point to be plotted on normalized OPSpecs charts. Or you can do the math yourself – it's just a little multiplication and division.

9. The steps of the manual planning process using normalized OPSpecs charts are summarized in the accompanying diagram.

Manual Quality-Planning Process

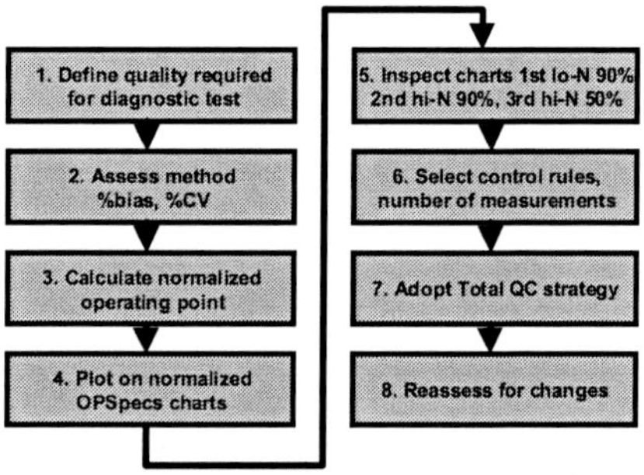

- Define the quality requirement at a medically important decision level using the format of an allowable total error, such as given by the CLIA criteria for acceptable performance or a calculated total biologic error.
- Assess method inaccuracy as the %bias and method imprecision as the %CV at the medically important decision level.
- Calculate the y-coordinate [(%bias/%TE_a)*100] and x-coordinate [(%CV)/%TE_a)*100] for the normalized operating point.
- Plot the normalized operating point on the OPSpecs charts selected for the number of control materials to be analyzed (2 materials or 3 materials).
- Inspect the normalized OPSpecs charts in the following order: low N 90% AQA, high N 90% AQA, and then high N 50% AQA.
- Select the control rules and total number of control measurements from the first chart that provides a solution (i.e., provides a QC procedure whose operating limits are above the operating point). Try to achieve 90% error detection with 5% or less false rejections. If no selection is found, use your maximum QC procedure.
- Adopt a Total QC strategy to balance the efforts expended on statistical QC and other non-statistical QC components. Adopt a HI-Ped TQC strategy when the QC selection is made from a 90% OPSpecs chart; adopt a MOD-Ped TQC strategy when the QC selection is made from a 50% OPSpecs chart; adopt a LO-Ped TQC strategy when a maximum QC procedure must be used.

The WHEN of quality planning

In a healthcare laboratory, quality planning should be an ongoing activity. It's never too late or too early to apply the quality planning process. You need to begin right away! Given that the quality-planning process can be fast and easy to perform – one minute or less – the biggest demand on your time will be the time needed to define the quality requirement for the test and the time needed to determine the imprecision and inaccuracy of your methods. Once you become proficient at using the quality-planning process, you can apply the process to accomplish the following:

- Establish method specifications for purchasing new analytical systems;
- Select QC procedures once you have determined the imprecision and inaccuracy from your initial method validation studies;
- Adapt the QC procedures (if necessary) to accommodate the performance of your methods under routine conditions, as characterized by estimates of imprecision from routine QC data and estimates of inaccuracy or bias from monthly peer-comparison results and periodic proficiency testing surveys;
- Identify tests and methods that need improved analytical performance;
- Prioritize purchases of new methods, instruments, and analytical systems on the basis of needed improvements in analytical quality;
- Assign experienced analysts to analytical systems that require technical expertise to assure quality;
- Determine which methods and instruments are best suited for cross-training and widespread rotations of analysts;
- Update the QC guidelines during the annual review of your procedure manuals.

The WHO of quality planning

In workshops and seminars, I often tell participants that I can teach fifth and six grade students to do quality planning in less time than it takes to teach adults. Why less time? The students don't raise any objections about who, what, when, and why – if you give them the how, they take the tools and use them.

The point of that statement is to emphasize that we have a well-defined quality-planning process and it's easy to do if you follow the directions. If given a quality requirement, the OPSpecs charts for that requirement, and the figures for the method bias and CV, any fifth or sixth grader can plot the operating point and identify the line or lines above the point. The mechanics of using an OPSpecs chart are that simple.

The things that are difficult in this process are (a) defining the quality requirement for the test and (b) determining the precision and accuracy of the method. Those steps require skilled and experienced laboratory scientists. In principle, the medical director of the laboratory has the responsibility for defining the quality requirements for the tests. In practice, that activity may be delegated to managers, supervisors, lead analysts, or quality specialists. In cases where CLIA has defined an allowable total error, that requirement can be used as the starting point. Anyone familiar with the CLIA regulations can look up the requirements.

Reliable estimates of method imprecision and inaccuracy depend on proper statistical analysis of sets of experimental data, initially from method validation studies and later on from routine QC, monthly peer-review comparisons, and periodic proficiency testing surveys. Here's where training and experience with method validation studies and routine QC are important. Some statistical skills are needed – at least the knowledge of which experiments and statistics provide reliable estimates of different types of analytical errors. In many laboratories, these skills reside with QA or QC specialists, R&D technologists, senior analysts, or experienced managers and supervisors.

Example applications for practice

Cholesterol is my favorite test! I use cholesterol as an example over and over and over because it illustrates many of the problems and difficulties you can expect to encounter with other tests. As a clinical chemist, I've followed the evolution of cholesterol methodology and quality standards for over thirty years. In many ways, cholesterol provides a model system that illustrates the importance of analytical quality management in making test results commutable, i.e., interchangable from method to method and lab to lab [1].

Commutability should be our goal for all laboratory tests, not just cholesterol. This will require that each laboratory carefully plan its testing processes to assure the quality required by national standards and guidelines. The cholesterol story shows the importance of having methods that are highly specific, with excellent analytical performance (imprecision and inaccuracy), traceability of standards and calibrators, comparability between field methods and a national reference method, and statistical QC for assuring the quality of routine test results.

Few tests and methods are as well characterized and well studied as cholesterol. Therefore, we can expect there will be difficulties in assuring the quality of many of the other tests being performed in our laboratories. Even so, we will gain many useful insights into our quality management problems if we apply the quality-planning process to all our tests. To help get started with tests you're familiar with, the remaining chapters provide example applications in the following areas:

Automated chemistry applications (see chapter 10)
Blood Gas applications (see chapter 11)
Immunoassay applications(see chapter 12)
Coagulation applications (see chapter 13)

References

1. Wiebe DA, Westgard JO. Cholesterol - a model system to relate medical needs with analytical performance. Clin Chem 1993;39:1504-1513.

Online References:

Practice makes Proficient
http://www.westgard.com/qpbook/lesson57.htm

Remember to use the username and password provided at the beginning of this book to access the online materials.

Self-Assessment Questions:

- ❍ What organization has provided general guidelines for QC planning?
- ❍ What is the first step in the quality-planning process?
- ❍ What type of quality requirement can be used in the manual process?
- ❍ What error detection is considered to be ideal for a QC procedure?
- ❍ What false rejection is considered tolerable for a QC procedure?
- ❍ What graphic tool is used in the manual quality-planning process?
- ❍ When should you rely on non-statistical components of a quality system?
- ❍ How does quality-planning help you prioritize your equipment needs?
- ❍ How does quality-planning help you deploy your personnel?
- ❍ What are the most time-consuming steps in the quality-planning process?

10: Automated Chemistry Applications

This chapter describes detailed quality-planning applications for individual tests on an automated chemistry analyzer – cholesterol, glucose, chloride, and calcium. The individualized QC procedures for these tests represent the range of difficulties encountered for eighteen tests performed by the analyzer.

Objectives:

- ❍ Identify strategies for individualizing the design of QC procedures for chemistry tests in an automated analyzer.
- ❍ Identify strategies for implementing individualized QC designs for tests in a multitest analyzer.

Chapter materials:

- ❍ **Automated Chemistry Applications**

Things to do:

- ❍ Study the chapter.
- ❍ Identify how QC is being performed for a multitest analyzer in your laboratory.
- ❍ Determine whether individualized QC designs can be implemented in the software of the instrument, workstation, or laboratory information system.

Hagar the Horrible

I've been teaching – some might say preaching – about the importance of planning the analytical quality of laboratory tests for a long time; this chapter references one study I performed ten years ago about the financial savings that proper quality-planning can bring. Sometimes I worry, however, that people will change doctors rather than making the changes the doctor suggests, particularly when those changes seem to have unpleasant consequences. Lucky for us, the consequences of improved quality control are positive – fewer reruns, better detection of problems, ***AND LOWER COSTS****, as illustrated by this application for an automated multitest chemstry analyzer. Less waste, better performance – maybe this is advice we can all take!*

Automated Chemistry Applications

Quality-planning applications for clinical chemistry tests are perhaps the easiest to get started with because criteria for acceptable performance have been defined by CLIA for many of the routine chemistry tests and estimates of method imprecision and inaccuracy are generally available in the laboratory. It is also helpful that there are documented applications available in the literature. Finally, the high level of automation in chemistry analyzers has improved the performance of chemistry tests, particularly imprecision, thus careful selection of QC procedures can often reduce operating costs! Saving time and money should provide strong motivation for initiating your quality-planning applications in the clinical chemistry area.

Quality requirements

CLIA defines criteria for acceptable performance for 27 different chemistry tests as part of the proficiency testing guidelines. These criteria are in the form of an allowable total error and are presented as a statement of a target value plus and minus a certain amount. This amount is given in three different forms:

- A percentage, e.g., the acceptable performance for cholesterol is stated as "target value ± 10%."
- A concentration, e.g., target value ± 0.5 mmol/L for potassium.
- A interval based on the observed SD of the survey group, e.g., target value ± 3SD for blood gas pO_2. Laboratories can calculate these quality requirements on the basis of group SDs observed in peer review QC programs or previous proficiency testing events.

For some tests, it is necessary to define the medical decision level of interest to interpret the quality requirement, e.g., for glucose, acceptable performance is stated to be target value ± 6 mg/dL or 10%, whichever is greater.

- At a medical decision level of 50 mg/dL, the quality requirement would be 6 mg/dL or 12%.

- At a medical decision level of 120 mg/dL, the quality requirement would be 10% or 12 mg/dL.

Method imprecision and inaccuracy

Most clinical chemistry methods are classified as moderately complex via CLIA-88 guidelines, which require that the imprecision and inaccuracy of the method be validated through replication and comparison of methods experiments, respectively. Therefore, initial estimates of method imprecision and inaccuracy should be available in all laboratories. Ongoing estimates of method imprecision can be obtained from monthly or cumulative QC data and periodic estimates of method inaccuracy can be made from the difference between the laboratory mean and the group mean in inter-laboratory peer comparison programs, external quality assessment programs, and/or proficiency testing surveys.

Example applications

Some initial examples were presented in chapter 8 to illustrate the selection of QC procedures for glucose, cholesterol and calcium. Real-world applications for these tests have been described in the literature for a multitest chemistry analyzer [1], where the selection of QC procedures gave the following results:

- For 14 of 18 tests, a $1_{3.5s}$ rule with N=2 was selected for sodium, potassium, glucose, urea nitrogen, creatinine, phosphorus, uric acid, cholesterol, total protein, total bilirubin, GGT, ALP, AST, and LD;
- A single-rule, $1_{2.5s}$ with N=2, was selected for albumin;
- A multirule QC procedure was found useful for Cl and CO_2 tests;
- A special QC strategy was implemented for calcium by averaging the results of duplicate measurements.

This study was published in 1990 and therefore predates the 1992 publication of the CLIA-88 criteria for acceptable performance in proficiency testing surveys. Thus, the quality requirements were not exactly the same as those defined by CLIA. Note also that this study makes use of a different quality-planning tool – the critical-error graph – which preceded the OPSpecs chart that was introduced in 1991 [2,3].

Related to this study, we also documented the cost-savings that can be expected from optimized, individualized QC designs [4]. We had initially used a multirule QC procedure for all the tests on this analyzer because that's what was accepted practice on the earlier generation analyzer that was being replaced. Old QC practices are often carried over to new generation analyzers because we assume the new system will have similar performance characteristics. However, improvements in precision and stability may permit more cost-effective QC procedures to be implemented, as demonstrated in this application.

The initial changes in QC procedures provided a cost-savings of about $1,450 per month or $17,400 per year, which provided a total savings of $87,000 over the expected 5-year lifetime of the instrument. Later changes in the length of the analytical run increased the savings to $3,000 per month or $36,000 per year, which provided a total savings of $180,000 over the 5-year lifetime of the instrument.

Cholesterol

The method has an observed standard deviation of 2.7 mg/dL or 1.35% at a decision level of 200 mg/dL. Bias is assumed to be 0.0% because method validation studies show small systematic differences between comparative systems within the laboratory and ongoing comparison studies are used to maintain near-zero biases. Two control materials are to be analyzed each run to fulfill the CLIA requirement. TE_a *is defined as 20 mg/dL which is 10% at a medical decision level of 200 mg/dL (note if you look at the reference paper, the units used are actually mg/L rather than mg/dL, therefore the concentration values are all higher by a factor of 10).*

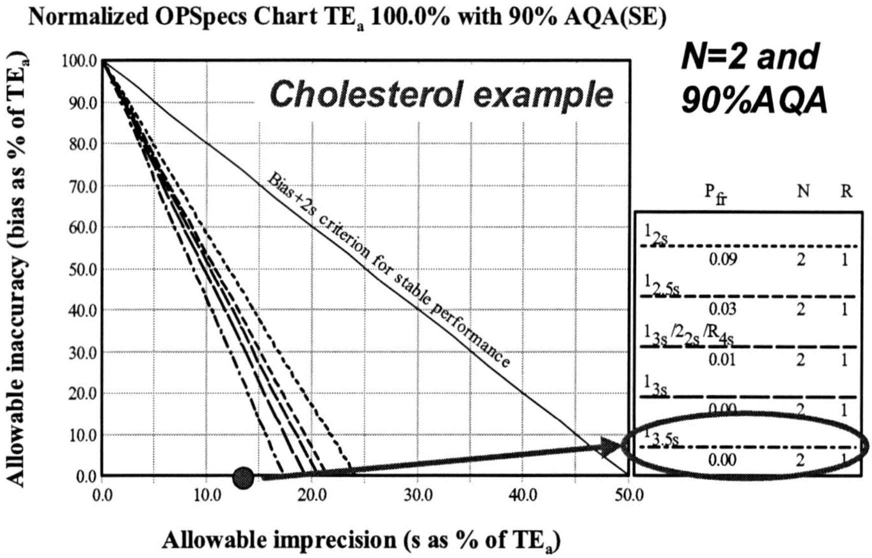

- The normalized operating point would have an x-coordinate of 13.5% [(1.35/10.0)*100] and a y-coordinate of 0.0%.
- When plotted on the normalized OPSpecs chart for 90% AQA and N=2, the validity of the $1_{3.5s}$ rule can be seen from the figure above. Any other QC procedure on the chart could also be used, but the advantage of using 3.5s control limits is that the false rejections would be essentially zero.
- The Total QC strategy can depend on statistical QC to detect problems because better than 90% detection is expected.

Glucose

The observed standard deviation is 1.2 mg/dL or 1.1% at a decision level of 110 mg/dL. Bias is assumed to be zero. TE_a was defined as 8.0 mg/dL, which would be 7.2% at a decision level of 110 mg/dL. This is somewhat more demanding than the CLIA requirement of 6 mg/dL or 10% (whichever is greater), which would be 10% at a decision level of 110 mg/dL. Two control materials are to be analyzed.

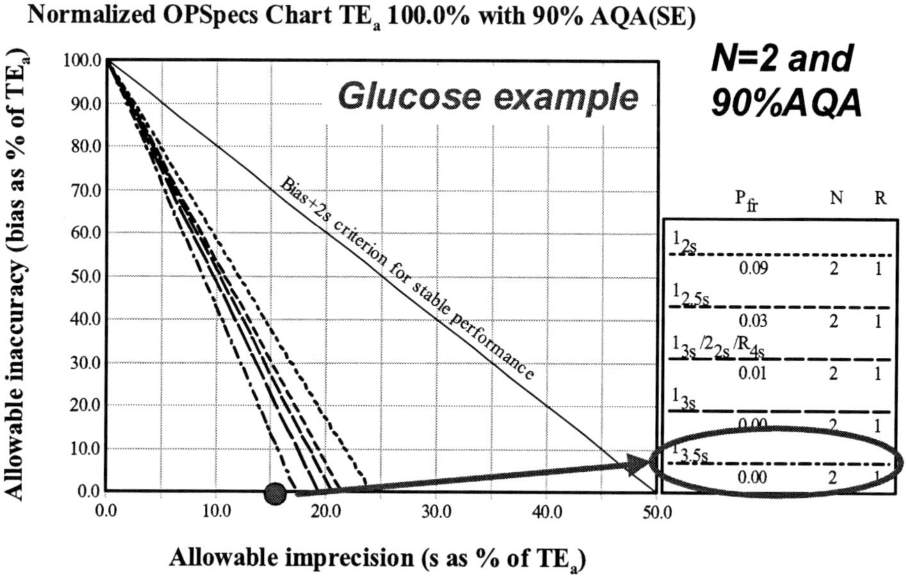

- The normalized operating point would have an x-coordinate of 15.3% [(1.1/7.2)*100] and a y-coordinate of 0.0%.
- When plotted on the normalized OPSpecs chart for 90% AQA and N=2, the results are the same as for the cholesterol example above – a $1_{3.5s}$ control rule will provide adequate error detection with essentially zero false rejections.
- The Total QC strategy is to depend on statistical QC to detect problems.

Chloride

The method SD was 1.04 mmol/L which is 1.04% at a decision level of 100 mmol/L. Bias is assumed to be zero. The CLIA requirement of 4.0 mmol/L corresponds to 4.0% at a decision level of 100 mmol/L. Two control materials are to be analyzed.

Normalized OPSpecs Chart TE_a 100.0% with 50% AQA(SE)

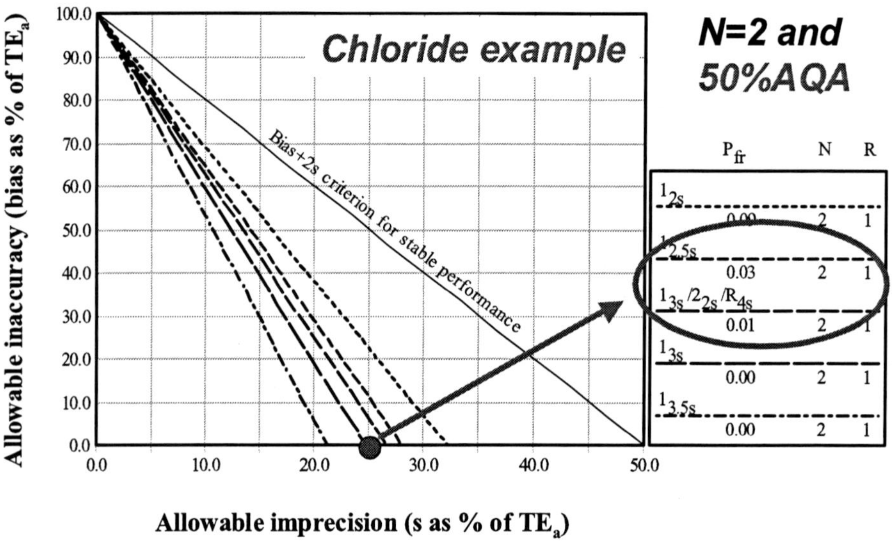

- The normalized operating point has an x-coordinate of 26% [(1.04/4.0)*100] and a y-coordinate of 0%.
- When plotted on a normalized OPSpecs chart for N=2 and 90%AQA, there is no appropriate QC procedure.
- When plotted on the chart for N=2 and 50%AQA, either a $1_{2.5s}$ single-rule or a multirule with $1_{3s}/2_{2s}/R_{4s}$ will provide at least 50% error detection (see figure above). Addition of a 4_{1s} rule to the multirule procedure ($1_{3s}/2_{2s}/R_{4s}/4_{1s}$) would be useful to maximize error detection across two runs.
- The Total QC strategy should provide more emphasis on preventive maintenance and specific instrument checks when only moderate error detection can be achieved within the first run. For this chloride test, frequent maintenance and cleaning of the chloride electrode is needed to prevent problems from occurring.

Calcium

The observed SD was 0.168 mg/dL, which is 1.68% at a decision level of 10.0 mg/dL. TE_a was defined as 0.5 mg/dL, which would be 5% at a medical decision level of 10.0 mg/dL (which is much more demanding than the CLIA requirement of 1.0 mg/dL or 10% at a decision level of 10.0 mg/dL).

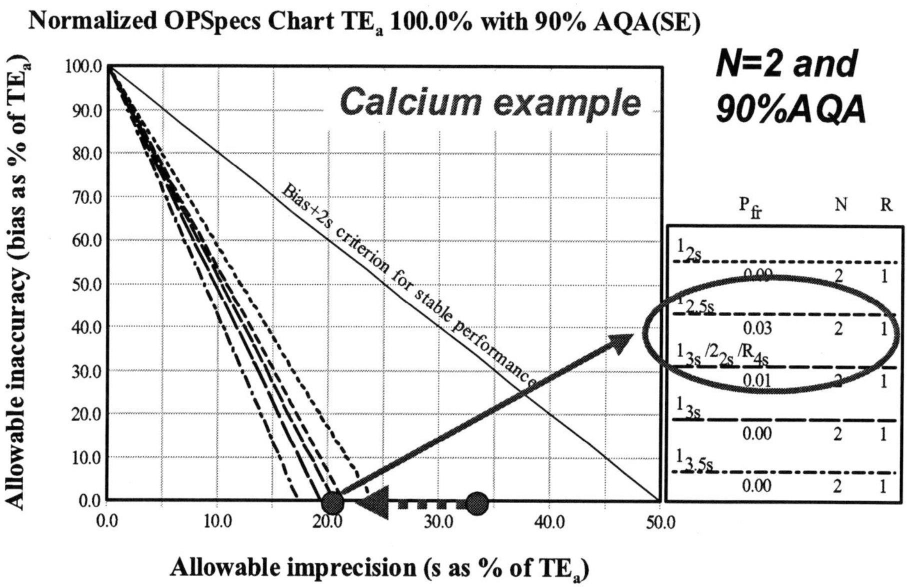

- The normalized operating point would have an x-coordinate of 33.6% [(1.68/5.0)*100] and a y-coordinate of 0.0%.
- When plotted on the N=2 with 90% AQA or N=2 with 50%AQA, no QC procedure can be selected. A maximum QC procedure could be selected, possibly a multirule procedure that includes a 4_{1s} rule to look-back at the control data in the previous run. However, the error detection for a single-rule QC procedure will be low to moderate, which is not very satisfactory.
- The Total QC strategy should emphasize improving method performance and preventing problems from occurring. If duplicate measurements were made to reduce the imprecision

of the method (which would change the x-coordinate to 33.6%/ 1.414 or 23.8%), then a multirule solution could be found on the N=2 50%AQA chart (gives essentially the same operating point as shown on the previous N=2 and 50%AQA chart for chloride). Further improvement to give an x-coordinate of 20% is needed to find a solution on the N=2 90%AQA chart, as shown in the figure on the previous page. This strategy of improving method performance by making replicate measurements was actually implemented in the laboratory by installing two calcium tests on the analyzer. Note, however, if the CLIA quality requirement of 10% were used, then the original operating point would have had a normalized x-coordinate of 16.8%, and the same QC procedure could have been selected as shown in the cholesterol and glucose examples above.

Planning and implementation strategies

There are lessons to be learned from quality-planning applications in all areas of the laboratory. Routine chemistry applications may be simpler than others, but are still a source of important insights and advice. You're more likely to solve complicated quality-planning problems if you have a good grasp of the solutions to simpler applications.

Manage quality in a quantitative manner to improve productivity and reduce costs. Cost-savings can be demonstrated when QC procedures are designed or selected on the basis of the quality required for the test and the imprecision and inaccuracy observed for the method. These savings will be particularly significant if your current laboratory QC practice is to utilize 2 SD control limits, which cause a high level of false rejections – about 9% when N is 2, 14% when N is 3, and 18% when N is 4. If multirule QC procedures are being used with 4th and 5th generation automation analyzers, it may be possible to simplify QC, reduce N, improve productivity, and reduce costs, as demonstrated for the example applications here [which have been documented in the scientific literature, references 1 and 4].

Begin with proficiency testing criteria as the quality requirements. For most routine chemistry tests, proficiency testing criteria will have been defined in the form of allowable total errors. Although these requirements represent the minimum level of quality that must be achieved by the laboratory, their availability will allow you to get started right away. Begin your quality-planning applications using these criteria, then repeat the process when you obtain better information about the quality requirements for your patient applications.

Use the best estimates of method performance available at the time. Laboratories always have current QC data that can be used to estimate the SD of a method, but may not have current comparison of methods data to estimate the bias of a method. There is nothing wrong with making an initial assumption that bias is zero in order to get started with your quality-planning applications. Use the best estimates of method performance that are available at the moment. You can always repeat the planning process when you have better information. Information about bias may be obtained from monthly peer-comparison programs or from periodic proficiency testing surveys.

Individualize the QC procedure for each test on a multitest system. Different tests have different quality requirements and different analytical performance, therefore, there will be different QC procedures that are appropriate for different tests on a multitest system.

Keep N constant and changes the rules to adjust QC performance. It will often be necessary to keep the number of control measurements the same for each test on a multitest analyzer and then vary the control rules to optimize QC performance for different tests. Usually only 3 to 5 different QC designs will be needed to handle all the tests; when we planned for our multitest chemistry analyzer, ultimately 14 of the 18 tests could be controlled using 3.5s limits, 1 with 2.5s limits, 2 others with multirule procedures, and 1 required a special QC procedure.

Adjust the TQC strategy to deal with tests with poor performance. It is not unusual to encounter a few tests for which error detection is less than ideal, therefore efforts are needed to improve analytical performance and/or to prevent problems from occurring. Sources of errors and causes of instability need to be identified and preventive maintenance schedules adjusted to prevent problems from occurring with these tests.

Implement individualized QC designs via computer. With automated systems, it is generally necessary to computerize QC to keep up with the production of test results. Flexible QC software is needed, particularly the ability to select different control rules for different tests that are performed on the same analytical system. Test-specific QC is an important feature in computer software to help you manage and operate your automated systems in the most cost-effective way.

References

1. Koch DD, Oryall JJ, Quam EF, Feldbruegge DH, Dowd DE, Barry PL, Westgard JO. Selection of medically useful quality-control procedures for individual tests done in a multitest analytical system. Clin Chem 1990;36:230-233. [also available as PDF file at http://www.westgard.com/multchem.htm]

2. Westgard JO, Hyltoft Petersen P, Wiebe DA. Laboratory process specifications for assuring the quality in the US National Cholesterol Education Program. Clin Chem 1991;37:656-661.

3. Westgard JO, Wiebe DA. Cholesterol operational specifications for assuring quality required by CLIA proficiency testing. Clin Chem 1991;37:1938-1944.

4. Westgard JO, Oryall JJ, Koch DD. Predicting effects of QC practices on the cost-effective operation of a multitest analytical system. Clin Chem 1990;36:1760-1764. [also available as PDF file at http://www.westgard.com/multchem.htm]

Online References:

Automated Chemistry Applications
http://www.westgard.com/qpbook/lesson58.htm

Selection of medically useful quality-control procedures for individual tests done in a multitest analytical system. [PDF]
http://www.westgard.com/multchem.htm

Predicting effects of QC practices on the cost-effective operation of a multitest analytical system. [PDF]
http://www.westgard.com/multchem.htm

Remember to use the username and password provided at the beginning of this book to access the online materials.

Self-Assessment Questions:

- ❍ What is meant by "individualized QC design"?
- ❍ How can improved QC lead to cost savings?
- ❍ How can you individualize QC designs for each test on a multitest analyzer if the number of control measurements must be kept constant?
- ❍ In general, how many different QC designs would be expected for a multitest analyzer?
- ❍ What flexibility is needed in your QC software?

11: Blood Gas Applications

This chapter considers the selection of QC procedures for the basic blood gas parameters – pH, pCO_2, and pO_2. The application is for a Point-of-Care (POC) analyzer and makes use of the typical precision performance expected for a new analyzer, as documented by a published evaluation report.

Objectives:

- ❍ Apply the quality-planning process to blood gas parameters and a POC situation.
- ❍ Identify special factors that are critical for blood gas parameters.

Chapter materials:

- ❍ **Blood Gas Applications**

Things to do:

- ❍ Study the chapter.
- ❍ Review how QC is performed for a blood gas analyzer in your laboratory.
- ❍ Review the POC blood gas application in your institution.
- ❍ Determine the CLIA quality requirement for pO_2 on the basis of survey information available in your laboratory.

Hagar the Horrible

One area that needs careful planning for quality is the Point-of-Care testing field. Unfortunately, some of the recommended QC procedures, such as "electronic" QC, are simplistic and won't provide correct readings on the control status of the method. POC tests should be subject to the same quality standards and the same quality-planning process. This chapter illustrates how it can be done for a POC blood gas analyzer. The method performance figures used in these applications are representative of a new POC analyzer, as documented in a method evaluation study published in 1999.

Blood Gas Applications

Blood gas measurements are often performed in Point-Of-Care (POC) settings as well as larger clinical or pulmonary laboratories. Patients may be monitored during surgery and in the recovery room via the POC tests. Later, when the patients are moved back to their hospital rooms, they may be monitored by measurements performed in a central clinical laboratory or pulmonary function laboratory. The comparability and consistency of test results will be important.

When a new POC analyzer is obtained, the performance of the analyzer should be evaluated by comparison to the measurements being performed in an established laboratory, such as the central clinical chemistry laboratory or the pulmonary function laboratory. Method validation studies will provide estimates of imprecision and bias that can then be used for planning QC procedures.

Quality requirements

The US CLIA criteria for acceptable performance in proficiency testing are as follows:

Blood gas pH	Target Value ± 0.04 pH unit
Blood gas pCO_2	Target Value ± 5 mm Hg or +/- 8% (greater)
Blood gas pO_2	Target Value ± 3 SD

To quantify the requirement for pO_2, results from an AACC/CAP proficiency testing survey during 1999 showed the following SDs and CVs for pO_2 for "all" analyzers, which represent approximately 3500 laboratories that participated in the survey:

At 145 mm Hg, SD=6.7 mm Hg, CV=4.6%
At 115 mm Hg, SD=7.1 mm Hg, CV=6.1%
At 118 mm Hg, SD=7.5 mm Hg, CV=6.4%
At 59 mm Hg, SD=14.7 mm Hg, CV=25.1%
At 144 mm Hg, SD=7.2 mm Hg, CV=5.0%

The SD and CV for the 4th specimen (59 mm Hg) appear to be inconsistent with the rest of the figures and further inspection showed that different manufacturers' systems provided large differences in their mean values, demonstrating that the "all" or overall SDs and CVs may reflect a large contribution from systematic errors between different types of analyzers. Averaging the results from the other four specimens gives an SD of 7.1 mm Hg and a CV of 5.5%. The CLIA requirement for pO_2 can therefore be estimated to be about ± 16.5%.

Method imprecision and inaccuracy

To estimate the imprecision of the analyzer, initial method validation studies should include a replication study performed over a period of 20 days. Typically, three different control materials would be analyzed and the SDs and CVs calculated for each level. To estimate inaccuracy or bias, a comparison of methods experiment should be performed on a minimum of 20 and preferably 40 fresh patient samples. The paired data should be analyzed by regression or t-test statistics.

Example applications

For the examples here, the estimates of method CVs are similar to the performance documented in a recently published evaluation study of a POC analyzer [1]. Three different levels of control materials are generally provided for blood gas measurements. Typical levels would be 7.20, 7.40, and 7.60 for pH; 60, 40, and 20 mm Hg for pCO_2, and 60, 100, and 140 mm Hg for pO_2.

As before, the Normalized OPSpecs charts used here are available in the book or on the Internet. The Normalized Operating Point calculations are shown in the examples.

pH

The average method SD for the three control materials is 0.005 pH unit and the method bias is 0.01 pH unit. The CLIA requirement is 0.04 pH units.

Normalized OPSpecs Chart TE_a 100.0% with 90% AQA(SE)

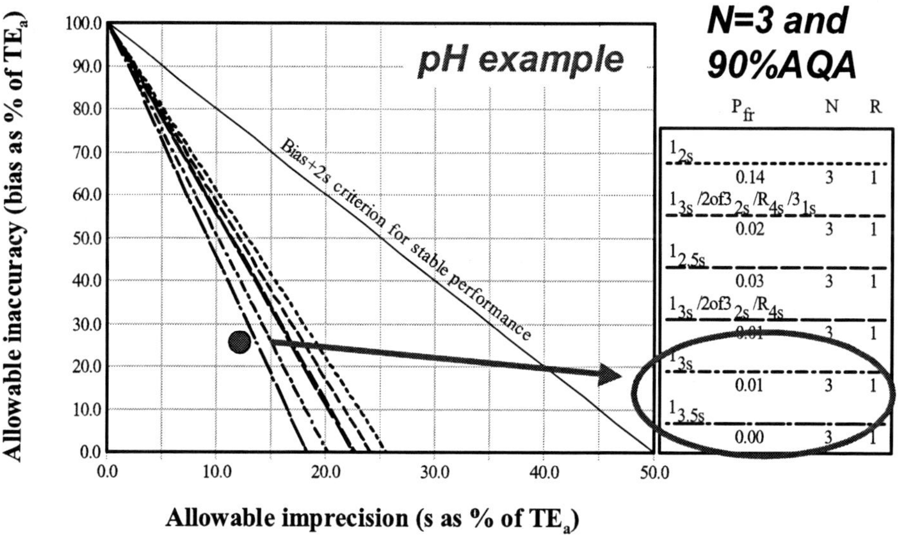

- The normalized operating point has an x-coordinate of 12.5% [(0.005/0.04)*100] and a y-coordinate of 25% [(0.01/0.04)*100].
- When plotted on the normalized OPSpecs chart for N=3 with 90% AQA, the operating limits of all the QC procedures are above the operating point (see figure above). Any control rule with N=3 can be used, but it would be best to select a 1_{3s} or $1_{3.5s}$ rule to keep false rejections very low.
- The Total QC strategy should depend on statistical QC to detect problems and include the minimum preventive procedures recommended by the manufacturer and by good laboratory practice.

pCO_2

The average CV for the three control materials is 2.5%. Method bias is observed to be 0.2 mm Hg at the mean of the comparison data (at approximately 40 mm Hg). The quality requirement at 40 mm Hg would be 5 mm Hg or 12.5%.

Normalized OPSpecs Chart TE_a 100.0% with 90% AQA(SE)

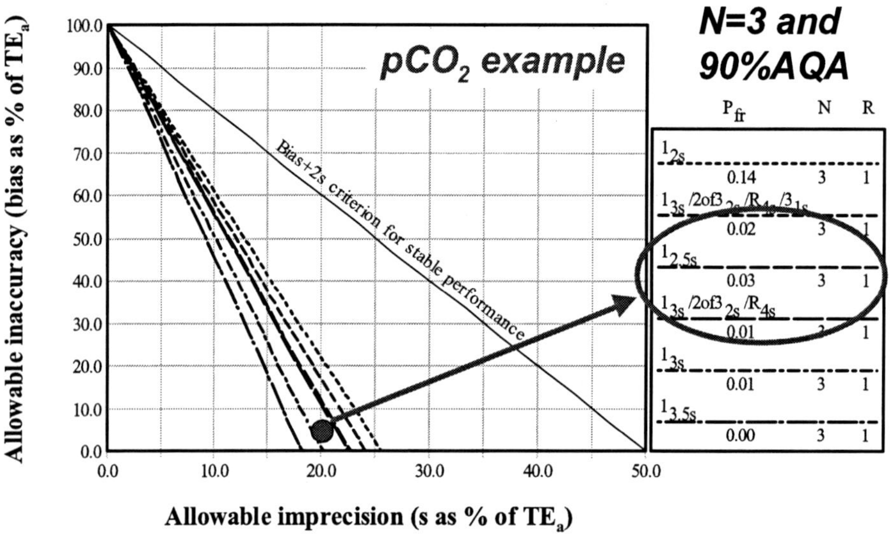

- The normalized operating point has an x-coordinate of 20% [(2.5%/12.5%)*100] and a y-coordinate of 4.0% [(0.2mm/5mm)*100].
- When plotted on the normalized OPSpecs chart for N=3 with 90% AQA, there are four possible QC procedures (see figure above). A multirule procedure with $1_{3s}/2of3_{2s}/R_{4s}$ rules or a single-rule QC procedure using a $1_{2.5s}$ rule could be selected. The multirule QC procedure is preferred because it will give fewer false rejections (1.0% vs 3.0%).
- The Total QC strategy can again depend on statistical QC to detect important problems whenever they occur.

pO_2

The average CV is observed to be 4.1% and the bias between methods is nearly zero. As shown earlier, the CLIA quality requirement is 16.5%, as calculated from results of a proficiency testing survey where the group CV is estimated as 5.5% on the basis of 4 different PT specimens.

Normalized OPSpecs Chart TE_a 100.0% with 50% AQA(SE)

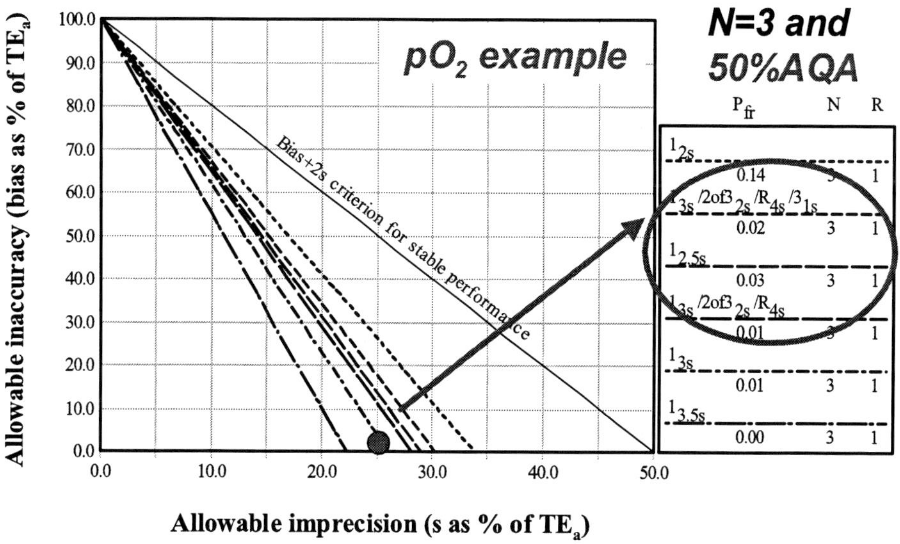

- The normalized operating point has an x-coordinate of 25% [(4.1%/16.5%)*100]. The y-coordinate is zero.
- When plotted on a normalized OPSpecs chart for N=3 and 90%AQA, the only solution is the 1_{2s} rule, which has an unacceptably high level of false rejections (approx. 14%).
- When plotted on a normalized OPSpecs chart for N=6 and 90% AQA, there are four solutions available. However, it's unlikely that POC testing sites will be willing or able to run 6 controls to monitor pO_2. Therefore, an N=3 solution will be needed.
- When plotted on a normalized OPSpecs chart for N=3 and 50%AQA, there are two multirule procedures that will provide at least 50% error detection (see figure above). The fact that

their operating lines are considerably above the operating point indicates that the error detection should be considerably higher than 50%. The best selection to give maximum error detection would be the multirule procedure that includes a 3_{1s} control rule.

- The Total QC strategy for pO_2 should include an aggressive preventive maintenance program to minimize the problems that occur. Additional QC checks such as the use of tonometered blood would be a valuable addition to monitor performance. Correlation with oxygen saturation may be useful to check the reliability of some specimens.

Planning and implementation strategies

It is not unusual to see a range of performance for different blood gas parameters – from excellent for pH, good for pCO_2, and marginal for pO_2. The method CVs used in the examples here are representative of the performance that can be expected from current portable blood gas analyzers [1], thus there is a need for well designed QC procedures to assure comparability of results between point-of-care and central laboratory applications. The problem of how to QC pO_2 measurements is further complicated by matrix effects of the control materials [2].

Use subsets of a multirule procedure to provide different QC designs. The differences in analytical performance and quality requirements will typically lead to different QC designs for each of these tests. One way to relate these different QC procedures is to select rules that are part of a particular multirule combination. In this case, select the $1_{3s}/2of3_{2s}/R_{4s}/3_{1s}$ combination and utilize the whole set of rules for pO_2, drop the 3_{1s} rule for pCO_2, and drop all but the 1_{3s} rule for pH. This provides a set of QC designs that are all related to a single multirule procedure, which will be the focus of in-service training.

Implement multistage designs for startup and monitoring. In situations where it is not possible to achieve the ideal performance of 90% error detection with less than 5% false rejections, implement two different QC designs – one having 90% error detection (with some increase in false rejections if necessary) and the other having low false rejections (with moderate error detection). Use the high error detection design to check carefully at "startup" and the low false rejection design to "monitor" performance after startup. For blood gas measurements, it may be useful to have an N=3 startup design that is performed once a day and an N=1 monitoring design that is performed by new operators and at eight-hour shift changes.

Accept lower error detection when there is frequent calibration. Many blood gas analyzers have automatic calibration functions that are scheduled at short intervals, often hourly. With this frequent calibration, most instrument sources of shifts or drifts are automatically corrected and therefore do not require detection by the QC procedure. Optimal QC performance then depends on maintaining a low level of false rejections. Moderate error detection – 50% or more – should be tolerable.

Utilize instrument function checks as part of TQC strategy. Again, because of the automatic checks programmed into many blood gas analyzers, the TQC strategy can support QC designs with moderate error detection. Instrument function checks, such as electronic QC, can be used to complement the detection capabilities of statistical QC procedures.

References

1. Lindemans J, Hoefkens P, van Kessel AL, Bonnay M, Kulpmann WR, van Suijlen JDE. Portable blood gas and electrolyte analyzer evaluated in a multiinstitutional study. Clin Chem 1999;45:111-117.

2. Olafsdottir E, Westgard JO, Ehrmeyer SS, Fallon KD. Matrix effects on the performance and selection of QC procedures to monitor PO_2 in blood gas measurements. Clin Chem 1996;42:392-6.

Online References:

Blood Gas Applications
http://www.westgard.com/qpbook/lesson59.htm

Remember to use the username and password provided at the beginning of this book to access the online materials.

Self-Assessment Questions:

- ❍ What information is needed to determine the CLIA criterion for acceptable performance of pO_2?
- ❍ What QC procedure would be appropriate for a pH measurement when the observed bias is zero and the observed SD is 0.005?
- ❍ What CV is needed for a pCO_2 method if bias were zero at a decision level of 40 mm Hg?
- ❍ Why is it often difficult to QC pO_2 methods?
- ❍ What is the meaning of the term "multistage QC"?

12: Immunoassay Applications

One of the most challenging areas for quality-planning applications is the selection of QC procedures for immunoassay methods. Examples are provided for thryoxine, cortisol, and thyroid stimulating hormone (TSH).

Objectives:

- ❍ Apply the quality-planning process to immunoassay tests.
- ❍ Identify strategies that are critical for implementing effective QC procedures.

Chapter materials:

- ❍ **Immunoassay Applications**

Things to do:

- ❍ Study the chapter.
- ❍ Review how QC is performed for immunoassay methods in your laboratory.
- ❍ Determine the CLIA quality requirement for TSH on the basis of survey information available in your laboratory.

Hagar the Horrible

Many times when I speak in front of audiences, someone will ask me what QC they should be doing. They're looking for one answer, one QC procedure, one set of rules that will work for everything. Unfortunately, there is no magic set of rules, not even the "Westgard Rules." QC procedures need to be carefully designed for the specific tests and methods in your laboratory. Immunoassay tests illustrate this need because the current generation of analytic instruments is less precise than the later generations of automated chemistry and hematology analyzers. The immunoassay applications in this chapter will introduce some more advanced planning and implementation strategies.

Immunoassay Applications

Quality planning for immunoassays poses some special difficulties because there are usually multiple decision levels, different quality requirements at these different decision levels, and different method CVs at different decision levels. The title of an April 2000 survey of immunoassay instruments in CAP TODAY makes the point – "Of all analyzers, immunoassay the trickiest" [1]. QC designs may be more complicated because immunoassay measurement procedures are generally not as precise as the highly automated chemistry and hematology methods, therefore it may be necessary to utilize multi-level or multistage designs, often with multirule control procedures and a higher number of control measurements.

Quality requirements

Endocrine tests and some toxicology tests are commonly performed by immunoassay methods. CLIA's list of regulated endocrine tests is short – only seven tests – cortisol, free thyroxine, human chorionic gonadotropin, T3 uptake, triiodothyronine, thyroid stimulating hormone, and thyroxine. For all but cortisol and thyroxine, the quality requirements are given as Target Value plus and minus 3 SD, where the SD here is estimated from the group of laboratories participating in the proficiency testing survey. For cortisol, the allowable total error is given as 25%; for thyroxine, the allowable total error is given as 20% or 1.0 mcg/dL, whichever is greater. CLIA's requirements for toxicology are generally stated as Target Value plus and minus 20 or 25%, the higher figure being used most often.

For other assays, it would seem appropriate to extend the 3 SD peer group concept and utilize the data from inter-laboratory peer comparison programs and external quality assessment programs as the starting point for defining the quality requirements. Clinical quality requirements may also be used, but their application requires access to more sophisticated planning tools utilizing a more complex clinical quality-planning model and computer support, such as the QC Validator program [2-3], to carry out the calculations.

Method imprecision and inaccuracy

Imprecision is estimated from replication studies that are typically carried out with three or more levels of control materials. The SDs observed and the CVs calculated are likely to vary widely from low to high end of the reportable range. CVs may be as large as 10 to 15% at one end of the range and typically will be about 5% in the most precise part of the range. Inaccuracy can be assessed from comparison of methods experiments, but the lack of reference methodology makes it difficult to assign systematic errors to one method or the other. Therefore, it is widespread practice to assess systematic errors by comparison to like methods in monthly peer-review programs or periodic proficiency testing surveys.

Example applications

A study published by Mugan et al [4] describes applications for 7 different tests that were performed on an automated analyzer – prolactin, Total β-hCG, CEA, FSH, LH, TSH, and β2-Microglobulin. Seth [5] has illustrated how QC procedures can be selected with the aid of critical-error graphs. Carey has provided some general QC planning guidelines, as well as some detailed examples for theophylline, cortisol, thyroxine, and folate, that are available on the Internet [6].

As before, Normalized OPSpecs charts are used to select the QC procedures. The calculations for the normalized operating point are shown.

Thyroxine

A method has a CV of 5.5% and a bias of 0.0% at a decision level of 5.0 ug/dL. CLIA defines the allowable total error as 20%. Given 3 control materials are to be analyzed, select an appropriate QC procedure and Total QC strategy.

Normalized OPSpecs Chart TE_a 100.0% with 90% AQA(SE)

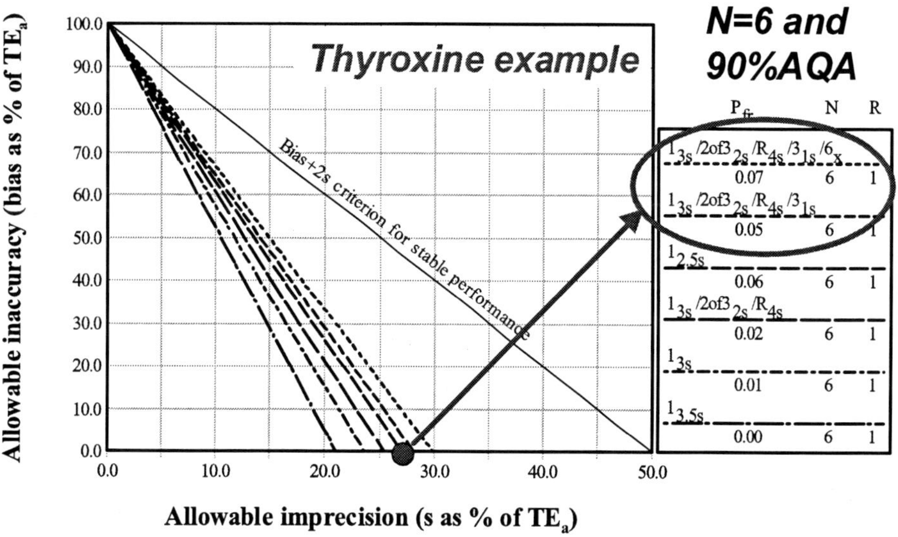

- The normalized operating point would have an x-coordinate of 27.5% [(5.5%/20.0%)*100] and a y-coordinate of zero.
- Two solutions are identified when the operating point is plotted on the normalized OPSpecs chart for N=6 and 90% AQA (see above). Multirule procedures are needed to provide the desired 90% detection of medically important systematic errors.
- The Total QC strategy could depend on the high error detection of the multirule QC procedure, however, it would be advantageous to improve method performance and reduce the number of control measurements from 6 to 3 per run. Inspection of the N=3 90% AQA chart shows that the x-coordinate can have a maximum value of about 23%, which corresponds to improving the method CV to 4.6%.

Cortisol

A method has a CV of 5.3% at a medical decision level of 30 ug/dL. Method bias is assumed to be zero. The CLIA PT criterion is 25%. Given 3 control materials are to be analyzed, select an appropriate QC rules, N, and TQC strategy.

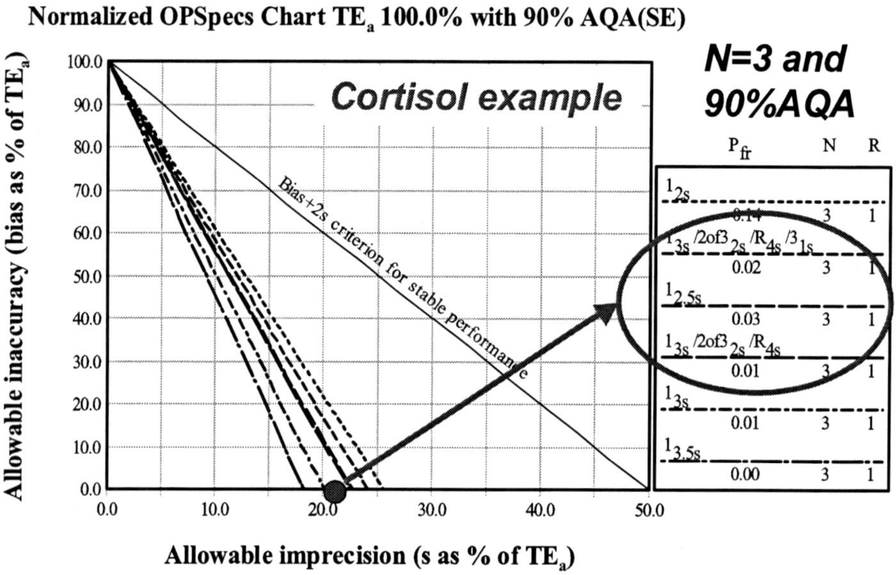

- The normalized operating point would have an x-coordinate of 21.2% [(5.3%/25%)*100] and a y-coordinate of 0%.
- The normalized OPSpecs chart for N=3 with 90%AQA shows 4 possible solutions (see above), but the 1_{2s} procedure should not be considered because of its high rate of false rejections, about 0.14 or 14%. A $1_{2.5s}$ single-rule procedure would be the simplest to implement and is perfectly adequate for detecting medically important systematic errors in the first run in which they appear.
- The Total QC strategy can depend on the statistical QC procedure to detect problems.

Thyroid Stimulating Hormone

The method CV is 7.5% at a level of 0.8 uIU/mL, 6.0% at 4.8 uIU/mL, and 6.0% at 26.6 uIU/mL. Method bias is assumed to be zero. TSH is a regulated analyte with a CLIA PT requirement in the form of TV ± 3SD. Data available from a CAP peer-review program yields calculated TE_a values of 28% at 1.0 uIU/mL, 19% at 5.0 uIU/mL, and 19% at 25 uIU/mL. Given three control materials are to be analyzed, select an appropriate QC rules, N, and TQC strategy.

A multilevel QC design would be useful here to provide one QC procedure for monitoring performance in the range of 5 to 25 uIU/mL and another to monitor performance at the low end. The two highest control materials can be used in one design and the lowest material in the other.

Upper control level

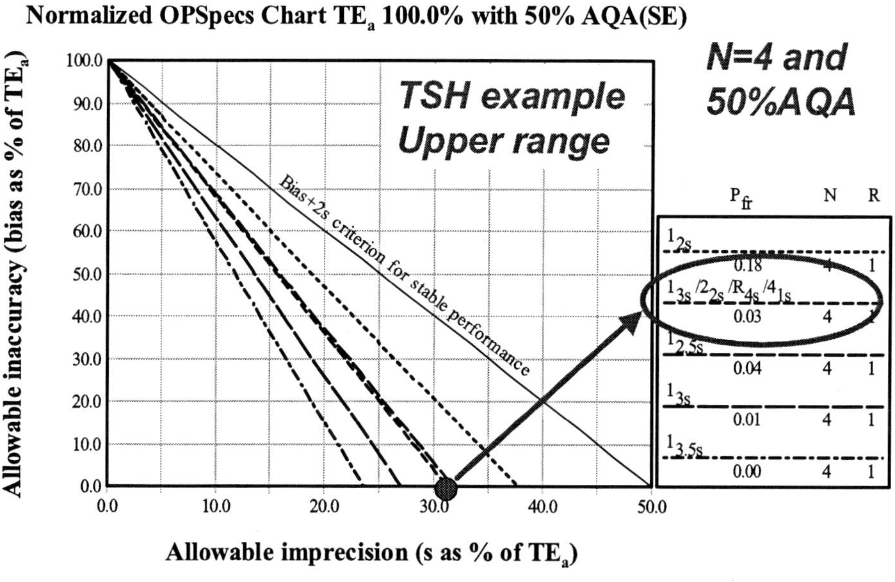

- To select a QC procedure to monitor the middle to upper end of the reportable range, the normalized operating point would have an x-coordinate of 31.6% [(6.0/19)*100] and a y-coordinate of zero.

- OPSpecs charts for Ns of 2 and 4 are used because the quality requirements and the CVs are the same for control materials at 5.0 and 25.0 uIU/mL. Three possible solutions are found on the normalized OPSpecs chart for N=4 with 50%AQA (see previous figure). A multirule procedure is the best choice here and the 8_x rule should be added to permit application across two runs.

Lower control level

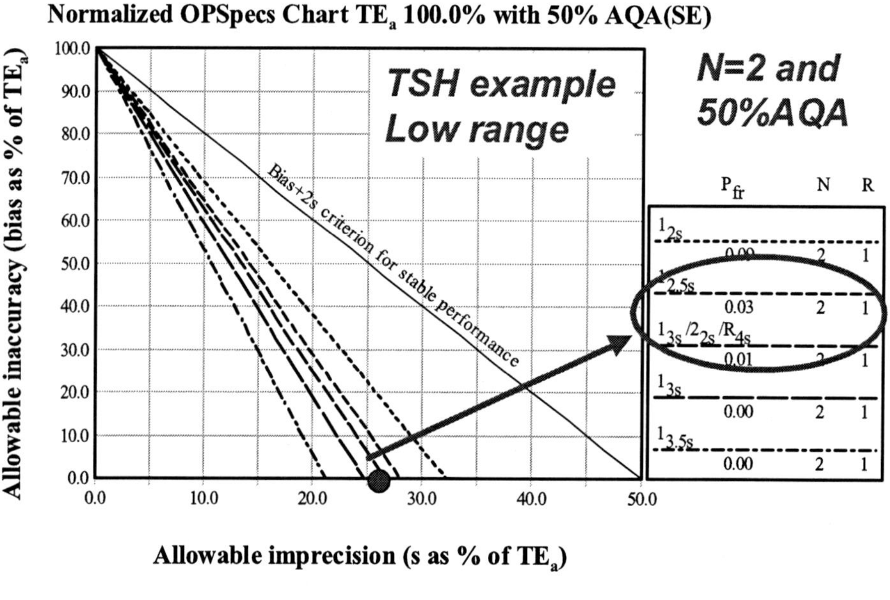

- To monitor the low range of the reportable range using the control material whose mean is 1.0 uIU/dL, the normalized operating point would have an x-coordinate of 26.8% [(7.5/28)*100] and a y-coordinate of zero.

- No solution can be found on the normalized OPSpecs chart for N=2 with 90%AQA. However, the N=2 chart with 50%AQA shows that a multirule procedure with $1_{3s}/2_{2s}/R_{4s}$ will provide at least 50% error detection. The 4_{1s} rule can be added to look-back at control data from a previous run, which should provide nearly 90% error detection over two runs. Two observations would be collected on the low control material each run and the multirule procedure applied to the data from the current and immediate previous run.

- The TQC strategy should take into account that less than 50% error detection is available in a single run. Considerable attention must be paid to non-statistical QC procedures to prevent problems from occurring.

Planning and implementation strategies

Quality-planning skills and experience are needed to deal with immunoassays. Basic quality-planning tools will get you started, help you develop your skills, and motivate you to learn about clinical quality requirements and the more advanced planning tools that support their use.

Start with peer group SDs to calculate quality requirements. The use of peer group SDs to calculate an allowable total error is a rational starting point in US laboratories because of the way that CLIA initially sets quality requirements.

Consider more advanced quality-planning tools that can utilize clinical quality requirements. An alternate approach would be to use clinical quality requirements in the form of medically important changes in test results that lead to changes in interpretation and treatment. The use of clinical quality requirement also requires knowledge of intra-individual biologic variation to account for an important preanalytic factor that affects test results. Incorporating that information also means a more complicated quality-planning model, which in turn complicates the calculations enough that computer support is needed, such as provided by the QC Validator program.

Utilize multilevel QC designs for different performance and different quality at different levels. When the quality requirements and method CVs are similar across the whole reportable range, a single QC design can be used and all levels of control materials incorporated in that design. This premise is less likely to hold for immunoassay tests than for general chemistry and hematology tests, therefore it may be effective to design different QC procedures for different medical decision levels or different parts of the reportable range. However, implementation of two different QC designs may be difficult with the current generation of QC software.

Utilize higher N multirule procedures to increase error detection. Achieving adequate error detection may often require a higher number of control measurements. Multirule designs have been optimized for up to 8 control measurements to maximize error detection and minimize false rejections [7]. A $1_{3s}/3of8_{2s}$ multirule with N=8 provides very high error detection while keeping false rejections at 2-3%.

Utilize multistage QC designs to monitor regular system changes. In situations where it is difficult to achieve high error detection AND low false rejection, two different QC designs can be employed – one for high error detection (with some increase in false rejection – a startup design) and another for low false rejection (with moderate error detection – a monitor design). Weekly changes in reagent lots might be checked at the beginning of the week using the startup design (high error detection and moderate false rejection), then followed throughout the week using the monitor design (low false rejection and moderate error detection).

References

1. Aller RD, Smalley D. Of all analyzers, immunoassay the trickiest. CAP TODAY 2000;14(4):30-64.

2. Westgard JO, Stein B, Westgard SA, Kennedy R. QC Validator 2.0: a computer program for automatic selection of statistical QC procedures for applications in healthcare laboratories. Comput Methods Programs Biomed. 1997;53:175-186.

3. Westgard JO, Stein B. Automated selection of statistical quality-control procedures to assure meeting clinical or analytical quality requirements. Clin Chem 1997;43:400-403.

4. Mugan K, Carlson IH, Westgard JO. Planning QC procedures for immunoassays. J Clin Immunoassay 1994;17:216-222.

5. Seth J. Quality Assurance. Chapter 10 in Principles and Practice of Immunoassay, 2nd ed., Price CP, Newman DJ, eds. Macmillan Reference Ltd, London, 1997, pp 211-241.

6. Carey RN. Tips for managing the quality of immunoassays. http://www.westgard.com/guest4.htm.

7. Westgard JO, Haberzettl CA. QC for immunoassays. Diagnostic Endocrinology and Metabolism: An AACC Inservice Training & Continuing Education Program 1996;14:239-243. See also http://www.westgard/com/qcapp4.htm

Online References:

Immunoassay Applications
http://www.westgard.com/qpbook/lesson60.htm

Tips for managing the quality of immunoassays, by R. Neil Carey, PhD
http://www.westgard.com/guest4.htm

QC for immunoassays
http://www.westgard.com/qcapp4.htm

Remember to use the username and password provided at the beginning of the book to access the online materials.

Self-Assessment Questions:

- ❍ What information is needed to determine the CLIA criterion for acceptable performance for TSH?
- ❍ What CV would be necessary for a thyroxine method in order to utilize only 3 control measurements?
- ❍ In the cortisol example, why is it okay to select a single-rule procedure rather than a multirule procedure?
- ❍ Why is it useful to consider two different QC designs for TSH?
- ❍ What is the meaning of the term "multilevel QC"?

13: Coagulation Applications

The quality-planning process can be applied to tests other than chemistry. This chapter provides examples for prothrombin time, partial thromboplastin time, and fibrinogen.

Objectives:

- Apply the quality-planning process to coagulation tests.
- Identify strategies that are critical for implementing effective QC procedures.

Chapter materials:

- **Coagulation Applications**
- **QC Planning online tool**
- **Method Planner online tool**

Things to do:

- Study the chapter.
- Review how QC is performed for coagulation tests in your laboratory.
- Practice using the online QC Planner and Method Planner tools with the examples in this chapter.

Hagar the Horrible

It's commonly believed that all this QC theory is meant only for chemistry and is completely out-of-place in areas like hematology and coagulation. This chapter is intended to make believers out of others, particularly those who are working in core laboratories that now include chemistry, hematology, and coagulation. The new coagulation analyzers are very similar to the automated chemistry analyzers and the same quality-planning approach can be applied, as we will see here.

Coagulation Applications

I've saved the best till last! Here are some quality-planning applications for coagulation tests performed on an automated coagulation analyzer that provides three levels of controls and on-line support for data calculations, display of control charts, and flagging by selected QC rules. Looks like an automated chemistry analyzer to me, which makes it easy to apply similar planning and implementation strategies!

Another important aspect of these applications is the availability of new online tools that can be used to prepare the OPSpecs charts. These online tools are very simple to use – you just put your numbers in the data-entry boxes and click the button to prepare the OPSpecs charts. As with our online tools that support QC training and Method Validation calculations and plotting, these tools demonstrate the power and usefulness of the Internet for education and training in analytical quality management.

Online quality-planning tools

Two tools are available – the Method Planner and the QC Planner. These tools run on the Westgard Web server, which means that the input data are sent back to another computer (the server) to be processed, then results are returned to your screen.

The **Method Planner** can be used to prepare OPSpecs charts for purposes of establishing specifications for imprecision and inaccuracy. You enter the allowable Total Error (which is your quality requirement: TE_a in %) and the number of control materials to be analyzed (two or three). The QC procedures available for two materials are 1_{2s}, $1_{2.5s}$, $1_{3s}/2_{2s}/R_{4s}$, 1_{3s}, and $1_{3.5s}$, all with a total N of 2. The QC procedures available for three materials are 1_{2s}, $1_{3s}/2of3_{2s}/R_{4s}/3_{1s}$, $1_{2.5s}$, 1_{3s}, and $1_{3.5s}$, all with a total N of 3. You determine the maximum allowable CV for a method by reading the x-intercept of the operating line of your preferred QC procedure. You determine the allowable CV for any specified allowable bias by locating the bias on the operating line, then reading the corresponding x-value.

Try it! ***http://www.westgard.com/qpbook/qptools.html***

Enter an allowable total error of 15% and select three control materials. Click the button to get the OPSpecs chart. For a 1_{3s} *control rule, you'll see the x-intercept defines the maximum allowable CV as 3.0%.*

The **QC Planner** can be used to prepare OPSpecs charts for two and three control materials and to plot the method's operating point (observed imprecision as x, observed inaccuracy as y). You enter the allowable Total Error (which is your quality requirement: TE_a in %), observed imprecision (which is your CV: s_{meas} in %), observed inaccuracy (which is your bias: $bias_{meas}$ in %), and the number of control materials (two or three). The tool will then prepare an OPSpecs chart and plot your operating point. You select a QC procedure by identifying the control rules and N that correspond to a line above your operating point. The tool will step you through a series of three OPSpecs charts – 1st the N=2 or 3 with 90%AQA(SE), 2nd the N=4 or 6 with 90%AQA(SE), and 3rd the N=4 or 6 with 50%AQA(SE) – in the same order as with the manual planning process that utilizes normalized OPSpecs charts.

Try it! ***http://www.westgard.com/qpbook/qptools.html***

Enter an allowable total error of 15%, method imprecision of 5% and bias of 1%, and three control materials. You'll find a solution on the 3rd chart which is the N=6 OPSpecs chart having 50% AQA(SE).

Now let's see how we can use these online tools for coagulation tests.

Quality requirements

CLIA includes criteria for acceptable performance for three coagulation tests in its hematology category:

Prothrombin time Target value ± 15%
Partial thromboplastin time Target value ± 15%
Fibrinogen Target value ± 20%

Method imprecision and inaccuracy

The example tests presented here are being performed by an automated coagulation analyzer. Routine QC data are available from four different control materials. One material is used for all three tests, two materials are used only for PT and PTT, and one material is used only for fibrinogen.

Material 1 CV_{PT}=2.6%, CV_{PTT}=2.3%, $CV_{fibrinogen}$=3.2% (at 273 mg/dL)
Material 2 CV_{PT}=3.3%, CV_{PTT}=2.3%
Material 3 CV_{PT}=3.7%, CV_{PTT}=2.6%
Material 4 $CV_{fibrinogen}$=5.2% (at 96 mg/dL)

The average CV for PT is 3.2%, the average CV for PTT is 2.4%, and the average CV for fibrinogen is 4.2%.

The laboratory has two of the automated coagulation analyzers, which are routinely compared to minimize any biases between them. Therefore, for practical purposes, the inaccuracy can be considered as zero.

Example applications

If you are looking at these examples on the Internet, you can access the QC Planner tool directly, enter the values, and work through the OPSpecs charts. For hardcopy documentation and off-line study, the normalized OPSpecs charts are shown.

Prothrombin time

The quality requirement is 15%, the observed CV is 3.2%, the observed bias is 0.0%, and three control materials are to be used.

You can enter these values directly into the QC Planner tool.

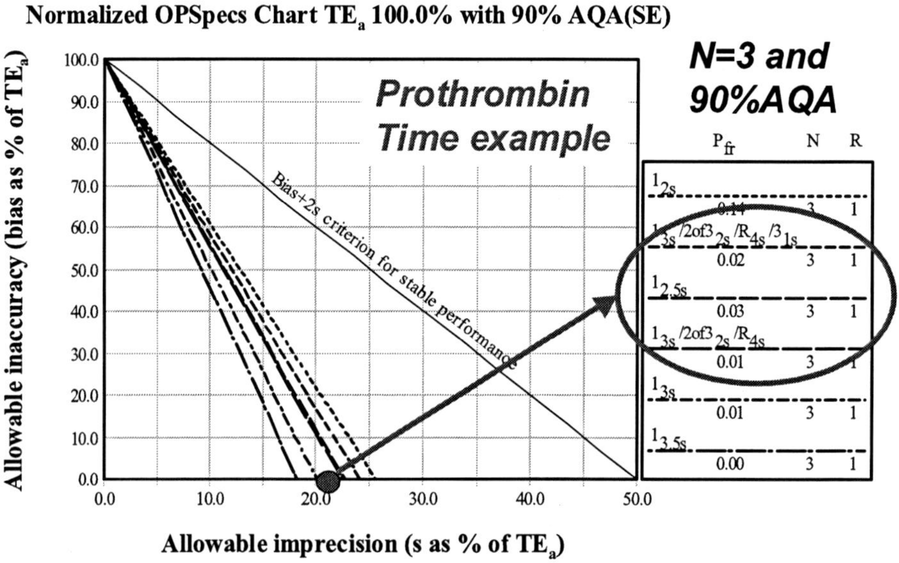

- The normalized operating point would have an x-coordinate of 21.3% [(3.2%/15%)*100] and a y-coordinate of zero.
- The normalized OPSpecs chart identifies four possible QC procedures, but the 1_{2s} rule with N=3 should be eliminated from consideration because of its high false rejection rate (about 14%). The $1_{2.5s}$ rule may be preferred over the multirule procedure for simplicity, but both provide the necessary error detection.
- The Total QC strategy can depend on the high error detection from statistical QC and should also include the preventive maintenance, instrument function checks, etc., as recommended by the manufacturer, regulatory and accreditation guidelines, and by good laboratory practices.

Partial Thromboplastin Time

The quality requirement is 15%, the observed CV is 2.4%, the observed bias is 0.0%, and three control materials are to be used.

You can enter these values directly into the QC Planner tool.

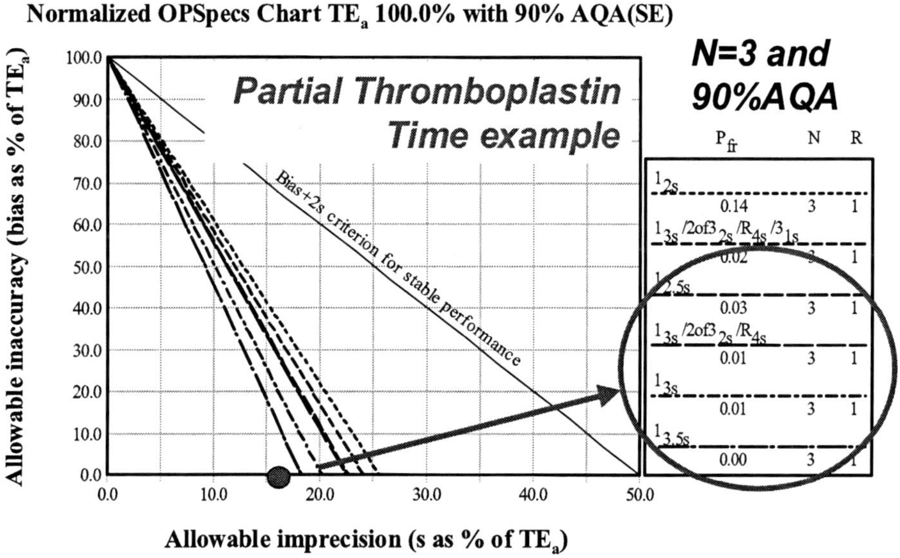

- The normalized operating point would have an x-coordinate of 16% [(2.4%/15%)*100] and a y-coordinate of zero.
- The normalized OPSpecs chart shows that all the possible QC procedures would provide adequate error detection. Again, the 1_{2s} rule with N=3 should be eliminated from consideration because of its high false rejection rate (about 14%). The 1_{3s} rule may be preferred over a multirule procedure for simplicity.
- The Total QC strategy can depend on the high error detection from statistical QC and should also include the preventive maintenance, instrument function checks, etc., as recommended by the manufacturer, regulatory and accreditation guidelines, and by good laboratory practices.

Fibrinogen

The quality requirement is 20%, the observed CV is 4.2%, the observed bias is 0.0%, and TWO control materials are to be used.

You can enter these values directly into the QC Planner tool.

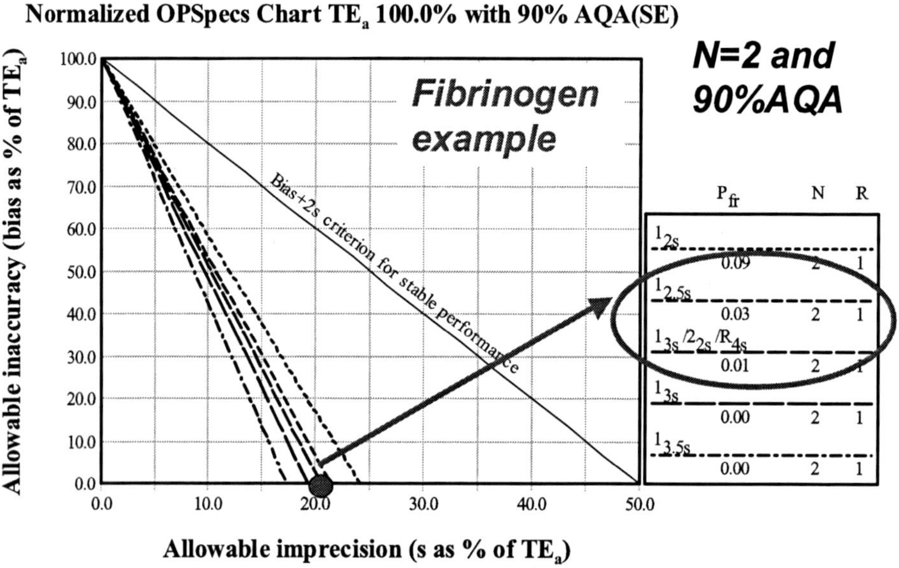

- The normalized operating point would have an x-coordinate of 21% [(4.2%/20%)*100] and a y-coordinate of zero.

- The normalized OPSpecs chart shows two possible solutions, but the 1_{2s} rule with N=2 should be eliminated from consideration because of its high false rejection rate (about 9%). The single rule $1_{2.5s}$ should be used; the $1_{3s}/2_{2s}/R_{4s}$ multirule procedure is a close second and could be used if it were easier to implement.

- The Total QC strategy can depend on the high error detection from statistical QC and should also include the preventive maintenance, instrument function checks, etc., as recommended by the manufacturer, regulatory and accreditation guidelines, and by good laboratory practices.

Planning and implementation strategies

The results from the QC Planner tool and the Normalized OPSpecs charts are the same. [Note, however, that there is one additional multirule QC procedure being considered on the normalized OPSpecs charts for three materials.]

Unify the QC procedure and TQC strategy when possible to provide simplicity in operation. All three tests here could be controlled using a $1_{2.5s}$ rule, which might make it easier for implementation and training. Not only can the same control rule be used, but also the same TQC strategy.

Utilize instrument QC software to implement individualized QC designs. Most automated analyzers provide online QC support, but may not include all the control rules considered here. For example, if the $1_{2.5s}$ rule is not available, but multirule support is provided, you could implement QC procedures that provide similar performance. Implement a $1_{3s}/2of3_{2s}/R_{4s}$ for PT, 1_{3s} for PTT, and $1_{3s}/2_{2s}/R_{4s}$ for fibrinogen.

Utilize online quality-planning tools to simplify the applications. The simplest tools to use are Internet tools that provide a data-entry form, then a button for executing the next step in the process. For periodic use and infrequent users, Internet tools may be the most practical.

Online References:

Coagulation Applications
http://www.westgard.com/qpbook/lesson61.htm

Online Quality-Planning Tools.
http://www.westgard.com/qpbook/qptools.html

Remember to use the username and password provided at the beginning of this book to access the online materials.

Self-Assessment Questions:

- ❍ If you were to use only two control materials for Prothrombin time (and the method performance given in the chapter), what control rule(s) should be selected?
- ❍ What CV would be necessary for the Prothrombin Time method in order to utilize 2 control measurements with a 1_{3s} control rule (hint – use the Method Planner tool here)?
- ❍ In the Partial Thromboplastin Time example, what bias could be tolerated if you were to utilize a 1_{3s} control rule and N=3?
- ❍ What bias could you tolerate for the fibrinogen method and $1_{2.5s}$ N=2 QC procedure?
- ❍ What are the advantages of the online quality-planning tools over the "manual" normalized OPSpecs charts?

14: What's wrong with statistical quality control?

This chapter discusses some of the complaints about statistical QC and identifies the importance of the quality-planning process for improving current QC practices.

Objectives:

- ❍ Summarize the current issues with statistical QC applications.
- ❍ Identify the opportunities to improve current QC practices by applying the quality-planning process.

Chapter materials:

- ❍ **Improving QC through quality planning**

Things to do:

- ❍ Study the chapter.
- ❍ Identify issues that limit the effectiveness of QC in your laboratory.

Hagar the Horrible

You may have noticed my emphasis on quality planning as "enlightenment" about how to improve QC, rather than a cursing of the present darkness of QC practices. I admit I do some of the latter, but it's done in an attempt to point out what is wrong and how we can improve. There are plenty of others in our field who are professional QC "cursers" who offer no useful or scientifically valid suggestions for replacing the practice of QC. This chapter provides some responses to the common complaints, while stressing that there is a better way.

Improving QC through quality planning

There's a lot of sentiment for changing current QC practices – getting rid of statistical QC and doing something different, whatever that might be. Here we will examine some of the frequently-made-complaints. As you'll see, many of these apparent problems or limitations can be overcome by applying the quality-planning process that has been described in this book. I hope this discussion will confirm the importance of applying the quality-planning process in your own work.

QC is not patient-focused!

Today's quality control practices are indeed arbitrary and should properly be called "arbitrary control" rather than quality control. Laboratories need to take responsibility for improving analytical quality management, as discussed in chapter 1 (*A Wake-up call for Quality Management*). Improvements are needed because most laboratories base their QC practices on regulatory, accreditation, and professional recommendations (chapter 3: *Complying with Regulations, Standards, and Practice Guidelines*), instead of selecting control rules and numbers of control measurements on the basis of the quality that is required for the test.

Patient focus requires an understanding of Total Quality Management (chapter 2: *Assuring Quality through Total Quality Management*), the recognition of the importance of defining the quality required by a test, and the need to implement a quality-planning process. No QC technique can be patient-focused until you define the quality needed and select the QC procedure to assure that quality is achieved by the methods in your laboratory. Chapter 5 *(Defining Quality Requirements)* discusses the current recommendations for quality requirements and identifies available sources of information to help you get started.

Defining the quality required for a test is the first step in the quality-planning process recommended here (chapter 4: *Devising a Practical Process*). I have long advocated the need to plan the quality of laboratory testing processes. The general steps of a quality-planning process were first outlined in a book on *Cost-Effective Quality Control* that was published in 1986 [1]. Development of the chart of operating specifications in the early 90s made the planning process much more practical [2]. The use of normalized OPSpecs charts makes it possible for any laboratory to implement a manual quality-planning process that is quick and easy to perform.

Statistical QC procedures can be patient-focused if a laboratory defines the quality required for its patient services and selects appropriate methods and appropriate QC procedures. The problem is not the fault of statistical QC. The fault is the laboratory's lack of planning!

QC doesn't consider improvements in instrument performance!

Later generations of instruments have better precision and better stability than those in the past. It's correct to question whether we should do QC the same old way on these new instrument systems. The answer again is to plan the QC procedure properly and take instrument performance into account. The new NCCLS guidelines [3, document C24-A2, described in chapter 3] outline the steps for planning a QC procedure as follows:

- Define the quality requirement
- Determine method performance - imprecision and bias
- Identify candidate SQC strategies
- Predict QC performance
- Set goals for QC performance
- Select appropriate QC

The 2nd step considers improvements in instrument performance and should lead to simpler QC procedures for highly automated 4th and 5th generation analyzers.

The quality-planning process devised here in chapter 4 follows the steps of the NCCLS guidelines. The observed imprecision and inaccuracy of a method is accounted for in the 2nd step of the process. It clearly impacts on the QC procedures that are selected.

We documented this ten years ago when describing how we changed from multirule QC procedures to single-rule procedures with wide limits ($1_{3.5s}$ rule) for 14 out of 18 tests on a multitest chemistry analyzer [4,5] (as discussed in chapter 10: *Automated Chemistry Applications*). The strategy is to individualize the QC design for each individual test on an instrument, rather than use a single QC procedure on all tests. To do that, you need a quick and easy quality-planning process, such as the manual process that utilizes normalized OPSpecs charts (chapter 8: *Using Normalized OPSpecs Charts*).

"One size fits all" QC is not appropriate!

True, you should select the control rules and number of control measurements that are appropriate for each test by implementing a QC planning process. You should establish run length and frequency of control analysis on the basis of the stability of the method and its susceptibility to problems. That will allow you to "size" or "individualize" the QC procedure for the quality required by your customers and for the performance observed for the methods in your laboratory. Follow the general NCCLS C24-A2 guidelines or follow the more detailed planning process described in chapter 8.

The applications shown here for automated chemistry tests (chapter 10), blood gas tests (chapter 11), immunoassays (chapter 12), and coagulation tests (chapter 13) demonstrate the different "sizes" of QC that might be expected.

QC is not appropriate for unit devices!

There are both technical and business aspects to this argument. The technical argument is that unit devices can't be monitored by QC because each device is separate and different. Sampling one device doesn't assure the next one is okay, therefore, it's argued that QC can't be used. However, all manufacturers claim that these unit devices are uniform, otherwise, they couldn't sell them at all! If they *are* uniform, then QC can be applied to monitor the general stability and performance of the devices, as well as operator proficiency in using the devices.

The business argument is that different QC is needed because the personnel involved in POC testing have little laboratory training and no experience with QC. The solution offered by NCCLS in the proposed guideline on "Quality Management for Unit Use Testing" is to develop a "sources of errors" matrix and identify specific methods for controlling each potential error [6]. This is consistent with our formulation of a Total QC strategy as described in chapter 7 *(Formulating TQC Strategies)*. However, it is always most efficient to monitor as many of the individual error sources as possible by statistical QC, therefore our planning for a TQC strategy takes into account the error detection capability provided by statistical QC.

One important limitation of the NCCLS approach is that the "method of control" for many of the individual error sources is often found to be operator training and competency, which is very difficult to evaluate and verify. Statistical QC may actually be the most quantitative way to monitor operating training and competency, as well as important operator variables in the testing process [7].

QC is too expensive!

Compared to what? Certainly there are techniques like instrument function checks and electronic QC that are less costly to perform, but are they actually less expensive? Function checks and electronic QC typically monitor only a few instrument variables and steps in the measurement process. What about the failure costs from errors in other steps that go undetected and impact negatively on patient treatment and outcome? We documented cost-savings from improved statistical QC designs for an automated chemistry analyzer (chapter 10) by considering the laboratory failure-costs due to repeat runs alone. The cost-savings would be even greater if we were to consider the failure-costs due to improper patient treatment because of incorrect test results. But that more complicated assessment of outside costs isn't even necessary. There are sufficient savings within the laboratory to justify improvements in statistical QC.

Electronic QC and related techniques may be cheap for the laboratory, but expensive for patient care. The detailed checking of individual error sources, as recommended by the NCCLS unit use guidelines, is also likely to be costly because it is an inefficient technique, at least as compared to the efficiency of statistical QC for monitoring many steps in the total testing process [8].

QC takes too much time!

What time are we talking about here – the time to analyze controls, the time to interpret control results, or the time for dealing with out-of-control signals? The real concern should be the turnaround time for reporting test results, where the QC problem in many laboratories is due to "false rejections" that require repeat analysis of controls, analysis of new controls, and re-runs of patient samples. Again, proper planning of QC procedures is critical to minimize false rejections and to provide appropriate detection of medically important errors. When this is done, a rejection signal should lead to trouble-shooting that eliminates analytical problems, rather than the wasteful re-work without improvement [9]. Problem-solving is a good investment in time because, in the long run, there will be fewer problems, fewer out-of-control situations, more rapid and effective problem-solving, and fewer delays in reporting patient test results.

The time that will be saved by careful selection of QC procedures will more than offset the time required to carry out the planning. With the quality-planning process recommended here (chapter 8), it takes only a few minutes to do the planning. It will actually take more time to define the quality needed for the test and obtain the estimates of imprecision and inaccuracy for the method. The savings come only after the planning, therefore you must make the initial investment in planning to achieve the savings in routine operation.

QC is too complicated!

There are at least two different issues here – one dealing with the difficulty in training personnel and the other the difficulty in implementing QC in a proper manner. The solutions for both are new technologies – in the first case Internet technology to support training and in the second computer technology to automate the QC process. Basic QC training is already available on the Internet through the American Society for Clinical Laboratory Science (http://www.ascls.org/wqc/). These materials are also available in hardcopy format for laboratories that have limited access to the Internet [10].

The comprehensive solution for implementation is to automate the whole QC process, from planning through implementation. An example of software that automates the QC selection process is provided by the QC Validator program [11,12], which makes use of OPSpecs charts to show the relationship between the quality required, the imprecision and inaccuracy observed for the measurement procedure, and the error detection capabilities of different QC procedures.

It would be ideal, of course, to integrate the automatic QC selection function into the QC software in an instrument system, a QC workstation, or a laboratory information system. The laboratory could then specify the quality required for the test and the automated QC process would select the appropriate QC procedure, load and sample the control materials, acquire the necessary control data, interpret the control data, and release or reject patient test results. Rather than worrying about which rules to use, the laboratory's responsibility would be focused on the quality needed for the application of the tests.

QC is old!

As someone who has been around for a while, I am beginning to take personal offense to the comment that "old" implies "no longer useful." I think experience is beneficial and leads to dependability. Statistical QC was derived from industrial statistical process control, which was developed in the 1930s. It continues to be the cornerstone of industrial production worldwide because it's a dependable, proven technique. Statistical QC has also been a fundamental technique for improving the quality of test results in healthcare laboratories. It takes time to become a "tried and true" technique, therefore we shouldn't discard this well-established technique without careful evaluation of any new technique. And what is the new technique that's going to replace statistical QC? Where's the documentation of effectiveness? You shouldn't have to "trust me" or the manufacturer! Statistical QC gives you a dependable, proven, and independent technique for managing and controlling the quality of your work.

What's right with statistical QC?

There are lots of things that are wrong with the way we have implemented statistical QC in laboratories in the past, but these things can be corrected. Here's what's right about statistical QC – it's still the best technique available for managing the analytical quality in laboratory tests. The biggest potential for improving QC systems in laboratories today is to plan statistical QC procedures carefully, implement them properly, and perform them correctly.

References

1. Westgard JO, Barry PL. Cost-effective quality control: Managing the quality and productivity of analytical processes. AACC Press, Washington DC, 1986.

2. Westgard JO. Charts of operational process specifications ("OPSpecs Charts") for assessing the precision, accuracy, and quality control needed to satisfy proficiency testing performance criteria. Clin Chem 1992;38:1226-1223.

3. NCCLS C24-A2. Statistical quality control for quantitative measurements: Principles and definitions; Approved guideline - second edition. NCCLS, Wayne, PA, 1999.

4. Koch DD, Oryall JJ, Quam EF, Feldbruegge DH, Dowd DE, Barry PL, Westgard JO. Selection of medically useful quality-control procedures for individual tests done in a multitest analytical system. Clin Chem 1990;36:230-3.

5. Westgard JO, Oryall JJ, Koch DD. Predicting effects of quality-control practices on the cost-effective operation of a stable, multitest analytical system. Clin Chem 1990;36:1760-4.

6. NCCLS EP18-P. Quality management for unit use testing; Proposed guidelines. NCCLS, Wayne, PA, 1999.

7. Westgard JO. Taking care of point-of-care QC. Clin Lab News Viewpoint, August 1997.

8. Westgard JO. Electronic QC and the total testing process. http://www.westgard.com/essay17.htm.

9. Hyltoft Petersen P, Ricos C, Stockl D, Libeer JC, Baadenhuijsen H, Fraser C, Thienpont L. Proposed guidelines for the internal quality control of analytical results in the medical laboratory. Eur J Clin Chem Clin Biochem. 1996;34:983-99.

10. Westgard JO. Basic QC Practices. Westgard QC, Madison, WI, 1998.

11. Westgard JO, Stein B, Westgard SA, Kennedy R. QC Validator 2.0: a computer program for automatic selection of statistical QC procedures for applications in healthcare laboratories. Comput Methods Programs Biomed 1997;53:175-86.

12. Westgard JO, Stein B. Automated selection of statistical quality-control procedures to assure meeting clinical or analytical quality requirements. Clin Chem 1997;43:400-403.

Online References:

What's wrong with statistical quality control?
http://www.westgard.com/qpbook/lesson62.htm

Remember to use the username and password provided at the beginning of this book to access the online materials.

Self-Assessment Questions:

- ❍ How do you make statistical QC patient-focused?
- ❍ How can you adapt statistical QC to new technologies that have improved performance?
- ❍ What's the meaning of the term "unit device"?
- ❍ What's the fallacy of the argument that statistical QC can't be used with unit devices?
- ❍ How might new QC technology improve current QC practices?

15: What questions do you have about quality planning?

This chapter summarizes common or frequently-asked-questions (FAQ's) about quality planning and even gives answers to them.

Objectives:

- ❍ Review common questions about the quality-planning principles and process.

Chapter materials:

- ❍ **FAQ's about Quality Planning**

Things to do:

- ❍ Study the chapter.
- ❍ Identify issues that limit the effectiveness of QC in your laboratory.

Hagar the Horrible

How do you get on top of problems with quality? You have to start at the bottom and know something about the technical aspects of quality management. That's what these lessons have been about. Start at the beginning with quality requirements, then plan method specifications and QC procedures that will assure that quality will be achieved in the end. This chapter gives a quick review of some of the important questions and issues.

Frequently-Asked-Questions about quality planning

Why oh why do I have to worry about quality planning?

Someone needs to worry about the quality of the test results being produced in your laboratory. Don't assume that manufacturers have solved all the problems! Don't assume that methods work perfectly in the real world! Someone in your laboratory has to assume responsibility for managing quality in a quantitative manner. Quality planning is the ingredient that is missing in most laboratories. We can learn how to do it ourselves, improve our own skills, and contribute that expertise to our laboratory.

The first step in the quality-planning process is to define the quality required for the test. Where can I find that information?

To get started, it's easiest to use the acceptability criteria from proficiency testing programs or external quality assessment programs. These criteria are generally in the form of an allowable total error, such as Target Value plus or minus a certain percentage or a fixed concentration. For example, the acceptability criterion for a cholesterol test is TV ± 10%; the criterion for calcium is TV ± 1.0 mg/dL. For US laboratories, about 80 different tests are covered by the CLIA acceptability criteria (For tests not covered by these CLIA criteria, see below).

Aren't the CLIA PT limits too wide to be useful?

We hear that comment from people who are only considering the stable performance of the method, i.e, comparing the imprecision and inaccuracy to the CLIA criterion using a total error equation for stable method performance, such as TE = bias + 2SD. When you want to consider QC performance, another term must be added to account for the "sensitivity" or error detection of the control rules and number of control measurements being used. This term is in the neighborhood of 2 to 3 times the SD for common QC procedures with low numbers of control measurements. Therefore, a quality-planning model that includes QC performance is more demanding and requires that the allowable total error encompass bias plus 4 to 5 times the SD of the method.

What should I do if CLIA doesn't include acceptability criteria for my test?

There are other sources of information about quality requirements, such as the European recommendations for allowable SDs (or CVs) and allowable bias. You can calculate an allowable total error as the sum of the bias plus 1.65 times the SD (be careful that everything is in the same units). Ricos has recently provided a database that includes 316 different quantities for which total error criteria have been calculated from biologic data. That database is included Appendix 3 of this book and is also posted on the westgard.com website.

You can also use another type of quality requirement, called the clinical decision interval, which can be thought of as the grey zone for interpreting a test result or the medically important change in a test result. However, you will need access to a computer program, such as the QC Validator program, which can be used to prepare a chart of operating specifications from a clinical decision interval type of requirement.

How are the method's bias and SD determined?

Initially, the estimates of inaccuracy and imprecision can be made from the method validation studies performed when a test system is being installed. Bias would be estimated from a comparison of methods experiment and the method SD or CV would be determined from a replication experiment. Later on, during the routine operation of a method, bias could be determined from peer comparison programs or from proficiency testing surveys and the method SD or CV could be determined from routine quality control data.

What should I do if there isn't any data on method bias?

Begin by assuming method bias is zero. You should always be able to estimate method imprecision from routine QC data or by performing a replication experiment. That's the essential data. Remember that you can always "replan" the QC procedure when you have better estimates of method performance.

Don't all QC procedures detect errors?

They all detect large errors, but have different sensitivities for small errors. For many tests, the errors that are medically important fall into the small error classification, therefore the choice of control rules and the number of control measurements is very important for assuring the quality of the tests.

What characteristics describe the performance of a QC procedure?

Two terms – the probability of false rejection (P_{fr}) and the probability of error detection (P_{ed}) – are important for describing the performance of a QC procedure. For practical purposes, we aim for a probability of 0.90 or a 90% chance of detecting medically important errors and a probability of 0.05 or a 5% or less chance of a false rejection.

What QC procedures provide high error detection?

Error detection depends on the control rules and number of control measurements. The narrower the control limits, the higher the rejection rate – both for error detection and false rejection. The more rules in a multirule combination, the higher the error detection. The higher the number of control measurements, the higher the error detection. Multirule procedures with Ns of 4 to 6 provide the maximum performance QC procedures that are practical for most laboratories.

What QC procedures have high false rejection rates?

The most serious problem is with the 1_{2s} control rule, which applies when a Levey-Jennings control chart has 2 SD control limits. When N=1, P_{fr} is 0.05 or 5%, which corresponds to the 1 out of 20 points that we expect to see outside of 2 SD control limits. When N=2, P_{fr} is 0.09 or 9%, which means that approximately 2 out of every 20 runs are expected to be judged out-of-control. When N=3, P_{fr} is 0.14 or 14%. When N=4, P_{fr} is 0.18 or 18%, which is approximately 1 out of 5 runs that will be observed to be out-of-control when everything is working *perfectly*. Since CLIA requires a minimum of 2 control materials or a minimum N of 2, the use of 2 SD control limits leads to nearly 10% false rejections, 10% repeat runs, and 10% waste. The frequent false rejections that result from use of 2 SD control limits are a BAD SITUATION, which is why the use of 2 SD control limits should generally be avoided.

Does the OPSpecs chart provide information about probabilities of rejection?

Yes, the probability of error detection is given in the title of the chart in terms of percent, e.g., 90%AQA indicates 90% error detection. The probability for false rejection will be found in the key area of the chart, next to the control rules.

Is the OPSpecs chart the only quality-planning tool available?

No, the OPSpecs chart isn't the only quality-planning tool – just the best tool. You can also use a critical-error graph, which has the size of a medically important error drawn on power curves of QC procedures to show exactly the error detection that will be available. Many analysts find that it is initially easier to understand the critical-error graph and therefore prefer this tool in the beginning. In the long run, however, the OPSpecs chart is a more useful tool and is actually easier to use, even though it is harder to understand because of all the information available on a single chart.

Why are the units on an OPSpecs chart given in percent, rather than concentration?

If concentration units were used, a different OPSpecs chart would be needed for every test application. By presenting the quality requirement, method imprecision, and method inaccuracy all as percentages, a single OPSpecs chart can be used for all tests that have the same quality requirement. This is an advantage for manual applications where a set of OPSpecs charts can be preprinted to cover a wide range of potential applications.

Since the units are already in percent, why is a normalized OPSpecs chart needed?

The original OPSpecs chart must be prepared for a specific quality requirement, e.g., 10%, 15%, or 20%. The chart can only be used for a test having that quality requirement, therefore you need a whole workbook of preprinted charts – an atlas of maps to provide guidance in the different states of the country. The normalized OPSpecs chart displays the allowable bias and allowable imprecision as a percent of the quality requirement, which allows the chart to be used with *any* quality requirement. The advantage is you only need a small number of charts. The disadvantage is you have to make some calculations to convert the observed bias and observed imprecision into a percent of the quality requirement.

What's the meaning of the "90%AQA(SE)" in the title of an OPSpecs chart?

The "%AQA" means percent **A**nalytical **Q**uality **A**ssurance, which corresponds to the expected error detection in percent, rather than as a probability. Therefore, 90%AQA means there is a 90% chance of detecting a medically important error. The "(SE)" in the title stands for **S**ystematic **E**rror, therefore an OPSpecs chart with 90%AQA(SE) describes the conditions necessary to provide 90% detection of medically important systematic errors.

Isn't 50% AQA too low to be useful?

It's always best to achieve 90% AQA whenever possible in order to detect medically important errors in the first run. However, there are situations where it may be too costly to provide 90% AQA because of the high number of control measurements that would be needed. In such cases, a different strategy is needed, such as using a multistage QC procedure that has a startup design that provides 90% AQA (with moderate false rejections if necessary) and a monitoring design that provides moderate error detection with a very low chance of false rejections. Achieving 50% AQA would be okay for a monitoring design.

How does the Total QC strategy compare to the quality-system approach that is being widely touted by NCCLS in its document for QC of unit use devices?

The quality system approach is to identify all the potential sources of errors or problems in a process, then select an appropriate quality monitor or method of control. NCCLS provides an example "sources of error matrix" that identifies over 100 possible error sources. The resulting quality system makes use of those quality monitors that are necessary to monitor the potential sources of error of an individual method. The Total QC strategy is similar in that it includes other quality monitors or methods of control, but it makes maximum use of statistical QC to monitor as many error sources as possible. In contrast, the NCCLS unit use guidelines attempt to avoid or minimize the use of statistical QC.

Can I make copies of the worksheet and normalized OPSpecs charts for my own applications?

Yes, your purchase of this book provides you the permission to make copies of quality-planning worksheet, flowchart, and normalized OPSpecs charts for use in your own applications. You can make xerox copies from the forms and charts in this book or you can download them from the westgard.com website to your computer and then print copies as needed.

Is Hagar really your relative?

Yes!

Does Hagar really believe in quality planning?

You bet!

Hagar the Horrible

Just thinking about planning is a start, but it's not the solution. You need to do it for real on applications that are of interest to you. If you've gotten this far, you've now got the background, resources, skills, and materials to do it for real. It will be a waste if you don't try it for real. Promise me you'll try quality planning on one test in your laboratory, then I'll rest easier.

Online References:

Frequently-Asked-Questions about Quality Planning
http://www.westgard.com/qpbook/lesson63.htm

Remember to use the username and password provided at the beginning of this book to access the online materials.

16. Glossary

Definitions of important terms are obtained from documents of professional societies and organizations such as the International Federation of Clinical Chemistry [IFCC], the American Society for Quality [ASQ], and the National Committee for Clinical Laboratory Standards [NCCLS], or, in some cases, are based on the use of these terms in the context of the approach to analytical quality management recommended here.

Accuracy. "Agreement between the best estimate of a quantity and its true value. It has no numerical value. See inaccuracy" [IFCC].

Allowable total error, TE_a. An analytical quality requirement that sets a limit for both the imprecision and inaccuracy that are tolerable in a single measurement or single test result.

Analyte. The substance to be measured.

Analytical error. "Difference between the estimated value of a quantity and its true value. This difference (positive or negative) may be expressed either in the units in which the quantity is measured, or as a percentage of the true value" [IFCC]. Used here to mean the difference between a patient's test result produced by the analytical process and the true or correct value for that sample.

Analytical quality assurance (AQA). Used with charts of operating specifications (OPSpecs charts) to indicate the level of assurance for detecting critical sized errors. For example, 90% AQA(SE) means there will be at least a 90% chance of detecting the critical systematic error when operating within the allowed limits for imprecision and inaccuracy for the given control rules and total number of control measurements (N).

Analytical quality requirement. Used here to refer to a quality requirement in the form of an allowable total error (TE_a). Often defined on the basis of proficiency testing criteria for acceptable performance, such as the CLIA requirements for regulated analytes.

Analytical run. Defined by CLIA as an interval within which the accuracy and precision of a testing system is expected to be stable. Cannot be longer than 24 hours. This definition is based on that given in NCCLS document C24A that defines a run as an interval, period of time, or number of specimens, for which the precision and accuracy of the method is expected to remain stable; between which events may occur that could cause errors that are important to detect.

Assayed control material. A control solution or control material for which the manufacturer defines the results expected for different tests and different methods. These "bottle values" are summarized on assay sheets and are useful for selecting control materials, however, they should not generally be used for setting the control limits because the values usually include a between-laboratory component of variation that makes the control limits too wide for use in an individual laboratory.

Bias. A systematic difference between an observed value and some measure of the truth. Generally used to describe the inaccuracy of a method relative to a comparative method in method evaluation or to a comparative group in proficiency testing.

$Bias_{meas}$. Used here to represent the bias of a measurement procedure relative to a comparative method or a comparative group in proficiency testing.

Biologic variation. A pre-analytical source of variation of a test result due to the changes in the patient. Studies of within-subject biologic variation are a source of information for setting biologic goals for allowable imprecision and allowable bias.

CLIA. Refers to the Clinical Laboratory Improvement Amendments, which are the regulations that govern US laboratories. Often called CLIA-88 because the regulations were passed in 1988.

Clinical quality requirement. Used here for a quality requirement that states the medically important change in a test result or describes the gray zone or decision interval for interpreting a test result.

Coefficient of variation, CV. The relative standard deviation, i.e., the standard deviation expressed as a percentage of the mean:

$$CV=100(s/\bar{x})$$

Control chart. "A graphical method for evaluating whether a process is or is not in a 'state of statistical control.' The determinations are made through comparison of the values of some statistical measure(s) for an ordered series of samples, or subgroups, with control limits" [ASQ]. In healthcare laboratories, the Levey-Jennings chart is commonly used to plot the result observed for a stable control material versus time, usually the day or run number.

Control limits. "Limits on a control chart which are used as criteria for signalling the need for action, or for judging whether a set of data does or does not indicate a 'state of control'" [ASQ]. Used here to refer to the defined limits or ranges of results expected due to the random error of the method, and beyond which some course of action should be taken. It is common in clinical laboratories to use Levey-Jennings control charts with limits set as either the mean plus and minus 2 standard deviations, or the mean plus and minus 3 standard deviations.

Control material, control product. A control solution that is available, often commercially, liquid or lyophilized, and packaged in aliquots that can be prepared and used individually.

Control measurements, control observations. The analytical results obtained for control solutions or control materials (that are analyzed for purposes of quality control).

Control procedure, QC procedure. The protocol and materials that are necessary for an analyst to assess whether the method is working properly and patient test results can be reported - that part of an analytical process that is concerned with testing the quality of the analytical results, in contrast to the measurement procedure, which produces the result. A control procedure can be described by the number of control measurements and the decision criteria (control rules) used for judging the acceptability of the analytical results.

Control rule. A decision criterion for interpreting control data and making a judgement on the control status of an analytical run. Symbolized here by A_L, where A is the abbreviation for a particular statistic or states the number of control measurements, and L is the control limit. An analytical run is rejected when the control measurements fulfill the stated conditions, i.e., when a certain statistic or number of control measurements exceeds the specified control limits.

Criteria for acceptability. CLIA's term for the decision criteria applied to assess the validity of an analytical run. Another name for QC procedure, with emphasis on definition of the decision criteria or control rules for interpreting control measurements.

Critical-error graph. A power function graph on which is imposed the critical-error that needs to be detected. Facilitates the estimation and comparison of the probability for error detection by different QC procedures.

Critical random error, ΔRE_{crit}. The size of random error that needs to be detected to maintain a defined quality requirement. Calculated as

$$(TE_a - bias_{meas})/1.65s_{meas}$$

where TE_a is the allowable total error, $bias_{meas}$ is the inaccuracy, and s_{meas} is the imprecision (standard deviation) of the measurement procedure.

Critical systematic error, ΔSE_{crit}. The size of the systematic error that needs to be detected to maintain a defined quality requirement. Calculated as

$$(TE_a - bias_{meas})/s_{meas}] - 1.65$$

where TE_a is the allowable total error, $bias_{meas}$ is the inaccuracy, and s_{meas} is the imprecision (standard deviation) of the measurement procedure.

Cumulative control limits. Control limits calculated from estimates of the mean and standard deviation that represent a time period longer than a month. Common practice is for laboratories to calculate monthly control statistics. Cumulative statistics can be easily calculated from monthly statistics that tabulate the sum of the individual values and the sum of the squares of those values.

Decision Interval, D_{int}. Used here to represent the gray zone, or interval of uncertainty, in interpreting a test result. An example is the NCEP (National Cholesterol Education Program) guidelines that indicate a cholesterol of less than or equal to 200 mg/dL is okay and that a value of more than or equal to 240 should have followup testing, which defines a gray zone of 40 mg/dL between 200 to 240, which is 20% at a decision level of 200 mg/dL. D_{int} can also be defined more generally by the change in a test result that is judged to be medically significant.

Decision level for critical interpretation (X_c). See medical decision level.

Distribution. Refers to the spread and shape of a frequency curve of some variable. A histogram is one way to graphically display the distribution of test results by showing the frequency of observations on the y-axis versus the magnitude on the x-axis. The normal or gaussian curve is one form of a distribution.

Error detection. See probability for error detection.

False rejection. See probability for false rejection.

Frequency of errors, frequency of occurrence of analytical errors, f. A performance characteristic of a measurement procedure that describes how frequently analytical errors are expected to occur. Related to the stability of the measurement procedure.

Gaussian curve. Gaussian distribution. Normal curve. Normal distribution. Refers to a symmetrical bell-shaped distribution whose shape is given by a specific equation (called the normal equation) in which the mean and standard deviation are variables. It is commonly assumed that the random error of an analytical method fits the Gaussian distribution and therefore can be characterized by calculating the standard deviation. The standard deviation is not a valid statistic if a distribution is not Gaussian.

High complexity tests. A CLIA category of tests that has the most demanding QC requirements. Includes any tests developed by the laboratory, modified by the laboratory, or manufacturer's tests that have been classified as high complexity.

Imprecision. "Standard deviation or coefficient of variation of the results in a set of replicate measurements. The mean value and number of replicates must be stated, and the design used must be described in such a way that other workers can repeat it. This is particularly important whenever a specific term is used to denote a particular type of imprecision, such as between-laboratory, within-day, or between day" [IFCC]. We use the term s_{meas} to represent a measurement procedure's stable standard deviation and express it as a percent, or coefficient of variation, on OPSpecs charts.

Inaccuracy. "Numerical difference between the mean of a set of replicate measurements and the true value. This difference (positive or negative) may be expressed in the units in which the quantity is measured, or as a percentage of the true value" [IFCC]. We use the term $bias_{meas}$ to describe the average systematic difference between a measurement procedure and a comparative method and express it in percent on OPSpecs charts.

Inherent imprecision, inherent random error. The standard deviation or coefficient of variation of the results in a set of replicate measurements obtained when the measurement procedure is operating under stable conditions.

Levey-Jennings control chart. A commonly used control chart in which individual control measurements are plotted directly on a control chart with limit lines drawn either as mean ± 2s or mean ± 3s. Time is displayed on the x-axis usually in terms of days or runs.

Matrix. Refers to the physical and chemical nature of the specimen, the substances present, and their concentrations. The matrix of a control material is an important consideration in selecting and implementing a QC procedure. In this context, the matrix refers to the substances and base from which the control material is prepared, in addition to all the additives such as spiking materials, preservatives, etc., necessary to make the product useful.

Mean, x. The arithmetic average of a set of values. A measure of central tendency of the distribution of a set of replicate results. Often abbreviated by an x with a bar over it.

Medical decision level, decision level, X_c. A concentration of analyte where medical interpretation is critical for patient care. There may be several different medical decision levels for a particular analyte. X_c should provide guidance for selecting relevant estimates of stable imprecision, and stable inaccuracy, and also the concentrations of analytes in control materials. This is analogous to identifying a critical Target Value (TV) for assessing test performance and validating QC design.

Medically important errors. Used here to indicate errors that, when added to the inherent imprecision and inaccuracy of a measurement procedure, cause the quality requirement to be exceeded. Medically important random errors are those increases in the standard deviation of the measurement procedure that cause the error distribution to exceed the quality requirement (see critical random errors). Medically important systematic errors are those shifts in the mean of the error distribution that cause the error distribution to exceed the quality requirement (see critical systematic error).

Method validation. The process of testing a measurement procedure to assess its performance and to validate that performance is acceptable. The magnitudes of the analytical errors are experimentally determined and their acceptability for the application of the method is judged versus defined requirements for quality in the form of maximum allowable errors.

Model. A mathematical equation that describes the behavior of a process as a function of its important characteristics.

Moderate complexity tests. A CLIA category of tests that includes about 75% of all tests performed by healthcare laboratories, including most automated analytical systems. This category has more stringent QC requirements than for "waived tests" or "provider performed microscopy."

Multirule quality-control procedure. A control procedure that uses two or more control rules for testing control measurements and determining control status. At least one rule is chosen for its ability to detect random errors and one to detect systematic errors.

NCCLS. Stands for National Committee for Clinical Laboratory Standards, which is an organization devoted to development of consensus standards for healthcare laboratories.

Normalized OPSpecs chart. A form of the OPSpecs chart in which the scales on the x and y axes are given as a percent of the quality requirement. This "normalization" allows the chart to be used with any quality requirement, rather than having to prepare the OPSpecs chart for a specific quality requirement.

Number of control measurements, N. Used here to indicate the total number of control measurements available for use in assessing the quality of an analytical run. We consider N to be the total number of control measurements available for inspection when using common Levey-Jennings type QC charts or multirule type QC procedures where it is possible to combine the measurements from different materials to accumulate a higher N (and higher error detection) for evaluating control status. These measurements may be replicates on one level or material, individual measurements on two or more materials, or replicate measurements on two or more materials. For example, if you assay a single material and make two measurements on that material, N is 2. If you assay two materials (as required by US CLIA regulations) and make single measurements on each, N is 2. If you assay two materials and make duplicate measurements on each, N is 4. If you assay three materials and make single measurements on each, N is 3. If you assay three materials and make duplicate measurements on each, N is 6. With the use of mean/ range or cusum type of QC procedures where it is more difficult to combine the measurements from different control materials, N is more likely to be the number of replicates on an individual material.

Operating point. A point that is plotted on an OPSpecs chart to represent a method's inaccuracy or bias as the y-coordinate and the method's imprecision or CV as the x-coordinate. A QC procedure can be selected by observing the location of the operating point relative to the lines that represent the allowable limits of imprecision and inaccuracy for different QC procedures. An appropriate QC procedure is one whose operating limits are above the method's operating point.

Operating specifications (OPSpecs). Used here to describe the imprecision and inaccuracy that are allowable and the QC that is necessary to assure, at a stated level, that a defined quality requirement will be achieved in routine operation.

OPSpecs chart. A plot of the inaccuracy (on the y-axis) and the imprecision (on the x-axis) that are allowable for different QC procedures. The chart is prepared for a defined quality requirement and for a stated level of analytical quality assurance (AQA). Readily available in workbook format in the OPSpecs Manual and also easily prepared by the QC Validator computer program.

Performance characteristics. Those properties that describe how well a procedure performs. For a control procedure, the performance characteristics are the probabilities for error detection and false rejection, or the average run lengths for rejectable and acceptable quality. For a measurement procedure, the performance characteristics include analytical range, precision, accuracy, interference, recovery, and also the frequency and duration of analytical errors.

Power curve. A line on a power function graph that describes the performance of a certain control rule and N.

Power-function graph. A graphical presentation of the performance characteristics of QC procedures that describes the probability for rejection (on the y-axis) versus the size of analytical error occurring (on the x-axis) for stated control rules and numbers of control measurements.

Precision. "The agreement between replicate measurements. It has no numerical value" [IFCC, NCCLS]. See also Imprecision.

Preventive maintenance. The renewing or refurbishing of critical parts of a method on a regular basis to prevent malfunctions.

Probability, p. The likelihood an event will occur, usually stated as a decimal fraction between 0 and 1, 0 meaning that the event will never occur and 1 meaning that the event will always occur. For example, p=0.05 means there is a 5% chance that an event will occur. Commonly used in quality control to describe the chance that a run will be rejected.

Probability for error detection, P_{ed}. A performance characteristic of a QC procedure that describes how often an analytical run will be rejected when results contain errors in addition to the inherent imprecision of the measurement procedure. Ideally, P_{ed} should be 1.00 for errors that are medically significant. In practice, we generally aim for a P_{ed} of 0.90 when selecting and designing QC procedures.

Probability for false rejection, P_{fr}. A performance characteristic of a QC procedure that describes how often an analytical run will be rejected when there are no errors occurring, except for the inherent imprecision of the measurement procedure. Ideally, P_{fr} should be 0.00. In practice, we generally aim for a P_{fr} of 0.05 or less.

Process capability. An industrial term used to describe how the inherent variability of a production process under stable operation compares to the allowable variation. ΔSE_{crit} is an index of process capability for an analytical testing process.

Process stability. Used here to characterize the performance of the measurement procedure in terms of the frequency of analytic runs having medically important errors (f) that invalidate the medical usefulness of test results.

Proficiency testing, PT. Used in the US to describe a program of external quality assessment whereby specimens are submitted to laboratories for their analysis with the purpose of grading the performance of the laboratory.

Proficiency testing criteria for acceptable performance, PT criteria. Defined limits about a target value (TV) that are used to classify analytical performance as acceptable or not. CLIA defines PT criteria for about 80 regulated analytes, using a format of TV ± a stated %, TV ± a fixed concentration, or TV ± 3 SD, where the SD is usually a group standard deviation from a PT survey. These PT criteria should be interpreted as total error criteria because only single measurements can be made on PT specimens and the test result is subject to both random and systematic errors.

Provider performed microscopy, PPM. A special subset of moderately complex tests that may be performed by physicians, dentists, nurse practioners and midwives, and physician assistants as part of a patient examination.

QC acceptability criteria. The term used by CLIA to indicate the decision criteria or control rules used to monitor test performance during a run of patient specimens.

Quality Function Deployment, QFD. The industrial technique for planning products and production processes to achieve the desired quality characteristics. Principles of QFD are the basis for the quality-planning approach that has been developed for laboratory applications.

Quality planning process. The steps to be followed to select control rules, N, and a Total QC strategy that are appropriate for the quality needed and the imprecision and inaccuracy observed for a laboratory test.

Quality planning model. Term used to describe an equation that shows the additive effects of different factors that influence the variation of a test result. The analytical model relates the imprecision and inaccuracy of the measurement procedure and the sensitivity of the control procedure to the total analytical error that is allowable. The clinical model includes the analytical components plus pre-analytical components, such as within-subject biological variation, etc., and relates them to the clinical decision interval or gray zone for interpreting a test result.

Random error, RE. An error that can be either positive or negative, the direction and exact magnitude of which cannot be exactly predicted. In contrast, systematic errors are always in one direction.

Run. See analytical run.

Sample. "The appropriate representative part of a specimen which is used in the analysis." [IFCC]

Specimen. "Material available for analysis." [IFCC]

Standard. "Material or solution with which the sample is compared in order to determine the concentration or other quantity. The compound term calibration standard should be used whenever needed to avoid confusion with other technical or colloquial meanings of the word standard." [IFCC]

Standard deviation, s. A statistic that describes the dispersion or spread of a set of measurements about the mean value of a gaussian or normal distribution. Calculated from the equation:

where n is the number of measurements, and x_i is an individual measurement.

Standard deviation index, SDI. Generally used in reports from proficiency testing (PT) surveys to describe how far a PT result is

$$s = \sqrt{\frac{\Sigma(x_i - \bar{x})^2}{(n - 1)}}$$

from the target value (TV). An SDI of +2.0 means that the laboratory's reported result is 2 standard deviations of the group above the target value or mean of the group.

Statistical quality control. Those aspects of quality control in which statistics are applied, in contrast to the broader scope of quality control which includes many other procedures, such as preventive maintenance, instrument function checks, and performance validation tests. Statistical QC procedures are often used to monitor routine performance of a method and to alert the laboratory when the performance of a method changes.

Statistical control limits. As used with Levey-Jennings and Westgard multirule types of QC procedures, these are the lines drawn on control charts to define the range of results expected due to the random error of the method. The limits are often obtained from a group of 20 or more measurements on a particular control material by calculating the mean and standard deviation, then using multiples such as the mean plus and minus 3s, 2s, or 1s to establish control limits for different control rules.

Statistical process control. A general term used to describe those aspects of a control system in which statistics are applied to determine whether observed measurements fall within the range expected due to the random variation of the process. Industrial process control procedures provided the basis for introduction of statistical control in healthcare laboratories, however, industrial process control procedures often use the mean and range of a group of control measurements (e.g., Shewhart mean and range charts), whereas healthcare applications tend towards the use individual measurements or individual-value control charts, such as the Levey-Jennings chart.

Systematic error, SE. An error that is always in one direction and is predictable, in contrast to random errors that may be either positive or negative and whose direction cannot be predicted.

Test complexity. Refers to the CLIA system of classifying tests into categories on the basis of the difficulty of measurement and interpretation. Categories include waived, provider performed microscopy, moderate complexity, and high complexity.

Total Biologic Goal, TE_b. An allowable total error that is calculated from biologic goals as the sum of the allowable bias plus 1.65 times the allowable imprecision.

Total error, TE. The net or combined effect of random and systematic errors.

Total error requirement. See allowable total error.

Total imprecision. The random error observable over a period of many runs and many days.

Total QC strategy. The balance of the efforts expended on statistical QC, preventive maintenance, instrument function checks, method performance tests, and quality improvement.

Total Quality Management, TQM. A management philosophy and strategy that is based on W. Edward Deming's teachings that the priority in management is to improve quality, which will in turn improve productivity and lead to lower costs. Employs the scientific method as represented by Plan-Do-Check-Act (PDCA). The PDCA cycle is the basis for the laboratory quality-management model that is made up of components of Quality Planning (QP), Quality Laboratory Processes (QLP), Quality Control (QC), Quality Assessment (QA), and Quality Improvement (QI).

True value. Generally used to indicate that this is the correct analytical concentration or result.

Variable. A quantity of interest, whose value or magnitude fluctuates or changes.

Variance. The standard deviation squared. If there are independent sources of errors, the variance of the total error is the sum of the variances due to the individual sources of error.

Waived tests. A specific category of tests defined by CLIA, such as dipstick tests, fecal occult blood, urine pregnancy tests, erythrocyte sedimentation rates, blood glucose monitoring devices, etc., which are subject to the lowest level of regulation. The main requirement for QC is to follow the manufacturer's directions.

Westgard rules, Westgard multirule control procedure. A control procedure that uses a series of control rules to test the control measurements. A 1_{2s} rule is used as a warning, followed by use of 1_{3s}, 2_{2s}, R_{4s}, 4_{1s}, and 10_x as rejection rules.

Within-run imprecision. The random error observable within the time period of a single analytical run.

z-score, z-value. A calculated number that tells how many standard deviations a control result is from its mean value, e.g., a control result of 112 on a material having a mean of 100 and a standard deviation of 5 has a z-score of +2.4, i.e., it is 2.4 standard deviations above its mean.

17: Reference List

2000-2001 Comprehensive Accreditation Manual for Pathology and Clinical Laboratory Services. Joint Commission on Accreditation of Healthcare Organizations, Oakbrook Terrace, IL, 1999.

Aller RD, Smalley D. Of all analyzers, immunoassay the trickiest. CAP TODAY 2000;14(4):30-64.

Barnett RN. Medical significance of laboratory results. Am J Clin Pathol 1968;50:671-676.

Burnett RW, Westgard JO. Selection of measurement and control procedures to satisfy HCFA requirements and provide cost-effective operation. Arch Pathol Lab Med 1992;116:777-782.

Carey RN. Tips for managing the quality of immunoassays. http://www.westgard.com/guest4.htm.

Cotlove E, Marris E, Williams G. Biological and analytical components of variation in long-term studies of serum constituents in normal subjects: III. Physiological and medical implications. Clin Chem 1970;16:1028-1032.

Fraser CG. The application of theoretical goals based on biological variation data in clinical chemistry. Arch Pathol Lab Med 1988;112:404-15.

Fraser CG. Biological variation in clinical chemistry. An update: collated data, 1988-1991. Arch Pathol Lab Med 1992;116:916-23.

Fraser CG, Hyltoft Petersen P, Ricos C, Haeckel R. Proposed quality specifications for the imprecision and inaccuracy of analytical systems for clinical chemistry. Eur J Clin Chem Clin Biochem 1992;30:311-317.

Groth T, Falk H, Westgard JO. An interactive computer simulation program for the design of statistical control procedures in clinical chemistry. Comp Prog Biomedicine 1981;13:73-86.

Health Care Financing Administration (HCFA) and Public Health Service (PHS), US Dept of Health and Human Services (HHS). Medicare, Medicaid and CLIA Programs. Regulations implementing the Clinical Laboratory Improvement Amendments of 1988 (CLIA) and Clinical Laboratory Improvement Act program fee collection. Fed Regist 1993;58:5215-37.

Howanitz PJ, Tetrault GA, Steindel SJ. Clinical laboratory quality control: a costly process now out of control. Clin Chim Acta 1997;260:163-174.

Hyltoft Petersen P, deVerdier C-H, Groth T, Aronsson T. Clinically based quality goals; a NORDKEM project. Eur J Haematol. 1990;45(Suppl 53):6-8.

Hyltoft Petersen P, Ricos C, Stockl D, Libeer JC, Baadenhuijsen H, Fraser C, Thienpont L. Proposed guidelines for the internal quality control of analytical results in the medical laboratory. Eur J Clin Chem Clin Biochem 1996;34:983-999.

Klee GG. Tolerance limits for short-term analytical bias and analytical imprecision dervied from clinical assay specificity. Clin Chem 1993;39:1514-1518.

Koch DD, Oryall JJ, Quam EF, Feldbruegge DH, Dowd DE, Barry PL, Westgard JO. Selection of medically useful quality-control procedures for individual tests done in a multitest analytical system. Clin Chem 1990;36:230-233. [also available as PDF file at http://www.westgard.com/multchem.htm]

Lindemans J, Hoefkens P, van Kessel AL, Bonnay M, Kulpmann WR, van Suijlen JDE. Portable blood gas and electrolyte analyzer evaluated in a multiinstitutional study. Clin Chem 1999;45:111-117.

Mugan K, Carlson IH, Westgard JO. Planning QC procedures for immunoassays. J Clin Immunoassay 1994;17:216-222.

National Cholesterol Education Program Laboratory Standardization Panel. Current status of blood cholesterol measurement in clinical laboratories in the United States. Clin Chem 1988;34:193-201.

NCCLS C24-A2. Statistical Quality Control for Quantitative Measurements: Principles and Definitions; Approved Guideline - Second Edition. National Committee for Clinical Laboratory Standards, Wayne PA, February 1999.

NCCLS EP18-P. Quality management for unit use testing; Proposed guidelines. NCCLS, Wayne, PA, 1999.

Olafsdottir E, Westgard JO, Ehrmeyer SS, Fallon KD. Matrix effects on the performance and selection of QC procedures to monitor PO2 in blood gas measurements. Clin Chem 1996;42:392-6.

Parvin CA, Gronowski AM. Effect of analytical run length on quality-control (QC) performance and the QC planning process. Clin Chem 1997;43:2149-2154.

Ricos C, Alvarez V, Cava F, Garcia-Lario JV, Hernandez A, Jimenez CV, Minchinela J, Perich C, Simon M. Current databases on biologic variation: pros, cons and progress. Scand J Clin Lab Invest 1999;59:491-500

Seth J. Quality Assurance. Chapter 10 in Principles and Practice of Immunoassay, 2nd ed., Price CP, Newman DJ, eds. Macmillan Reference Ltd, London, 1997, pp 211-241.

Skendzel LP, Barnett RN, Platt R. Medically useful criteria for analytical performance of laboratory tests. Am J Clin Pathol 1985;83:200-205.

Tonks DA. A study of the accuracy and imprecision of clinical chemistry determinations in 170 Canadian laboratories. Clin Chem 1963;9:217-233.

U.S. Department of Health and Social Services. Medicare, Medicaid, and CLIA Programs: Regulations implementing the Clinical Laboratory Improvement Amendments of 1988 (CLIA). Final Rule. Fed Regist 1992 (Feb 28);57:7002-7186.

Wiebe DA, Westgard JO. Cholesterol - a model system to relate medical needs with analytical performance. Clin Chem 1993;39:1504-1513.

Westgard JO, Groth T. Power functions for statistical quality control rules. Clin Chem 1979;25:863-869.

Westgard JO, Barry PL. *Cost-effective quality control: Managing the quality and productivity of analytical processes.* AACC Press, Washington DC, 1986.

Westgard JO, Barry PL. Beyond quality assurance: Committing to quality improvement. Laboratory Medicine 1989;20:241-247.

Westgard JO, Barry PL. Total Quality Control: Evolution of quality systems in health care laboratories. Laboratory Medicine 1989;20:377-84.

Westgard JO, Burnett RW, Bowers GN. Quality management science in clinical chemistry: A dynamic framework for continuous improvement. Clin Chem 1990;36:1712-16.

Westgard JO, Oryall JJ, Koch DD. Predicting effects of QC practices on the cost-effective operation of a multitest analytical system. Clin Chem 1990;36:1760-1764. [also available as PDF file at http://www.westgard.com/multchem.htm]

Westgard JO, Quam EF, Barry PL. QC selection grids for planning QC procedures. Clin Lab Science 1990;3:271-278.

Westgard JO, Hyltoft Petersen P, Wiebe DA. Laboratory process specifications for assuring quality in the U.S. National Cholesterol Education Program. Clin Chem 1991;37:656-61.

Westgard JO, Wiebe DA. Cholesterol operational process specifications for assuring the quality required by CLIA proficiency testing. Clin Chem 1991;37:1938-44.

Westgard JO. Assuring analytical quality through process planning and quality control. Arch Pathol Lab Med 1992;116:765-9.

Westgard JO. Charts of operating specifications (OPSpecs charts) for assessing the precision, accuracy, and quality control needed to satisfy proficiency testing criteria. Clin Chem 1992;38:1226-33.

Westgard JO, Seehafer JJ, Barry PL. Allowable imprecision for laboratory tests based on clinical and analytical test outcome criteria. Clin Chem 1994;40;1909-14.

Westgard JO, QA: Are laboratories assuring, assessing, or assuming the quality of clinical testing today? Proceedings of the CDC 1995 Institute on Critical Issues in Health Laboratory Practice: Frontiers in Laboratory Practice Research. CDC, Atlanta, GA, 1996, pp 179-189.

Westgard JO. Error budgets for quality management: Practical tools for planning and assuring the analytical quality of laboratory testing processes. Clin Lab Manag Review 1996;10:377-403.

Westgard JO, Haberzettl CA. QC for immunoassays. Diagnostic Endocrinology and Metabolism: An AACC Inservice Training & Continuing Education Program 1996;14:239-243. See also http://www.westgard/com/qcapp4.htm

Westgard JO. Taking care of point-of-care QC. Clin Lab News, August 1997.

Westgard JO, Stein B. Automated selection of statistical quality-control procedures to assure meeting clinical or analytical quality requirements. Clin Chem 1997;43:400-3.

Westgard JO, Stein B, Westgard SA, Kennedy R. QC Validator 2.0: a computer program for automatic selection of statistical QC procedures for applications in healthcare laboratories. Computer Method Programs Biomed 1997;53:175-86.

Westgard JO. *Basic QC Practices.* Westgard QC, Madison, WI, 1998.

Westgard JO. Myths of Quality. Chapter1 in *Basic Method Validation.* Westgard QC, Madison, WI 1999, pp. 3-8.

Online References:

Online materials on Westgard Web can be accessed by using the username and password provided at the beginning of this book.

CLIA Total Error Requirements
http://www.westgard.com/clia.htm

Electronic QC and the total testing process
http://www.westgard.com/essay17.htm

European Biologic Goals and calculated total allowable biologic error
http://www.westgard.com/europe.htm

Mapping the Road to Quality with OPSpecs Charts
http://www.westgard.com/scotland.htm

Myths of quality
http://www.westgard.com/essay2.htm

Normalized OPSpecs calculator
http://www.westgard.com/qpbook/normcalc2.htm

Normalized OPSpecs charts (PDF Download)
http://www.westgard.com/qpbook/normcharts.html

Online Quality-Planning Tools.
http://www.westgard.com/qpbook/qptools.html

Predicting effects of QC practices on the cost-effective operation of a multitest analytical system. [PDF]
http://www.westgard.com/multchem.htm

QC for immunoassays
http://www.westgard.com/qcapp4.htm

QP 1: A Wake-up Call for Analytical Quality Management
http://www.westgard.com/qpbook/lesson49.htm

QP 2: Assuring Quality through Total Quality Management
http://www.westgard.com/qpbook/lesson50.htm

QP 3: Complying with Regulations, Standards, and Practice Guidelines
http://www.westgard.com/qpbook/lesson51.htm

QP 4: Devising a Practical Process
http://www.westgard.com/qpbook/lesson52.htm

QP5: Defining Quality Requirements
http://www.westgard.com/qpbook/lesson53.htm

QP 6: Adopting the OPSpecs Chart as your quality-planning tool
http://www.westgard.com/qpbook/lesson54.htm

QP 7: Formulating a Total Quality Control Strategy
http://www.westgard.com/qpbook/lesson55.htm

QP 8: Using Normalized OPSpecs charts
http://www.westgard.com/qpbook/lesson56.htm

QP 9: Practice makes Proficient
http://www.westgard.com/qpbook/lesson57.htm

QP 10: Automated Chemistry Applications
http://www.westgard.com/qpbook/lesson58.htm

QP 11: Blood Gas Applications
http://www.westgard.com/qpbook/lesson59.htm

QP 12: Immunoassay Applications
http://www.westgard.com/qpbook/lesson60.htm

QP 13: Coagulation Applications
http://www.westgard.com/qpbook/lesson61.htm

QP 14: What's wrong with statistical quality control?
http://www.westgard.com/qpbook/lesson62.htm

QP 15: Frequently-Asked-Questions about Quality Planning
http://www.westgard.com/qpbook/lesson63.htm

Quality-planning worksheet (PDF Download)
http://www.westgard.com/qpbook/qcplanworksheet.html

Selection of medically useful quality-control procedures for individual tests done in a multitest analytical system. [PDF]
http://www.westgard.com/multchem.htm

Tips for managing the quality of immunoassays, by R. Neil Carey, PhD.
http://www.westgard.com/guest4.htm

18: Answers to Self-Assessment Questions

Chapter 1: Is quality still an issue in the new millenium?

1. What is a consent decree?

In the context of laboratory testing, a consent decree is a legal agreement between the US government and a manufacturer to resolve an issue about the quality of products or the quality of the manufacturing process. The agreement may impose restrictions on the sale and distribution of products and the corrective action needed to keep products on the market.

2. What are Quality System Regulations?

These are the regulations that apply to manufacturing practices and define good manufacturing practices. Just like laboratories must follow CLIA rules, manufacturers must follow QSR rules.

3. What laboratory management activities are often bundled into the purchase of new methods and systems?

It is common for manufacturers to perform the initial validation studies, provide operator training, establish means and SDs on control materials, provide recommendations for routine QC, and provide the standard operating protocol (or method procedure).

4. How do you maintain an independent quality management system when you have to buy everything from a manufacturer"

First, it is important to define quality requirements on the basis of what is needed for your own patient care services. Use those requirements to judge whether method performance is acceptable. Establish QC procedures on the basis of those same quality requirements and estimates of method performance obtained from evaluation studies in your laboratory. Obtain QC materials from at least two different sources for use with your analytical systems. Determine the means and SD for each material and test from data generated in your own laboratory. Implement appropriate QC designs using available software that allows you to select the control rules and Ns that are needed for each test.

Chapter 2: Why is quality planning still important?

1. What are the five components in a TQM process?

The components include Quality Laboratory Processes (QLP), Quality Control (QC), Quality Assessment (QA), Quality Improvement (QI), and Quality Planning (QP). These components fulfill the steps of scientific management as defined in Deming's PDCA cycle (Plan, Do, Check, Act). The Check step consistes of both the QC and QA components.

2. What's the TQM process centered on?

TQM focuses on customer needs or quality requirements, which in the case of laboratory tests involves a number of dimensions of quality, such as analytical quality, turnaround time, specimen type and size, etc. Requirements for analytical quality need to be defined to operate laboratory testing processes in a cost-effective way.

3. What is the name for the industrial approach to quality planning?

Industry uses the term Quality Function Deployment, or QFD. There are whole books, workshops, and courses available on QFD.

4. How does "listening" to the customer differ from doing what the customers say?

Customers may complain about laboratory services and tell you what to do – usually that comes down to doing things faster. While they experience the outcome from the laboratory process, they don't necessarily understand all the steps in the process, some of which are outside the laboratory. Listening is important to gain an understanding of the customer's problem. The solution to the problem requires your understanding of the process. In short, you need to translate the customer's complaint or problem into the changes that are needed to improve the process.

5. What are "operating specifications"?

The concept comes from Deming's definition of an operating specification, which is supposed to describe what needs to be done and how to know if it's done properly, e.g., answer the telephone in three rings. In the laboratory, we need to have bench-level specifications for the method's imprecision and inaccuracy to be able to get the correct test results. We need a QC procedure so the analysts will know if the test results are correct. Operating specifications are the imprecision and inaccuracy that are allowable and the QC that is necessary.

6. **How do quality goals differ from operating specifications?**

Quality goals seldom consider the need for QC, therefore they don't provide the complete information that is needed for routine operation of a testing process. Quality goals need to be translated into operating specifications! That's what quality planning is all about.

Chapter 3: What guidelines exist for quality planning?

1. **Is quality planning explicit or implicit in the CLIA regulations?**

CLIA doesn't mention the words "quality planning", however, CLIA does require that *appropriate* QC procedures be used to monitor the performance of a method. CLIA does define minimum requirements for quality by the proficiency testing criteria for acceptable performance, but it remains up to the manufacturer and the laboratory to assure those requirements are achieved. This is where quality planning is needed to be sure that the quality required by CLIA PT criteria is achieved in routine service.

2. **What specific CLIA rules relate to quality planning?**

CLIA states that for methods whose QC instructions have not been cleared by FDA, "the laboratory must evaluate the instrument and reagent instability and operator variance in determining the number, type, and frequency of testing calibration and control materials and establish criteria for acceptability used to monitor test performance during a run of patient specimen(s)." To accomplish this requires quality planning.

3. **What does CLIA mean by "clearance of QC instructions"?**

This refers to a provision in the original CLIA rules whereby FDA would review and approve manufacturers' directions for QC. Originally scheduled to be implemented in 1994, this provision has been postponed again and again. The most recent information is that the FDA QC clearance provision will be deleted from the final, final, final, final, final CLIA document that is due out by the end of 2000. It's not known whether the provision stated in the answer to #2 above will be modified. If not, laboratories are fully responsible.

4. **What is NCCLS?**

NCCLS stands for National Committee for Clinical Laboratory Standards. It's a consensus standards organization, which means it attempts to develop standard ways of doing things that are acceptable to the scientific community, laboratory users, and regulators and accreditors. One goal is to avoid regulations by development of consensus standards.

5. How is an NCCLS standard developed?'

NCCLS forms a committee composed of professional experts in that subject area, hospital users, manufacturers, and government representatives. The committee develops the standard document, which then must be approved by the hierarchy of NCCLS and finally by a vote of the membership.

6. What are the steps recommended by NCCLS for planning a QC procedure?

NCCLS document C24-A2 provides the guidelines for statistical QC. Section 5 of that document identifies the planning steps as follows: define the quality required for the test, determine the performance for the method, identify candidate QC procedures, assess the performance of those QC procedures, define what performance is needed for QC, then select an appropriate QC procedure.

Chapter 4: How is quality planning performed?

1. What applications are of interest in the laboratory?

The main interests are in setting purchase specifications and selecting appropriate control rules and numbers of control measurements.

2. What applications are of interest to a manufacturer?

The manufacturer's first need is to establish performance specifications for the precision and accuracy of the analytical methods and systems. Given the expected elimination of the FDA QC clearance process in the final CLIA rules, there is no requirement for manufacturers to provide detailed QC instructions. However, manufacturers may choose to assist their customers and users in implementing appropriate QC procedures.

3. What quality-planning tool is recommended here?

The chart of operating specifications or "OPSpecs chart" is the first choice.

4. Explain how this tool is like a map.

The OPSpecs chart delineates different areas of method performance. The location of your method depends on its observed imprecision (x-coordinate) and its observed inaccuracy (y-coordinate). You can see the implications for laboratory QC from the location of the operating point.

5. How do you use this map to select a QC procedure?

The OPSpecs chart describes an area of allowable imprecison and allowable accuracy for each QC procedure. If your operating point falls in that area, you can use that QC procedure.

6. How do you use this map to set method performance specifications?

The maximum allowable imprecision (for bias of zero) is given by x-intercept of the line that defines the operating limits of a QC procedure.

7. Where can you get these maps?

Preprinted OPSpecs charts are available in a workbook called the OPSpecs Manual. Computer generated charts can be provided from the QC Validator program. Normalized OPSpecs charts that are suitable for manual applications are provided in chapter 8. The charts can be also be prepared using commonly available spreadsheet programs with specifications found in the scientific literature.

Chapter 5: How are quality requirements defined for a laboratory test?

1. What's the CLIA PT criterion for glucose?

It's given as TV ± 10% or plus/minus 6 mg/dL, whichever is greater. This means that at a concentration of 110, the 10% criterion applies (11 mg/dL), whereas at a concentration of 50, the 6 mg/dL or 12% criterion applies.

2. What's the biologic goal for the imprecision of a glucose method?

The maximum allowable CV is given as 2.2% in the European recommendations for biologic goals (see *Appendix 2*).

3. What's the biologic goal for the inaccuracy of a glucose method?

The maximum allowable bias is given as 4.4% which is an interim goal that will ultimately be reduced to 1.1%

4. What's the biologic goal for the total error of a glucose test?

The allowable biologic total error can be calculated as the allowable bias plus 1.65 times the allowable CV. Given the figures above, the allowable biologic total error would be 8.0% for the interim recommendations, but will ultimately be reduced to 5.5%.

5. What's a medically important change in results for a glucose test?

Skendzel and Barnett define the medically important change to be 30% at a level of 100 mg/dL. Keep in mind that the within-subject biologic variation is 12.2% for glucose, i.e., a patient's own CV is expected to be 12.2%, therefore most of this 30% will get used up by the patient, leaving only a small part for the analytical factors of imprecision and inaccuracy.

6. What's the allowable imprecision for a glucose method if the allowable total error is 10% and there is no method bias?

The answer here depends on the total error criterion that is used. Most commonly, TE is calculated as the bias plus 2 SD (or 2CV). In this case where bias is zero, the 2SD TE criterion would lead to an allowable CV of 5%. If a TE criterion of bias plus 3CV were used, the allowable CV would be 3.3%.

Chapter 6: How do you translate quality requirements into process specifications?

1. What's the meaning of 90%AQA(SE)?

The AQA stands for Analytical Quality Assurance and the SE stands for Systematic Error. The 90% means that there should be at least a 90% chance of detecting a medically important systematic error. The 90% is a percentage expression that corresponds to a 0.90 probability for error detection.

2. Where do you find the probability of false rejection?

P_{fr} is found in the key area of the OPSpecs chart, the 2nd column.

3. How do you match the different lines to the different control rules?

There are two ways. The easiest is to match the top to bottom order on the graph with the top to bottom order in the key, e.g., the 2nd line from the top in the graph corresponds to the 2nd row from the top in the key. The other way is to match the dots and dashes of the different lines in the graph to the same in the key.

4. Given a TE_a of 10%, recommend a QC procedure for a glucose method having a CV of 1.5% and a bias of 2.0%.

If you use the OPSpecs chart on page 82, you'll find your operating point (the large dot below) is below all the operating lines. this means you could choose any one of these control rules, but probably you'll want to select the one with the least amount of work. The line immediately above the operating point corresponds to a $1_{3s}/2_{2s}/R_{4s}$ with N of 2 and 1% false rejections (P_{fr} = 0.01), but the line above that corresponds to a $1_{2.5s}$ rule with an N of 2, which would give 90% detection of medically important systematic errors and only 3% false rejections (P_{fr} = 0.03). In this case, the single-rule QC procedure may be simpler to implement than a multirule, but the decision is yours.

OPSpecs Chart TE_a 10.0% with 90% AQA(SE)

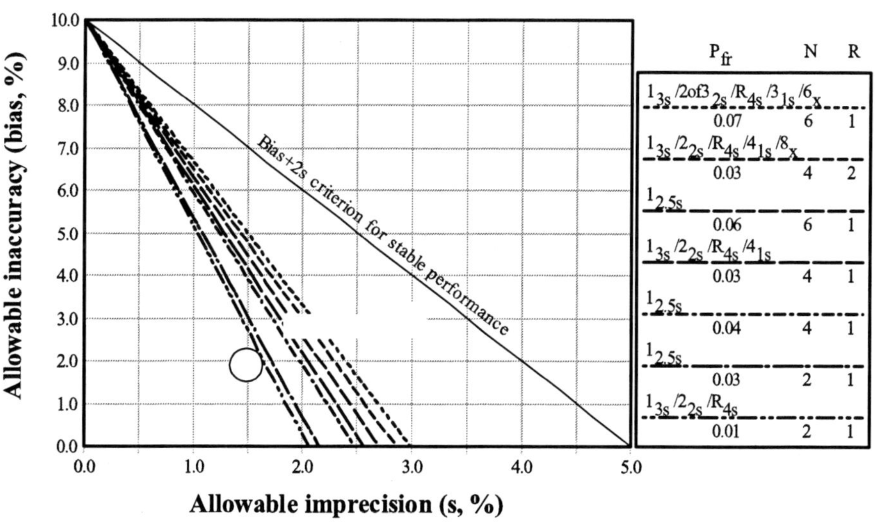

5. Given a TE_a of 10%, recommend the maximum CV for a glucose method if you are to implement a Levey-Jenning's control chart having 3 SD control limits and a minimum of 2 controls per run.

You can't use the same OPSpecs chart from question 4 because there's no 1_{3s} rule with N=2 in the graph. Instead, use the OPSpecs chart on page 79 (It's the chart in the section "How to select a QC procedure" with the pencil.) The 1_{3s} rule with N=2 is the line 2nd from the bottom. The x-intercept of that line gives the maximum allowable CV, which is about 1.9%.

OPSpecs Chart TE_a 10.0% with 90% AQA(SE)

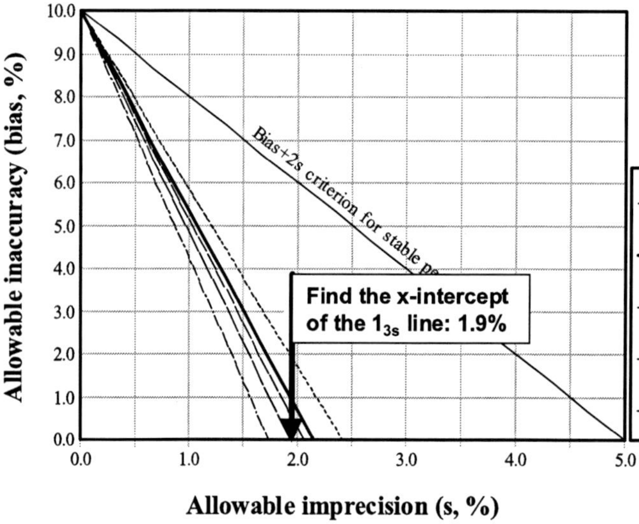

	P_{fr}	N	R
1_{2s}	0.09	2	1
$1_{2.5s}$	0.03	2	1
$1_{3s}/2_{2s}/R_{4s}$	0.01	2	1
1_{3s}	0.00	2	1
$1_{3.5s}$	0.00	2	1

Chapter 7: What do you do when quality isn't good enough?

1. What is the key parameter for deciding which TQC strategy to use?

The expected error detection of the QC procedure (%AQA or Ped) determines which TQC strategy to use. With high error detection, statistical QC is the best and most efficient way to check the process. With moderate or low error detection, you can't rely solely on statistical QC, therefore other components of the QC system become more important.

2. How can you minimize the cost of statistical QC?

Cost can be reduced by using the lowest number of control measurements necessary and by using the widest control limits possible. The number of control measurements affects the direct costs of materials and reagents. Wide control limits reduce the chances for false rejections, which saves repeat runs and operator time.

3. When might you reduce the amount of QC being performed?

Another factor to consider is the instability of the method or the frequency of problems. If experience with the method has demonstrated a very low number of problems, then you might consider operating with moderate error detection and making sure the false rejections are kept very low.

4. When is it appropriate to utilize multirule QC procedures with look-back rules?

If less than 90% error detection is available in the first run, then it makes sense to utilize a multirule procedure with a rule that encompasses the data from the current run and the immediate past run(s). If an error occurs that persists from run to run, you'll detect that error as soon as possible.

5. How can you identify methods or systems where staff can be rotated without any effect on the quality of testing?

For those methods and system where statistical QC procedure provides high error detection, SQC gives you a very powerful way to monitor the quality of the testing processes, including operator performance. These are the methods and systems that are most amenable to frequent change and rotation of operators.

6. When should you reduce staff rotations in order to improve quality?

For methods or systems whose performance permits only low error detection by statistical QC, you have to depend on other ways to check and monitor the testing process. One of the best detectors is an experienced operator, therefore it is advisable to staff those methods and systems with well-trained and experienced analysts. This will often mean that staff rotations should be kept at a minimum.

Chapter 8: Can you do quality planning by hand?

1. What's the advantage of using "normalized" OPSpecs charts?

The regular OPSpecs chart is prepared for the specific quality requirement of the test, therefore you need access to a whole atlas of maps or a computer program that can generate the individual maps when needed. The advantage of using "normalized" OPSpecs charts is that you only need 4 charts for 2 materials and 4 charts for 3 materials, which is a total of just 8 charts. Those 8 charts are readily available in this book or from the Internet, permitting you to implement a quality-planning process with minimal materials.

2. Given a quality requirement of 10% for a cholesterol test and a bias of 1% and CV of 2% for the method, what are the coordinates for plotting the operating point on a normalized OPSpecs chart?

The y-coordinate is the observed bias expressed as a percent of the quality requirement, which is [(1/10)*100] or 10%. The x-coordinate is the observed CV expressed as a percent of the quality requirement, which is [(2/20)*100] or 20%.

4. Given a triglycerides method with a CV of 5%, a bias of 4%, and two control materials, what control rules and N should be used?

For triglycerides, the CLIA criterion (see Appendix 1) for TE_a is 25%. The operating point has a y-coordinate of [(4/25)*100] or 16% and an x-coordinate of [(5/25)*100] or 20%. There's no good solution on the N=2 90%AQA chart – the 1_{2s} rule with N=2 has a false rejection probability of 0.09 or 9%, which is too high. The N=4 90%AQA chart shows that a multirule procedure or $1_{2.5s}$ procedure will give the desired error detection.

5. What performance is needed for a triglycerides method in order to use 2 control measurements and a Levey-Jennings chart with 3SD control limits?

The x-intercept of the 1_{3s} N=2 line on the normalized OPSpecs chart for 90%AQA is a little less than 20%, therefore the method CV should be better than 4% if there is no method bias.

Chapter 8, problem 4:

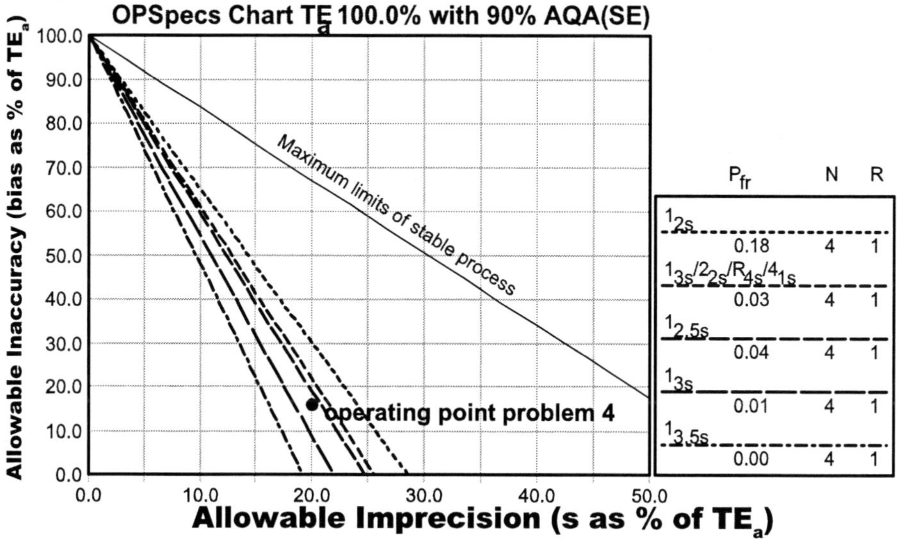

Chapter 8, problem 5:

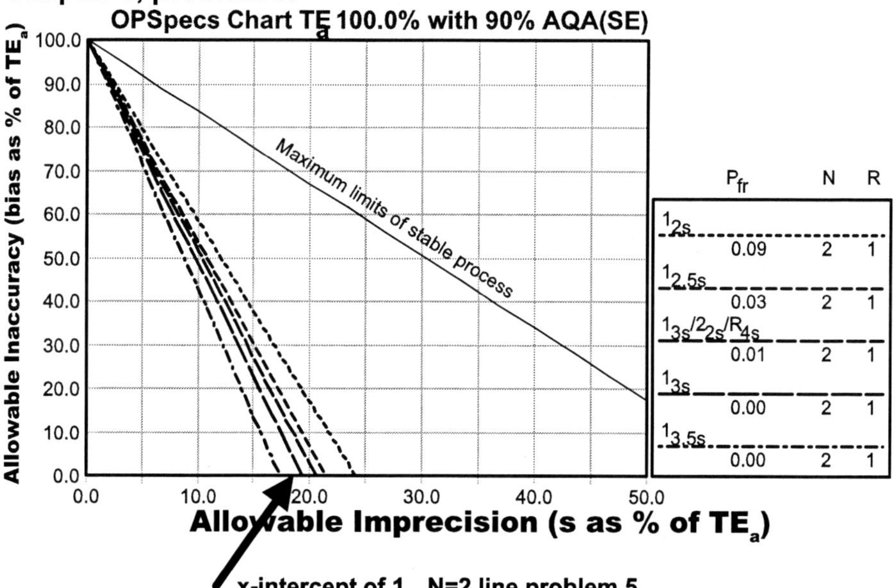

x-intercept of 1_{3s} N=2 line problem 5

Chapter 9: How do you become proficient at quality planning?

1. What organization has provided general guidelines for QC planning?

NCCLS, the National Committee for Clinical Laboratory Standards, has provided planning guidelines for statistical QC procedures in its C24-A2 document.

2. What is the first step in the quality-planning process?

Definition of the quality requirement for the test is the starting point for quality-planning applications. You can find them in *Appendices 1, 2, 3.*

3. What type of quality requirement can be used in the manual process?

A quality requirement in the form of an allowable total error (TE_a) is used in the manual planning process. This is the type of criterion provided by CLIA in defining acceptable performance in proficiency testing.

4. What error detection is considered to be ideal for a QC procedure?

The goal in the planning process is to achieve 90% or more detection of medically important errors, which corresponds to a probability of 0.90.

5. What false rejection is considered tolerable for a QC procedure?

The goal in the planning process is to limit false rejections to 5% or less, which corresponds to a probabilitiy of 0.05. Remember that a Levey-Jennings control chart with 2 SD limits gives a false rejection of 0.05 when N=1, which is okay. However, when N=2, P_{fr} is 0.09, meaning that 9% of the runs will be falsely rejected, when N=3 its 0.14 or 14% of the runs, and when N=4, its 0.18 or 18% of the runs. To reduce the costs of false rejections and rework, laboratories should almost never use 2 SD control limits.

6. What graphic tool is used in the manual quality-planning process?

A chart of operating specifications, or OPSpecs chart, is the quality-planning tool of choice. For a given quality requirement, this chart shows the bias and CV that are allowable for different QC procedures.

7. When should you rely on non-statistical components of a quality system?

In applications where statistical QC provides less than 50% detection of medically important errors, it will be important to prevent errors by instrument function checks, method performance tests, preventive maintenance, etc.

8. How does quality-planning help you prioritize your equipment needs?

You can identify those methods and analytical systems that need better analytical performance through your quality-planning efforts. The OPSpecs chart can actually show you the analytical performance that is needed for the most cost-effective operation of your testing processes.

9. How does quality-planning help you deploy your personnel?

Methods and systems which have high error detection by statistical QC are the best for rotating your personnel. SQC gives you an easy, yet quantitative way to assure the quality of the test results.

10. What are the most time-consuming steps in the quality-planning process?

Once the mechanics of the quality-planning process are mastered, it takes only a minute or two to perform the planning. The real problem timewise will be the time it takes to determine the quality requirements for the tests and to get the estimates of method performance (bias and CV).

Chapter 10: Automated Chemistry Applications

1. What is meant by "individualized QC designs"?

The idea is to design QC for each individual test in order to account for the quality required for that test and the observed performance of the method.

2. How can improved QC lead to cost savings?

One obvious cost savings is the reduction of false rejections, particularly if 2 SD control limits have been used previously. By reducing false rejects, you save the time and effort that was wasted on rerunning tests. Another savings is to minimize number of control measurements that are needed to detect medically imoprtnant errors. By optimizing error detection, you save the doctors from needless repeat testing while at the same time helping them make correct medical decisions. These savings are hard to quantify, but they are obvious benefits from high quality laboratory services.

3. How can you individualize QC designs for each test on a multitest analyzer if the number of control measurements must be kept constant?

Remember that error detection depends on the control rules and the number of control measurements that are used. If N is constant, then you need to change the control rule or rules from test to test. This might mean using rules such as $1_{2.5s}$, 1_{3s}, and $1_{3.5s}$ to adjust error detection by changing the control limit. Or, using subsets of rules from a multirule procedure, such as $1_{3s}/2_{2s}/R_{4s}/4_{1s}$, adjusting error detection by the changing the number of rules included.

4. In general, how many different QC designs would be expected for a multitest analyzer?

Even though there may be 20 or more tests on an analyzer, you will generally need only 3 to 5 different QC procedures. On highly automated analyzers, most of the tests will perform very well with minimum QC. There will be a few that are problematic and those are the ones that need special attention.

5. What flexibility is needed in your QC software?

The important capability is to be able to select the control rules for each test. Some QC software packages allow you to select the rules, but then apply those rules to all tests or all tests on an instrument system.

Chapter 11: Blood Gas Applications

1. What information is needed to determine the CLIA criterion for acceptable performance for pO_2?

The CLIA criterion is given as the target value (TV) ± 3 SD, where the SD here represents the group of laboratories in the proficiency testing program. Remember, you can look up the CLIA criteria in Appendix 1.

Chapter 11, problems 2 and 3:

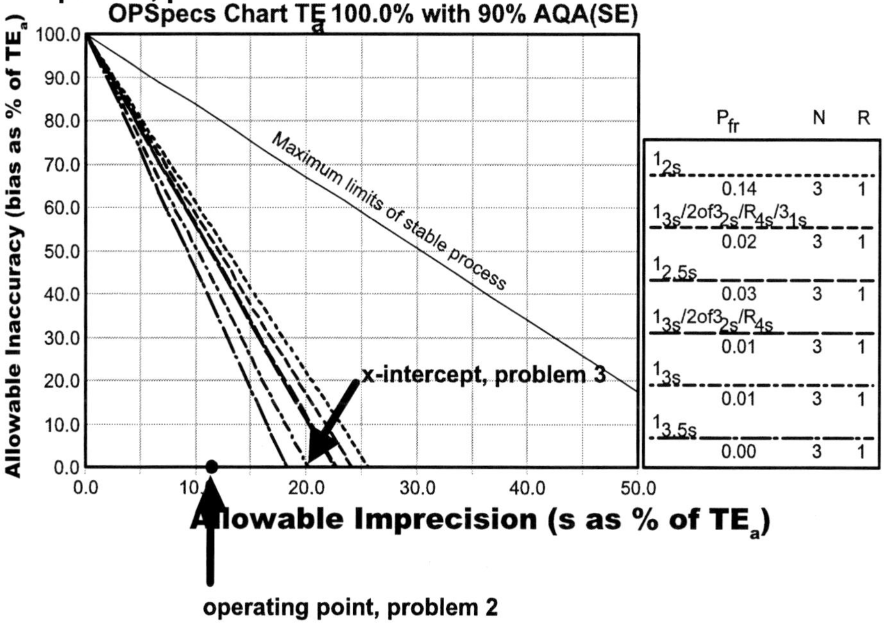

2. What QC procedure would be appropriate for a pH measurement when the observed bias is zero and the observed SD is 0.005?

The CLIA criterion is TV ± 0.04 pH unit. Using a normalized OPSpecs chart, the y-coordinate of the operating point would be zero and the x-coordinate would be 12.5%. With either two or three control materials, a $1_{3.5s}$ control rule could be used and would provide 90%AQA.

3. What CV is needed for a pCO_2 method if there were no bias at a decision level of 40 mm Hg?

The CLIA criterion is 5 mm Hg or 8%, whichever is greater. For mid-range performance at 40 mm Hg, which is the decision level we'll use, the quality requirement of 5 mm Hg is greater (12.5%). Since bias is zero, all we have to do is find the x-intercept of the control line. For three control materials, the normalized OPSpecs chart with 90%AQA for a 1_{3s} control rule shows an x-intercept of 20% which corresponds to [(12.5*20)/100] a CV of 2.5% or an SD of 1 mm Hg [(1/40)*100=2.5]. Note that this can be a little tricky; you have to take the normalized operating point value and reverse the calculations to get the desired number.

4. Why is it often difficult to QC pO_2 measurements?

Method imprecision is often not as good for pO_2. In addition, the control solutions themselves are generally unstable once opened, which leads to additional variability that is incorporated into the estimate of method imprecision and the SD used in calculating control limits.

5. What is the meaning of the term "multistage QC"?

Multistage QC refers to having different QC designs that are used at different stages of operation, e.g., a high error detection design for checking performance before starting the analysis of patient specimens and a low false rejection design for monitoring performance periodically during routine operation. When ideal error detection (>90%) and false rejection (<5%) can't be achieved with a single QC procedure, the multistage strategy is to select one design for high error detection (by using the most sensitive rules, providing higher N, or allowing somewhat higher false rejections) and another design for low false rejections (even if error detection is only moderate).

Chapter 12: Immunoassay Applications

1. What information is needed to determine the CLIA criterion for acceptable performance for TSH?

CLIA often uses a criterion based on 3 SD of the group variation for endocrine tests, which is the case for TSH. You will need access to CAP surveys or similar reports to get the group SDs needed to calculate the CLIA criteria.

2. What CV would be necessary for a thyroxine method in order to utilize only 3 control measurements?

The CLIA criterion for thyroxine is 20% or 1 mcg/dL. If you consider a concentration of 5 mcg/dL (where the two are equal), the normalized OPSpecs chart for 90%AQA shows x-intercepts of 18-23% for those QC procedures having acceptably low false rejection rates. The 18-23% normalized values correspond to CVs around 3.6% [(18*20)/100] to 4.6% [(23*20)/100]. Therefore, a method CV around 4% would be desirable when method bias is zero.

Chapter 12, problem 2:

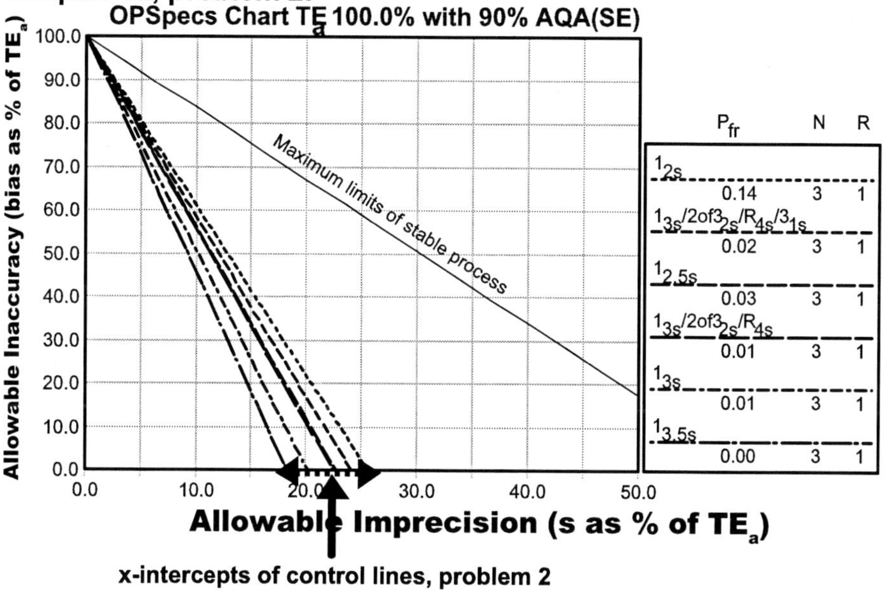

3. In the cortisol example, why is it okay to select a single-rule procedure rather than a multirule procedure?

When 90%AQA is achieved, the medically important systematic error should be detected in the first run in which it occurs. There's no need to look-back to an earlier run to maximize error detection, therefore there's no need for a multirule procedure. You can still use a multirule procedure, but if it's simpler to implement a single-rule procedure, that's fine.

4. Why is it useful to consider two different QC designs for TSH?

In situations where there are different quality requirements, different medical applications, and/or different analytical performance at different concentrations, it may be useful to design different QC procedures for different medical decision levels. In the TSH example, differences in quality requirements and method performance led to the development of a multilevel QC design.

5. What is the meaning of the term "multilevel QC design"?

Multilevel QC design refers to establishing different QC procedures at different medical decision levels. See the TSH example for an illustration.

Chapter 13: Coagulation Applications

1. If you were to use only two control materials for Prothrombin Time (and the method performance given in this lesson), what control rule(s) should be selected?

Recall that the quality requirement is 15% (see Appendix 1), the observed CV is 3.2%, and the observed bias is 0.0%. The normalized operating point has an x-coordinate of 21.3% [(3.2/15)*100]. Using the normalized OPSpecs chart for N=2 and 90%AQA, we find that the control lines for $1_{3s}/2_{2s}/R_{4s}$, $1_{2.5s}$ and 1_{2s}, all with N=2, are above the operating point. We immediately discount the 1_{2s} because of its high false rejection, and then we have a choice between the $1_{2.5s}$ rule and the multirule. The $1_{2.5s}$ might be simpler to implement than the multirule; it will depend on what your laboratory can and prefers to implement.

Chapter 13, problems 1 and 2:

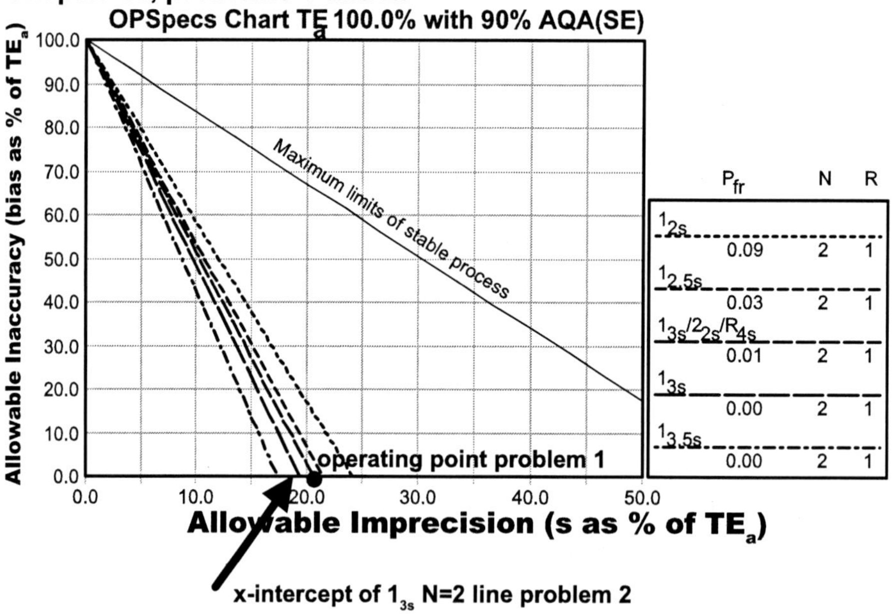

2. What CV would be necessary for the Prothrombin Time method in order to utilize 2 control measurements with a 1_{3s} control rule?

The x-intercept for the line representing a 1_{3s} rule with N=2 is approximately 19%, which converts [(19*15)/100] to a CV of 2.9%.

3. In the Partial Thromboplastin Time example, what bias could be tolerated if you were to utilize a 1_{3s} control rule with N=3?

Given an x-coordinate of 16% from the example, the y-coordinate could be 20% and still keep the operating point below the line for the 1_{3s} rule with N=3. The 20% value corresponds to a bias of 3.0% [(20*15)/100].

Chapter 13, problem 3:

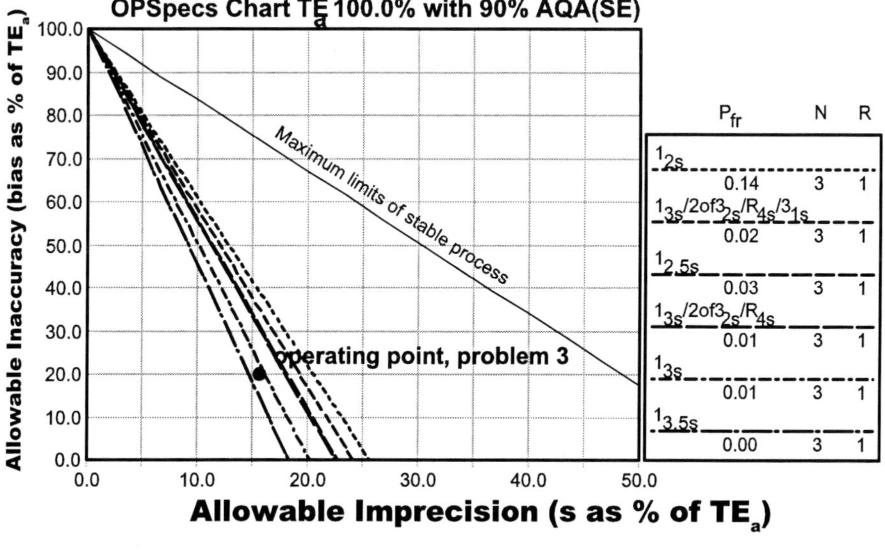

4. What bias could you tolerate for the fibrinogen method and a $1_{2.5s}$ N=2 QC procedure?

Given the observed CV of 4.2%, essentially no bias can be tolerated if the operating point is to be kept below the line for the $1_{2.5s}$ rule.

Chapter 13, problem 4:

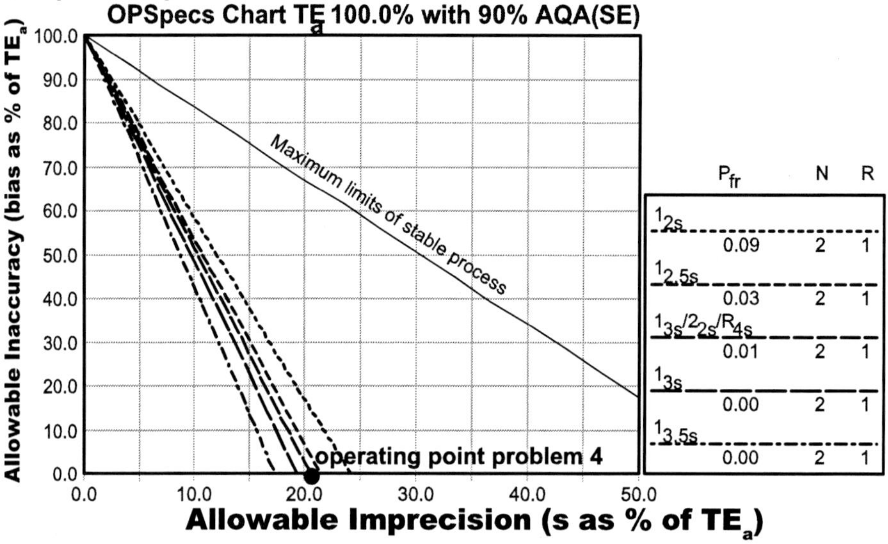

As you can see, any increase in bias would move the operating point up on the graph, above the line of the $1_{2.5s}$ rule. If CV were improved, there would be more room for bias.

5. What are the advantages of the online quality-planning tools over the "manual" normalized OPSpecs charts?

The biggest advantage is the elimination of the calculation of the normalized operating point. It's also handy to be able to print out the OPSpecs charts for documentation.

Chapter 14: What's wrong with statistical quality control?

1. How can you make statistical QC patient-focused?

By defining the quality required for patient services and designing your processes to achieve and assure that level of quality, statistical QC truly becomes patient-oriented and patient-focused. Contrast this to the current practices of "arbitrary control" where the quality needed has *never* been defined. Quality planning is the answer!

2. How can you adapt statistical QC to new technologies that have improved performance?

By taking the method imprecision, inaccuracy, and instability into account, statistical QC procedures can be adapted for improvements in performance by new methods, instruments, and analytical systems. Quality planning is the answer!

3. What's the mean of the term "unit device"?

Unit device refers to an analytical testing device that has a reagent cartridge that is disposed of after one test. Each test consumes one unit device.

4. What's the fallacy of the argument that statistical QC can't be used with unit devices?

Unit devices have to be uniform to provide consistent performance, otherwise they couldn't be used to perform tests. Statistical QC can still be used to monitor the uniformity of the process and may be particularly useful to monitor operator proficiency.

5. How might new QC technology improve current QC practices?

Automation has been the major contributor to improvements in the measurement process. Likewise, automation is needed to improve the QC process. This includes automation of the quality-planning process and integration into the QC software of analytical instruments, computer workstations, and laboratory information systems.

Appendix 1: CLIA '88 Analytical Quality Requirements

Fundamental to quality control is knowing the quality that needs to be controlled. A quality requirement must be defined if the QC practice is to be rational and objective. Historically, quality control has been used in laboratories to monitor whatever quality was being achieved, not for controlling to a defined level of quality.

Analytical quality requirements

Analytical quality requirements have been defined by the CLIA-88 proficiency testing (PT) criteria for acceptable performance [Federal Register February 28, 1992;57(40):7002-7186]. These criteria are presented in three different ways:

- as absolute concentration limits, e.g., target value ± 1 mg/dL for calcium;
- as a percentage, e.g., target value ± 10% for albumin, cholesterol, and total protein;
- as the distribution of a survey group, e.g., target value ± 3 standard deviations (SD) for thyroid stimulating hormone.

In a few cases, two sets of limits are given, e.g., the glucose requirement is given as the target value ± 6 mg/dL or ± 10% (whichever is greater).

The CLIA PT criteria specify the total errors that are allowable. The total error format is implicit because the CLIA-88 rules specify that only a single test is to be performed for each PT specimen. Under such conditions, the observed analytical error will be the total error due to both inaccuracy and imprecision.

Following is a list of the CLIA proficiency testing criteria for the currently regulated analytes, based on the February 28, 1992, Federal Register.

Routine Chemistry

Test or Analyte	Acceptable Performance
Alanine aminotransferase (ALT)	Target value ± 20%
Albumin	Target value ± 10%
Alkaline phosphatase	Target value ± 30%
Amylase	Target value ± 30%
Aspartate aminotransferase (AST)	Target value ± 20%
Bilirubin, total	Target value ± 0.4 mg/dL or ± 20% (greater)
Blood gas pO_2	Target value ± 3 SD
Blood gas pCO_2	Target value ± 5 mm Hg or ± 8% (greater)
Blood gas pH	Target value ± 0.04
Calcium, total	Target value ± 1.0 mg/dL
Chloride	Target value ± 5%
Cholesterol, total	Target value ± 10%
Cholesterol, high density lipoprotein	Target value ± 30%
Creatine kinase	Target value ± 30%
Creatine kinase isoenzymes	MB elevated (present or absent) or Target value ± 3 SD
Creatinine	Target value ± 0.3 mg/dL or ± 15% (greater)
Glucose	Target value ± 6 mg/dL or ± 10% (greater)
Iron, total	Target value ± 20%
Lactate dehydrogenase (LDH)	Target value ± 20%
LDH isoenzymes	LDH1/LDH2 (+ or -) or Target value ± 30%
Magnesium	Target value ± 25%
Potassium	Target value ± 0.5 mmol/L
Sodium	Target value ± 4 mmol/L
Total protein	Target value ± 10%
Triglycerides	Target value ± 25%
Urea Nitrogen	Target value ± 2 mg/dL or ± 9% (greater)
Uric acid	Target value ± 17%

Toxicology

Test or Analyte	Acceptable Performance
Alcohol, blood	Target value ± 25%
Blood lead	Target value ± 10% or ± 4 mcg/dL (greater)
Carbamazepine	Target value ± 25%
Digoxin	Target value ± 20% or 0.2 ng/mL (greater)
Ethosuximide	Target value ± 20%
Gentamicin	Target value ± 25%
Lithium	Target value ± 0.3 mmol/L or ± 20% (greater)
Phenobarbital	Target value ± 20%
Phenytoin	Target value ± 25%
Primidone	Target value ± 25%
Procainamide (and metabolite)	Target value ± 25%
Quinidine	Target value ± 25%
Theophylline	Target value ± 25%
Tobramycin	Target value ± 25%
Valproic acid	Target value ± 25%

Hematology

Test or Analyte	Acceptable Performance
Cell identification	90% or greater consensus on identification
White cell differential	Target ± 3 SD based on percentage of different types of white cells
Erythrocyte count	Target ± 6%
Hematocrit	Target ± 6%
Hemoglobin	Target ± 7%
Leukocyte count	Target ± 15%
Platelet count	Target ± 25%
Fibrinogen	Target ± 20%
Partial thromboplastin time	Target ± 15%
Prothrombin time	Target ± 15%

Endocrinology

Test or Analyte	Acceptable Performance
Cortisol	Target value ± 25%
Free thyroxine	Target value ± 3 SD
Human chorionic gonadotropin	Target value ± 3 SD or (positive or negative)
T_3 uptake	Target value ± 3 SD by method
Triiodothyronine	Target value ± 3 SD
Thyroid stimulating hormone	Target value ± 3 SD
Thyroxine	Target value ± 20% or 1.0 mcg/dL (greater)

General immunology

Test or Analyte	Acceptable Performance
Alpha-1 antitrypsin	Target value ± 3 SD
Alpha-fetoprotein	Target value ± 3 SD
Antinuclear antibody	Target value ± 2 dilution or (pos. or neg.)
Antistreptolysin O	Target value ± 2 dilution or (pos. or neg.)
Anti-Human Immunodeficiency virus	Reactive or nonreactive
Complement C3	Target value ± 3 SD
Complement C4	Target value ± 3 SD
Hepatitis (HBsAg, anti-HBc, HBeAg)	Reactive (positive) or nonreactive (negative)
IgA	Target value ± 3 SD
IgE	Target value ± 3 SD
IgG	Target value ± 25%
IgM	Target value ± 3 SD
Infectious mononucleosis	Target value ± 2 dilution or (pos. or neg.)
Rheumatoid factor	Target value ± 2 dilution or (pos. or neg.)
Rubella	Target value ± 2 dilution or (pos. or neg.)

Appendix 2: European Biologic Goals

Recommendations for the allowable CV and allowable bias have been developed by a European working group on the basis of biologic variability.

This table provides proposed and interim (in parenthesis) quality specifications for total analytical imprecision (CV,%) and inaccuracy (as % maximum allowable deviation) for commonly analyzed quantities. [Reference: Frazer CG, Hyltoft Petersen P, Ricos C, Haeckel R. "Proposed quality specifications for imprecision and inaccuracy of analytical systems for clinical chemistry." Eur J Clin Chem Clin Biochem 1992;30:311-317]

The interim specifications are based on the state of the art achieved by the best 0.20 fractile of laboratories (i.e.the best 20% of laboratories).

The total biologic error is calculated from the equation TE = 1.65 (imprecision) + inaccuracy. [Reference: Hyltoft Petersen P, Ricos C, Stockl D, Libeer JC, Baadenhuijsen H, Fraser C, Thienpont L. "Proposed guidelines for the internal quality control of analytical results in the medical laboratory." Eur J Clin Chem Clin Biochem 1996;34:983-999]

Key to the tables

I(%)	Desired specification for Imprecision (CV)
B(%)	Desired specification for Bias (inaccuracy)
TE(%)	Desired specification for Total Error

How to use this information

If your laboratory isn't required to meet CLIA criteria for acceptability, and/or if you find quality requirements based on biologic variability more appropriate, you may consider the recommendations in this appendix as well as *Appendix 3*. The quality-planning process works with any total error requirement, whether set directly by CLIA or calculated from biologic goals.

Test or Analyte	Proposed and (Interim) Specifications		
	I (%)	B (%)	TE (%)
Albumin	1.4 (1.8)	1.1 (2.8)	3.4 (5.8)
Bicarbonate	2.3 (4.9)	1.6 (4.6)	5.4 (12.7)
Bilirubins	11.3	9.8	28.4
Calcium	0.9 (1.5)	0.7 (1.8)	2.2 (4.3)
Chloride	0.7 (1.0)	0.5 (1.4)	1.7 (3.0)
Cholesterol	2.7	4.1	8.6
Creatinine	2.2	2.8 (4.4)	6.4 (8.0)
Glucose	2.2	1.9 (4.4)	5.5 (8.0)
Iron	15.9	8.9	35.1
Lithium	3.6	4.2	10.1
Magnesium	1.1 (2.6)	1.6 (2.2)	3.4 (6.5)
Phosphate	4.0	3.1 (8.0)	9.7 (14.6)
Potassium	2.4	1.6 (4.8)	5.6 (8.4)
Proteins	1.4	1.5 (2.8)	3.8 (5.1)
Triacylglycols	11.5	15.6	34.6
Urea	6.3	5.3	15.7
Urate	4.2	4.0 (8.4)	10.9 (15.3)

Test or Analyte	Proposed and (Interim) Specifications		
	I (%)	B (%)	TE (%)
Acid phosphatase	4.5	2.1 (9.0)	9.5 (16.4)
Alanine aminotransferase	13.6	6.4	36.0
Alkaline phosphatase	3.4	6.4	12.0
Amylase	3.7	6.5 (7.4)	12.6 (13.5)
Aspartate aminotransferase	7.2	6.2	18.0
Creatine kinase	20.7	19.8	54.0
Gamma-Glutamyl transferase	7.4	21.8	34.0
Lactate dehydrogenase	3.9	4.1 (7.8)	10.5 (14.2)
Thyroxine (total)	3.4 (4.1)	4.1 (6.8)	9.7 (13.6)
Triiodothyronine	4.0 (4.7)	5.5 (8.0)	12.1 (15.8)
Digoxin	3.8 (4.7)	3.9	10.2 (11.7)
Transferrin	2.4 (4.0)	2.3 (4.8)	6.3 (11.4)
IgG	1.9 (3.7)	5.0	8.1 (11.1)
IgA	2.2 (3.8)	12.5	16.1 (18.8)
IgM	2.3 (5.4)	12.7	16.5 (21.6)

Appendix 3: Desired Specifications for Total Error, Imprecision, and Bias derived from Biologic Variation

The most recent and extensive listing of biologic goals has been provided by a Spanish group [Reference: Ricos C, Alvarez V, Cava F, Garcia-Lario JV, Hernandez A, Jimenez CV, Minchinela J, Perich C, Simon M. "Current databases on biologic variation: pros, cons and progress." Scand J Clin Lab Invest 1999;59:491-500]

This list includes over 300 quantities. Detailed references to the sources of information on biologic variability can be found on the internet at the address **http://www.westgard.com/biodatabase1.htm**

The total biologic error is calculated from the equation TE = 1.65 (imprecision) + inaccuracy. [Reference: Hyltoft Petersen P, Ricos C, Stockl D, Libeer JC, Baadenhuijsen H, Fraser C, Thienpont L. "Proposed guidelines for the internal quality control of analytical results in the medical laboratory." Eur J Clin Chem Clin Biochem 1996;34:983-999]

Key to the tables

B-	Blood
(B)Erthyr-	Erythrocyte
(B)Leuc-	Leukocyte
S-	Serum
P-	Plasma
I(%)	Desired specification for Imprecision (CV)
B(%)	Desired specification for Bias (inaccuracy)
TE(%)	Desired specification for Total Error

How to use this information

If your laboratory isn't required to meet CLIA criteria for acceptability, and/or if you find quality requirements based on biologic variability more appropriate, you may consider the recommendations in this appendix as well as appendix 2. The quality-planning process works with any total error requirement, whether set directly by CLIA or calculated from biologic goals.

Type	Test or Analyte	Desirable Specification I (%)	B (%)	TE (%)
S-	11-Deoxycortisol	10.7	9.5	27.1
S-	17-Hydroxiprogesterone	9.8	14.0	30.2
S-	5´Nucleotidase	11.6	7.6	26.8
U-	5-HIAA concentration, 24 h	10.2	9.7	26.5
S-	α1-Acid Glycoprotein	5.7	6.8	16.2
S-	α1-Antichymotripsine	6.8	5.7	16.8
S-	α1-Antitrypsin	3.0	4.3	9.2
S-	α1-Globulins	5.7	6.3	15.7
U-	α1-Microglobulin concentration overnight	16.5	16.7	43.9
P-	α2-Antiplasmin	3.1	—	—
S-	α2-Globulins	5.2	4.1	12.6
S-	α2-Macroglobulin	1.7	4.8	7.6
U-	α2-Microglobulin output, overnight	14.5	10.8	34.7
S-	α-Amylase	4.8	7.8	15.7
U-	α-Amylase concentration, random	47.0	26.2	103.7
S-	α-Amylase, pancreatic	5.9	8.0	17.7
S-	α-Carotene	17.9	—	—
S-	Acid phosp, tartrate-resistant	5.4	4.3	13.2
S-	Acid phosphatase (ACP)	4.5	3.0	10.3
S-	Acid phosphatase activity prostatic (PAP)	16.9	—	—
P-	Activated partial thromboplastin time	1.4	2.3	4.5
S-	ADA	5.9	7.0	16.7
S-	Alanine aminopeptidase	2.1	—	—
S-	Alanine aminotransferase	12.2	12.0	32.1
S-	Albumin	1.6	1.3	3.9
U-	Albumin concentration, first morning	18.0	16.4	46.1
S-	Aldosterone	14.7	12.4	36.7

Type	Test or Analyte	Desirable Specification I (%)	B (%)	TE (%)
U-	Aldosterone concentration, 24 h	16.3	12.7	39.6
S-	Alkaline phosphatase	3.2	6.4	11.7
S-	Alkaline phosphatase, bone isoform	3.3	9.1	14.5
S-	Alkaline phosphatase, placental	9.6	—	—
U-	Ammonia output, 24 h	12.4	9.2	29.6
S-	Androstendione	5.8	13.1	22.6
S-	Angiotensin converting enzyme	6.3	7.6	17.9
P-	Antithrombin III	2.6	4.0	8.3
S-	Apolipoprotein A1	3.3	3.7	9.1
S-	Apolipoprotein B	3.5	6.0	11.6
S-	Ascorbic acid	12.9	8.6	29.9
S-	Aspartate aminotransferase	6.0	5.4	15.2
S-	α-Tocopherol	6.9	4.8	16.2
S-	β2-Microglobulin	3.0	4.1	9.0
B-	Basophils, count	14.0	15.4	38.5
S-	β-Carotene	18.0	13.3	43.0
S-	β-Cryptoxanthin	18.4	—	—
S-	β-Globulins	5.1	3.4	11.7
S-	Bilirubin, conjugated	18.4	14.2	44.5
S-	Bilirubin, total	12.8	10.0	31.1
S-	C Peptide	4.7	4.1	11.7
U-	C Telopeptide type I collagen/Creat	17.6	—	—
S-	C Telopeptide type I procollagen	4.0	7.5	14.1
S-	C3 Complement	2.6	4.1	8.4
S-	C4 Complement	4.5	8.6	16.0
S-	CA 125	6.8	12.1	23.3
S-	CA 15.3	2.9	10.8	15.5

Type	Test or Analyte	Desirable Specification		
		I (%)	B (%)	TE (%)
S-	CA 19.9	12.3	24.0	44.3
S-	CA 549	4.6	8.7	16.2
S-	Calcium	1.0	0.8	2.4
U-	Calcium concentration, 24 h	13.8	11.4	34.1
U-	Calcium output, 24 h	13.1	9.4	31.0
S-	Carbohydrate deficient transferrin	3.6	9.8	15.7
S-	Carcinoembryonic antigen (CEA)	4.7	14.1	21.8
S-	Ceruloplasmin	2.9	3.1	7.8
S-	Chloride	0.6	0.5	1.5
S-	Cholesterol	3.0	4.1	9.0
S-	Cholinesterase	3.5	3.1	8.9
S-	Cholinesterase, immunoreactive	3.2	—	—
S-	Cholinesterase, catalitic activity	2.7	2.9	7.4
S-	CK MB %	3.5	10.8	16.5
S-	CK MB, activity	9.9	7.8	24.1
S-	CK MB, mass	9.2	16.0	31.2
P-	Copper	4.0	5.2	11.8
S-	Copper	2.5	3.6	7.7
S-	Cortisol	10.5	12.5	29.8
S-	C-Propeptide type 1 procollagen	4.1	4.9	11.6
S-	C-Reactive protein	26.3	24.9	68.3
S-	Creatin kinase	11.4	11.5	30.3
S-	Creatinine	2.2	3.4	6.9
Patient-	Creatinine clearance	6.8	4.8	16.0
U-	Creatinine concentration, 24 h	12.0	8.6	28.4
U-	Creatinine output, 24 h	5.5	6.4	15.4
P-	Cysteine	3.0	3.4	8.3

Type	Test or Analyte	Desirable Specification		
		I (%)	B (%)	TE (%)
S-	Dehydroepiandrosterone sulfate	1.7	7.5	10.4
U-	Deoxipyridinoline/Creatinine, 24 h	7.4	5.3	17.4
P-	Dipeptidyl-peptidase IV	4.1	4.2	10.9
P-	Elastase-PI	6.8	5.3	16.5
B-	Eosinophils, count	10.5	19.8	37.1
(B)Plat-	Epinephrine	12.7	—	—
P-	Epinephrine	24.2	—	—
B-	Erythrocytes, count	1.6	1.7	4.4
U-	Estradiol	15.2	—	—
S-	Estradiol	11.3	8.3	27.0
P-	Factor V	1.8	—	—
P-	Factor VII	3.4	5.1	10.7
P-	Factor VIII	2.4	4.9	8.9
P-	Factor X	3.0	—-	—-
S-	Ferritin	7.5	5.0	17.3
P-	Fibrinogen	5.4	4.8	13.6
S-	Follicle Stimulating Hormone	5.1	8.4	16.7
S-	Free Estradiol	11.4	—	—
U-	Free Estradiol	19.3	—	—
S-	Free Testosterone	4.7	—	—
U-	Free Testosterone	25.9	—	—
S-	Free Thyroxine (FT4)	3.8	3.6	9.9
S-	Free Triiodothyronine (FT3)	4.0	—-	—-
S-	Fructosamine	1.7	1.7	4.5
(B)Erythr-	G6PDH	16.4	11.4	38.5
S-	γ-Globulins	7.3	4.8	16.8
S-	γ-Glutamyltransferase	6.9	10.8	22.2

Type	Test or Analyte	Desirable Specification		
		I (%)	B (%)	TE (%)
S-	Globulins, total	2.8	3.5	8.0
S-	Glucose	2.5	2.3	6.3
B-	Glutathion Peroxidase	3.6	5.7	11.7
S-	Glycated albumin	2.6	2.9	7.2
S-	Glycated total protein	0.5	2.9	3.7
(B)Hb-	Glycohemoglobin	2.8	—	—
P,S-	Haptoglobin	10.2	10.4	27.3
S-	HDL Cholesterol	3.6	5.2	11.1
S-	HDL1 Cholesterol	2.8	6.9	11.5
S-	HDL2 Cholesterol	7.9	10.9	23.9
S-	HDL3 Cholesterol	3.5	4.0	9.8
B-	Hematocrit	1.4	1.7	4.1
B-	Hemoglobin	1.4	1.8	4.1
P-	Homocysteine	3.9	7.7	14.1
U-	Hydroxiproline/minute, night urine	18.1	13.2	43.0
S-	Hydroxybutyrate dehydrogenase	4.4	—	—
S-	Immunoglobulin A	2.5	9.3	13.4
S-	Immunoglobulin G	2.3	4.3	8.0
S-	Immunoglobulin M	3.0	11.9	16.8
S-	Insulin	10.6	15.5	32.9
(B)Leuc-	Interferon receptor	7.0	6.1	17.7
S-	Iron	13.3	8.8	30.7
S-	κ chains	2.4	4.0	8.0
S-	λ chains	2.4	4.7	8.6
B-	Lactate	13.6	8.0	30.4
S-	Lactate dehydrogenase (LDH)	4.3	4.3	11.4
P-	Lactoferrin	5.9	6.6	16.4

Type	Test or Analyte	Desirable Specification I (%)	B (%)	TE (%)
S-	LD1	3.2	3.0	8.2
S-	LD2	2.5	1.6	5.7
S-	LD3	2.4	1.8	5.8
S-	LD4	4.7	3.3	11.0
S-	LD5	6.2	4.6	14.8
S-	LDL Cholesterol	4.2	6.8	13.6
S-	LDL Cholesterol direct	3.3	—	—
B-	LDL receptor mRNA	10.8	6.4	24.1
B-	Leukocytes, count	5.5	5.6	14.6
S-	Lipase	11.6	10.1	29.1
S-	Lipoprotein (a)	4.3	21.6	28.6
S-	Lutein	11.9	—	—
S-	Luteinizing Hormone	7.3	7.8	19.8
S-	Lycopenen	21.6	—	—
B-	Lymphocytes, count	5.2	7.4	16.0
(B)Erythr-	Magnesium	2.8	3.2	7.8
(B)Leuc-	Magnesium	9.2	6.1	21.2
S-	Magnesium	1.8	1.8	4.8
U-	Magnesium concentration, 24 h	22.7	14.7	52.2
U-	Magnesium output, 24 h	19.2	13.4	45.0
(B)Erythr-	Mean corpuscular hemoglobin (HCM)	0.8	1.4	2.7
(B)Erythr-	Mean corpuscular hemoglobin conc (MCHC)	0.9	0.8	2.2
(B)Erythr-	Mean corpuscular volume (MCV)	0.7	1.2	2.3
(B)Plat-	Mean platelet volume (MPV)	2.2	2.3	5.8
B-	Monocytes, count	8.9	13.2	27.9
S-	Mucinous carcinoma-associated antigen (MCA)	5.1	10.1	18.5

Type	Test or Analyte	Desirable Specification		
		I (%)	B (%)	TE (%)
S-	Myoglobin	7.0	8.2	19.6
U-	N Telopeptide type I collagen/Creat	11.6	—	—
U-	N-Acetyl Glucosaminidase concentration,overnight	21.1	11.5	46.3
U-	N-Acetyl Glucosaminidase output,overnight	21.2	11.5	46.5
B-	Neutrophils, count	8.1	9.1	22.4
U-	Nitrogen, output	7.0	7.0	18.4
(B)Plat-	Norepinephrine	4.8	—	—
P-	Norepinephrine	9.8	—	—
S-	N-Propeptide type 1 procollagen	3.7	—	—
S-	Osmolality	0.7	0.4	1.5
S-	Osteocalcin	3.2	6.0	11.2
U-	Oxalate concentration, 24h	22.0	11.9	48.2
U-	Oxalate output, 24 h	21.3	11.7	46.8
B-	pCO2	2.4	1.8	5.7
B-	pH [H+]	1.8	1.0	3.9
B-	pH (pH units)	0.1	—	—
S-	Phosphate	8.5	9.4	4.3
U-	Phosphate concentration, 24 h	13.2	9.4	31.1
U-	Phosphate output, 24 h	9.0	7.2	22.1
Patient-	Phosphate tubular reabsorption	1.4	1.1	3.3
S-	Phospholipids	3.3	3.2	8.6
P-	Plasminogen	3.9	—	—
B-	Platelet distribution wide (PDW)	1.4	—	—
B-	Plateletcrit	6.0	—	—
B-	Platelets	4.6	5.9	13.4
(B)Leuc-	Potassium	6.8	4.8	16.0

Type	Test or Analyte	Desirable Specification I (%)	B (%)	TE (%)
S-	Potassium	2.4	1.8	5.8
U-	Potassium concentration, 24 h	13.6	8.9	31.3
U-	Potassium output, 24 h	12.2	8.2	28.4
S-	Prealbumin	5.5	5.5	14.5
S-	Prolactin (men)	3.5	15.4	21.1
P-	Prolyl Endopeptidase	8.4	5.5	19.3
S-	Prostatic specific antigen (PSA)	7.0	18.4	30.0
P-	Protein C	2.9	13.9	18.7
U-	Protein concentration, 24 h	19.8	10.9	43.5
U-	Protein output, 24 h	17.8	10.7	40.0
P-	Protein S	2.9	15.9	20.7
S-	Protein, total	1.4	1.2	3.4
P-	Prothrombin, time	2.0	2.0	5.3
U-	Pyridinoline/creatinine morning spot	4.4	4.9	12.1
B-	Pyruvate	7.6	5.0	17.5
B-	Red cell distribution wide (RDW)	1.8	1.7	4.6
S-	Retinol	7.4	5.9	18.1
S-	Rheumatoid factor	4.3	6.5	13.5
S-	SCC	19.7	13.3	45.8
B-	Selenium	6.0	4.2	14.1
P-	Selenium	6.0	4.6	14.5
S-	Sex Hormone binding globulin (SHBG)	6.1	11.1	21.1
(B)Erythr-	Sodium	0.9	3.1	4.6
(B)Leuc-	Sodium	25.5	15.7	57.7
S-	Sodium	0.4	0.3	0.9
U-	Sodium concentration, 24 h	12.0	9.0	28.8
U-	Sodium output, 24 h	14.4	8.3	32.0
S-	Superoxide dismutase	8.6	5.0	19.1

Type	Test or Analyte	Desirable Specification		
		I (%)	B (%)	TE (%)
(B)Erythr-	Superoxide dismutase	6.2	3.3	13.5
S-	T3-uptake	2.3	1.6	5.3
S-	Testosterone	4.4	5.8	13.0
Saliva-	Testosterone	8.7	7.2	21.4
U-	Testosterone	12.5	—	—
S-	Thyroglobulin	6.5	7.0	17.8
S-	Thyroid Stimulating Hormone (TSH)	9.9	8.4	24.6
S-	Thyroxin binding globulin (TBG)	3.0	2.1	7.1
S-	Thyroxine (T4)	3.0	3.4	8.3
S-	Tissue polipeptide specific antigen (TPS)	18.1	28.5	58.3
S-	Tissue polypeptide antigen (TPA)	14.4	12.4	36.1
U-	Total Catecolamines, conc, 24 h	12.0	10.0	29.8
S-	Transferrin	1.5	1.3	3.8
S-	Triglyceride	10.5	10.7	27.9
S-	Triiodothyronine (T3)	4.4	4.2	11.4
S-	Urate	4.3	4.8	11.9
U-	Urate concentration, 24 h	12.4	8.3	28.7
U-	Urate output, 24 h	9.3	5.9	21.1
S-	Urea	6.2	5.5	15.7
U-	Urea concentration, 24 h	11.4	8.6	27.3
U-	Urea output, 24 h	8.7	7.7	22.1
U-	Vanilmandelic Acid conc, 24 h	11.1	13.0	31.3
S-	VLDL Cholesterol	13.8	—	—
P-	Von Willebrand factor	0.0005	7.1	7.1
S-	Water	1.6	0.8	3.3
S-	Zeaxanthine	17.4	—	—
P-	Zinc	5.5	4.5	13.5
S-	Zinc	4.7	3.3	11.0

Appendix 4: The Financial Impact of Quality Planning

Yes, but...

At some point while reading this book, you (or your supervisor or manager or VP or CEO) may have the following reaction: "Doing better QC is all well and good, and we'd like to do it, but the bottom line is that we need to reduce our costs." You're thinking that (a) high quality and low cost aren't compatible, (b) improving QC must cost more than whatever you're doing now, and (c) your current QC is probably good enough – even though it's unlikely the actual quality needed for patient care has been defined for the tests being performed.

It's hard to believe, but improvements in QC can actually save you money! The Six Sigma results prove it! Careful planning of QC will reduce the false rejections of analytical runs which otherwise waste personnel time and laboratory materials. Reducing waste means saving money. Careful planning of QC will also save money for your healthcare organization by detecting medically important errors that would otherwise waste the time of physicians and nurses, as well as consume the resources of the hospital, in the improper diagnosis and treatment of patients.

Quality Costs – the costs of good quality and poor quality

These savings are understandable if you consider all the costs associated with quality. These costs are described by the industrial model for "quality-costs"[1], which includes the costs of good quality (preventive-costs and appraisal-costs) and the costs of poor quality (internal and external failure-costs), as shown in the next figure. In industry, the costs of good quality are the planning and design of the process, the training of the line workers, and the time and effort in measuring and monitoring the quality of the product. The costs of poor quality are the rework and waste of a production process – doing things over to get the product right, or scrapping the product altogether.

For a laboratory, the costs of good quality include the cost of planning for quality (a preventive-cost) and the cost doing QC (an appraisal-cost). The cost of doing QC is probably the only cost the laboratory keeps track of. The costs of poor quality include the wasted time, effort, and materials due to repeat analysis of controls, new controls, and patients (internal failure-costs) and the cost of repeat orders and additional test orders by the physician to confirm laboratory results, as well as the costs associated with the wrong diagnosis and treatment due to erroneous test results (external failure-costs). These failure-costs would be high if they were measured in laboratories and hospitals, but they usually aren't – another dragon that Hagar probably doesn't want to hear about!

Careful planning of QC will minimize internal failure-costs by reducing the false rejections of analytical runs and will reduce external failure-costs by assuring that medically important errors are detected. We adopted the industrial quality-costs model in the mid 1980s [2] and that concept is embedded in our thinking and also in the quality-planning process and tools that have been developed since then.

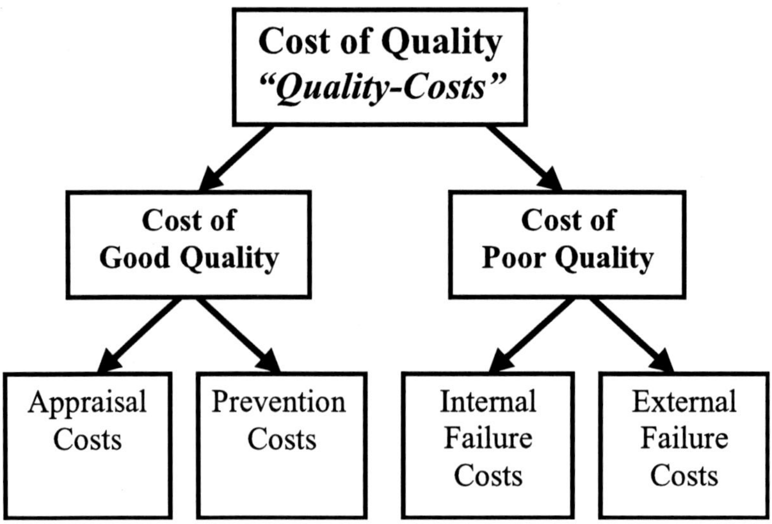

The Problem with High False Rejection

Poor QC is costing you money *right now*. There, I said it. It's a little known and oft-denied fact that most laboratories in the US and around the world are performing poor QC. I've heard too many personal anecdotes and read too many studies to say otherwise. I'm sorry to be the bearer of bad news, but someone has to speak out.

Before you protest, "not in my laboratory," answer these questions honestly: Does your laboratory still use 2 SD control limits? Does your laboratory repeat controls and patients again and again, analyze new controls, and then re-analyze the new controls until they're finally "in"? If so, most likely you have a false rejection problem that is costing you time and money. It's also a dangerous practice because analysts get accustomed to false alarms and no longer respond to *true* alarms, which leads to the reporting of erroneous test results. These actions are a result of poor quality planning, are costing you time and money, and are most likely giving your laboratory a bad reputation.

We must realize that many of the repeat runs, repeat controls, and new controls that we use to replace "bad" controls are the result of false rejection. The reason we don't immediately reject the run, but take these other actions first, is because we know instinctively that there really wasn't something wrong with the run in the first place. There isn't a problem with the samples – there's a problem with the control rules being used to detect the problem.

Here's a table with some hopefully eye-opening numbers about false rejection:

Control Rules	Number of Controls per Run			
	1	2	3	4
1_{2s}	5%	9%	14%	18%
$1_{2.5s}$	1%	2%	3%	4%
1_{3s}	0%	0%	1%	1%
$1_{3.5s}$	0%	0%	0%	0%
$1_{3s}/2_{2s}/R_{4s}$	0%	1%	2%	2%

Notice anything startling about the first row of this table? The 1_{2s} rule (i.e., 2 SD control limits) has a terribly high level of false rejections. There's no wonder this rule causes so many rejections and repeat runs. If you're running 2 controls and everything is working perfectly, you should be getting an out-of-control flag almost once in every ten runs (9%); with 3 controls, it's one out of every 6 or 7 runs; with 4 controls, it should be one out of every 5 runs. If there's actually a problem with the method, there will be even more flags, but who can tell a real rejection from a false rejection?

For those who aren't yet convinced that this is a serious problem, let's put the same condition into another context. If your laboratory has a fire alarm that goes off once a week even though there's no fire, would it save the laboratory time and money to get a better fire detector – one that only goes off when there's actually a real fire in the building? Obviously, a more reliable alarm or detector would save a lot of time if we've been evacuating the laboratory once a week. If we aren't evacuating the laboratory, then we're running the risk of a terribly high cost if a real fire occurs.

The Cost of False Rejections

If you're still not convinced, then maybe some actual figures in $$$$ will be persuasive.

Look at the next table, where the yearly costs of repeat runs have been calculated. The first column shows how many runs (from 1 to 4) are performed per day. The second column shows the total runs per year, assuming the laboratory operates all 365 days per year. The probability of false rejection is given in the 3rd column (0.09 for 2 control measurements per run and 0.14 for 3 per run) and is multiplied by the number of runs per year to give the extra runs needed, as shown in column 4. The remaining columns show the failure-costs or waste due to false rejections for 1 test or method, 5 methods, and 20 methods. The cost of analysis per sample is assumed to be $0.50. Sections A and B estimate the costs of repeating all patients and controls, assuming there is an average of 20 patients per run. Sections C and D show the costs if only the controls are repeated.

Runs/day	Runs/year	Pfr	Ex.runs/year	Cost/run	Waste or internal failure-costs per year 1 method	5 methods	20 methods
A. Cost of repeating run of 20 specimens and 2 controls when cost of each is $0.50							
1	365	0.09	32.85	$ 11.00	$ 361.35	$ 1,806.75	$ 7,227.00
2	730	0.09	65.7	$ 11.00	$ 722.70	$ 3,613.50	$ 14,454.00
3	1095	0.09	98.55	$ 11.00	$ 1,084.05	$ 5,420.25	$ 21,681.00
4	1460	0.09	131.4	$ 11.00	$ 1,445.40	$ 7,227.00	$ 28,908.00
B. Cost of repeating run of 20 specimens and 3 controls when cost of each is $0.50							
1	365	0.14	51.1	$ 11.50	$ 587.65	$ 2,938.25	$ 11,753.00
2	730	0.14	102.2	$ 11.50	$ 1,175.30	$ 5,876.50	$ 23,506.00
3	1095	0.14	153.3	$ 11.50	$ 1,762.95	$ 8,814.75	$ 35,259.00
4	1460	0.14	204.4	$ 11.50	$ 2,350.60	$11,753.00	$ 47,012.00
C. Cost of repeating 2 controls only when each control costs $0.50							
1	365	0.09	32.85	$ 1.00	$ 32.85	$ 164.25	$ 657.00
2	730	0.09	65.7	$ 1.00	$ 65.70	$ 328.50	$ 1,314.00
3	1095	0.09	98.55	$ 1.00	$ 98.55	$ 492.75	$ 1,971.00
4	1460	0.09	131.4	$ 1.00	$ 131.40	$ 657.00	$ 2,628.00
D. Cost of repeating 3 controls only when each control costs $0.50							
1	365	0.14	51.1	$ 1.50	$ 76.65	$ 383.25	$ 1,533.00
2	730	0.14	102.2	$ 1.50	$ 153.30	$ 766.50	$ 3,066.00
3	1095	0.14	153.3	$ 1.50	$ 229.95	$ 1,149.75	$ 4,599.00
4	1460	0.14	204.4	$ 1.50	$ 306.60	$ 1,533.00	$ 6,132.00

Let's assume that the laboratory adheres to the QC procedure religiously, i.e, both patients and controls are repeated whenever there's a rejection. For a small laboratory that performs only a single test or method once a day, the cost is $361 per year. If the laboratory performed 4 different tests, the cost would be $1,806; if there were 2 runs per day, the costs would increase to $3,613. For a laboratory that performed 20 different tests or for an instrument that performs 20 different tests, the cost per year is $7,227 for a single run per day, $14,454 if there are both morning and afternoon runs, and $28,908 if the laboratory operated around the clock, performing a third run on second shift and a fourth run on 3rd shift. For 3 controls per run instead of 2, the cost would be $47,012.

If you wondered why many laboratories don't repeat the patient samples when a run is out-of-control, now you know – the cost is too high. They keep the costs down by repeating only the controls, as shown in sections C and D of the table. But even those costs run into the thousands.

It would be better, of course, to utilize a QC procedure that has a lower false rejection rate. A multirule procedure with Ns of 2 and 3 would have only 1-2% false rejections, rather than the 9-14% for 2 SD control limits. You can see that a lot of money is wasted by common practice of using 2 SD control limits. At the same time, you can also see how the false rejection problem can be reduced by selecting other QC procedures, such as a 1_{3s}, $1_{2.5s}$, or multirule procedure. You can do the math and figure out the savings.

In summary, the costs of false rejections are a big problem in many laboratories. This cost can be reduced by selecting QC procedures that have a low probability for false rejection. Any laboratory that uses 2 SD control limits will experience false rejections; if not, they're somehow widening their control limits, perhaps by using the manufacturers' limits, bottle values that include lab to lab variation, supposedly clinical limits, or even drawing the CLIA total error criteria directly on control charts – all bad practices.

The Cost of Low Error Detection

Another problem is that many laboratories really don't know if their QC procedures will detect medically important errors. A lack of rejections may mean the method is working perfectly, or it may reflect that the QC procedure is *unable* to detect errors. If that occurs, the laboratory may be reporting erroneous test results, which could lead to improper diagnoses and treatments of patients. The potential cost of erroneous test results are hard to quantify – they might be small, but they could also be huge.

If we only consider the delay of effective treatment for patients due to erroneous test results and that the cost for an additional day in a hospital might be $1000 for a single patient, it's easy to see that analytical errors could cost the hospital tens or even hundreds of thousands of dollars. That cost shows up in the overall bottom line of the hospital, but doesn't show up in the laboratory operating statements. No one really knows that cost, but as Deming said, there are some figures that are important and must be considered – even if they are unknowable.

Laboratories should not knowingly operate with poor quality and poor quality control. The secret to knowing about quality is the Six Sigma techniques and the associated planning tools like the OPSpecs chart. The cornerstone of quality-planning is the selection of a QC procedure that will detect medically important errors. Built into the quality-planning tools, graphs, and calculations is the selection of a QC procedure on the basis of the quality required by the test and the imprecision and inaccuracy observed for the method; the process accomplishes this at the lowest cost by minimizing the probability for false rejection and the number of control measurements. Thus, the quality-planning process optimizes your QC so you aren't over-controlling a test and wasting resources, or under-controlling a test and suffering potentially high failure-costs. You do the right amount of QC for the test and for your method, with the assurance that you will detect analytical errors that would otherwise have a costly impact on patient care.

Optimizing your QC allows you to spend only the minimum amount on QC, while maximizing your "through-put" of tests. With fewer false rejects, you increase the productivity or "test-yield" of your processes; you can run more tests and have more staff time to devote to other tasks. With better error detection, you have fewer repeat tests ordered by puzzled physicians; you reduce medical errors and contribute to better patient care. If we could speak a moment in business terms, the quality-planning process leads to improved productivity, reduced costs, and dare we say, a competitive advantage.

In summary, the current QC practices in laboratories today contribute to two kinds of financial waste through high false rejection and low error detection. The quality-planning process will help you choose control rules that are high in error detection and low in false rejection, optimizing your quality and minimizing your costs.

Will Six Sigma save money for every test?

Just as there's no magic set of control rules for all tests and all laboratories, there's no one magic way to save money on all tests in all laboratories. Most likely there are tests that are being over-controlled (e.g., highly automated chemistry and hematology analyzers) and other tests that are being under-controlled (e.g., immunoassays, POC, manual assays). That's the outcome from using the same QC procedure on all the tests in the laboratory. With careful selection of QC procedure, you will save money in some areas while possibly spending more in other areas. Ultimately, what's important is that you'll be doing the right amount of QC on all of your tests, thereby making the optimal investment of time, effort, and materials.

There are some laboratories doing such poor QC, or so little QC, that the quality-planning process may require them to do more QC for all tests, which will inevitably cost them more than what they're spending now. But if a laboratory is operating that poorly, it's imperative to make an investment in better QC. There are also some tests that are very difficult to control because current analytical methods lack the desired performance. Those methods will require extra control measurements together with the most powerful control rules, implementation of non-statistical checks and an aggressive preventive maintenance schedule, increased education and training, staffing with more experienced analysts, and less rotation of staff.

Is it worth implementing a quality-planning process if you won't always save money? For most of us who have dedicated ourselves to clinical laboratory services, the knowledge of the quality of our tests is the key to managing the laboratory services effectively. There's no satisfaction in providing cheap test results if those results might be in error! We'd rather know if there are analytical problems so we have a chance to solve those problems. We'd rather assure the quality of the test results instead of assuming the quality is okay. We're healthcare professionals who take responsibility for the quality of our services!

Where to start?

Quality-planning is a big job in a laboratory that performs hundreds of different tests. Where should you start? Begin with tests where you can make the biggest impact, such as automated chemistry and hematology analyzers that perform a significant portion of the laboratory workload. Place a high priority on any tests where the current QC practice uses 2 SD control limits.

In the end, it's up to you!

I hope you're convinced that doing QC right is important and that the quality-planning process is the way to know what QC is needed. You have the tools (in this book and on the website). You know the process. You've seen how it's done. Now it's your turn!

References

1. Feigenbaum AV. Total quality control. Harvard Bus Rev 1954;34(6):93-101.

2. Westgard JO, Barry PL. *Cost-Effective Quality Control: Managing the Quality and Productivity of Analytical Processes.* Washington DC: AACC Press, 1986, pp 138-159.